Religion, the Courts, and Public Policy

RELIGION, THE COURTS, AND PUBLIC POLICY

BY ROBERT F. DRINAN, S.J.

GREENWOOD PRESS, PUBLISHERS
WESTPORT, CONNECTICUT

Library of Congress Cataloging in Publication Data

Drinan, Robert F
    Religion, the courts, and public policy.

    Reprint of the ed. published by McGraw-Hill, New York.
    Bibliography: p.
    Includes index.
    1. Church and state in the United States.
    2. Religion in the public schools--United States.
    3. Church and education in the United States.
    I. Title.
[BR516.D7 1978]   261.7'0973   78-6124
ISBN 0-313-20444-6

IMPRIMI POTEST:

John V. O'Connor, S.J.
Provincial, New England Province
Society of Jesus

NIHIL OBSTAT:

James A. O'Donohoe, J.C.D.
Diocesan Censor

IMPRIMATUR:

✠ *Richard Cardinal Cushing*
Archbishop of Boston

February 6, 1963

Reprinted with the permission of McGraw-Hill Book Company

Reprinted in 1978 by Greenwood Press, Inc.
51 Riverside Avenue, Westport, CT. 06880

Printed in the United States of America

10 9 8 7 6 5 4 3 2 1

Contents

Religion, the Courts, and Public Policy

CHAPTER ONE

Areas of Church–State Cooperation

GENERAL BACKGROUND OF CHURCH AND STATE IN AMERICA

The greatest problem confronting anyone who desires to lend some clarification to a discussion of church–state relations in America is the fact that the terms "church" and "state" have become heavily charged with emotional overtones. It might be desirable to substitute for these terms the words "religion" and "government." However, aside from the suspicion incurred by the writer who refuses to employ the consecrated terms of "church" and "state," the fact is that no more satisfactory terms are available.

It is true, nonetheless, that many writers and groups have read more into the unanalyzed phrase "the separation of church and state" than can reasonably be attributed to it. The word "separation" is not self-defining, and the terms, often capitalized, "church" and "state" are even less susceptible of precise definition.

Professor Paul G. Kauper of the University of Michigan Law School wrote perceptively about this basic problem of terminology in these words:

Separation of church and state is the symbolic language so often used as a beginning point of discussion. Actually this precise language does not have much relevancy to the American scene. It is borrowed from European history and tradition where the problem could be identified in terms of a single church and of a single state, or in later years of a single state and two churches, namely, Catholic and Protestant.[1]

Professor Franklin H. Littell, Chicago Theological Seminary, is even stronger in his depreciation of the "church–state" terminology customarily employed. In his uniquely incisive study of religion in America he states: "Many contemporary writers attempt to read back into the past 'a wall of separation' between church and state which in fact never has existed in the United States. Indeed the form of words, the shibboleth, is a *major impediment in the way of honest discussion.*" [Emphasis supplied.][2]

Canon Anson Phelps Stokes, in his exhaustive, three-volume treatise on church and state in America, illustrates an additional difficulty in the "church–state" terminology when he asserts that: "few of the more representative Protestant Churches, except Baptists and Lutherans, have a very clearly defined and consistent doctrine of the respective spheres of Church and State, and even the Lutheran doctrine is being modified under the stress of modern pressure."[3]

Catholics and, in fact, all non-Protestants have a particular problem in understanding the concept of the separation of church and state. The Catholic Church, for many centuries the foe of the "state" in the person of emperors anxious to usurp the rights of the "church," finds itself in a unique position in contemporary America. This uniqueness derives from the fact that America is the only nation ever established by persons of the Protestant faith in a land with no pre-existing Catholic tradition. In England, Holland, Germany, Scandinavia and elsewhere the Protestant Reformers were confronted with nations almost entirely Catholic in their population. The legal institutions and the church–state relations of these countries were, at the time of the Reformation, similarly Catholic in orientation.

In America, on the other hand, Protestants founded a nation where Catholics were almost unknown. The common law of England, however, which became the cornerstone of American legal institution, was to some extent the creation or at least the by-product of the work of Catholic jurists in the four centuries prior to the Reformation in England. In America, therefore, we behold a nation unique in history—the only land founded by Protestants with no prior Catholic population or tradition and the only Protestant land to adopt English legal institutions whose origins and out-look were influenced in a significant way by early medieval Catholic cleric-jurists.

In every attempt at generalization, therefore, concerning the relations of church and state in America, one is confronted with the realization that any over-all statement in this area is likely to contradict one of the Biblical, theological, moral and constitutional ideas which have entered into the present unwritten entente regarding church–state arrangements in America. Because of the unique origin of America's founding and America's correspondingly unique attitude toward the place of religion in our public law, the experience of other nations with respect to church–state problems is of limited value. In fact one of the greatest difficulties encountered in any intelligent "dialogue" about such relations in the United States is the initial decision about where to begin. Most persons are content to find refuge in the easiest area—in an analysis and discussion of what *precisely* the United States Supreme Court has said on the First Amendment's "establishment" and "free exercise" of religion clauses. Others will go beyond the law and argue public policy, but few, if any, observers can even outline what would be the wisest and fairest ultimate attitudes for the law to adopt.

The almost inevitable misunderstandings which arise in any discussion of church–state relations derive from the unavoidable intermingling of the Scriptural, theological, moral and constitutional concepts which have been woven into the debate over the question of whether the formula "separation of church and state" should be regarded as a secularistic shibboleth or as a near-sacred watchword.

It is an astonishing fact that the United States Supreme Court did not rule in any substantial way on the meaning of the "establishment" clause of the First Amendment until the year 1947. As will be described later, the *Everson* decision of 1947, which sustained the constitutionality of bus rides for parochial school children in New Jersey, was followed by five major decisions in the period between 1947 and 1962. Two of these decisions centered on released-time religious education—the *McCollum* opinion of 1948 and the *Zorach* ruling of 1952. A third decision, the *Torcaso* ruling in 1961, declared unconstitutional a Maryland law requiring an oath of belief in God as a prerequisite for public officeholders in that state. A fourth opinion, handed down in May, 1961, upheld the constitutionality of Sunday-closing laws while the fifth ruling, issued in June 1962, banned a nondenominational prayer from the public schools in the state of New York.

While all these rulings are of great importance, the fact is that for a century and a half the nation existed without a ruling from the nation's highest tribunal on the constitutional prohibition of an "establishment" of religion. Such a situation indicates the existence of a well-established and widely accepted church–state arrangement. It seems safe to assert that in the United States, more perhaps than in any European country, there existed until recent times an informally established "pan-Protestantism." It may be true to some extent that America is now a post-Protestant or even a post-Christian nation, but such a generalization becomes almost meaningless upon careful analysis.

What is certainly true, however, is that Americans have not yet found a way of communicating with each other concerning the place which religion should be granted in the public life of a newly pluralistic land. Catholics experience special difficulty in making known their convictions, since they must employ terminology not of their own creation and operate within a framework of statutory and decisional law which was designed to protect a pan-Protestant nation from non-Protestant influences.

Although new forces are in operation today seeking to change America's traditional church–state patterns, the remarks of Europe's most famous observers of America, de Tocqueville and Bryce, seem as true today as when they were penned. Wrote de Tocqueville: "There is no nation in the world in which the Christian religion retains a greater influence over the souls of men than in America. . . . In the United States religion exercises but little influence over the laws and the details of public opinion but it directs the manners of the community, and by regulating domestic life, it regulates the state." Fifty years later Bryce noted that: "Christianity is in fact understood to be, though not the legally established religion, yet the national religion. So far from thinking their Commonwealth godless, the Americans conceive that the religious character of a government consists in nothing but the religious beliefs of the individual citizens, and the conformity of their conduct to that belief. . . ."[4]

Although new forces now challenge our basic church–state customs, the importance and strength of these forces remains in doubt. Indeed, one might question whether the Sabbatarian's request to work on Sunday or the Catholic parent's desire for Federal funds for parochial schools are, in the final analysis, very serious challenges to the warm and cordial relationship between government and religion which exists in the United States. A very widespread revolution of ideas would be required to erode in any substantial way our remarkable relationship between religion and government, described as "symbiosis." This term, a biological concept meaning the living together of two dissimilar organisms, seems to convey more than any other single word both the profound interdependence and the complete independence of the secular and the sacred in American life.

A delicate distillation of Judaeo–Christian, Protestant, rationalist and French Revolutionary ideas has welded together a nation formed as the result of the greatest migration in the history of man. That distillation has always defied exact analysis, because it has merged into the inarticulate major premises by which Americans think and act.

Americans have traditionally been ill-equipped and characteristically reluctant to spell out their "public philosophy." Americans in fact have never done so. Now, confronted by the challenges of pluralism, they seem more than ever incapable of so doing, particularly if they start their explanation with an endorsement of the "separation of church and state" as one of their major dogmas.

The separation of church and state does, of course, exist in America, as it must in every nation where the spiritual needs of man and the dictates of his conscience are deemed to be superior to the temporal demands of the state. But to affirm and applaud the desirability of the separation of church and state—as all Americans and all Christians must do—is to say little or nothing about one's deepest views on the relation of the spiritual and temporal orders, or on the intertwining of law and morals, or on the relevance of religion to citizenship.

Many basic differences on fundamental legal and moral questions exist between religious groups in America. Such issues as birth-control legislation, the legal regulation of obscenity, American public policy on the population explosion and similar problems divide America's religionists and separate them more and more from the nation's non-religionists. None of these, however, has yet developed into a constitutional and legal question on which the Supreme Court has ruled. Although these basic problems of public morality may eventually become legal issues, it seems advisable to confine ourselves here to those problems which have already become legal and constitutional issues.

Three great problems dominate the church–state scene today and seem likely to continue to do so for the foreseeable future. These are: religious education in the public school, tax support of church-related schools and the request of Sabbatarians for the right to work on Sunday if they abstain from work on Saturday for religious reasons. Although each of these will be examined in detail later, a distorted picture of church–state relations might be conveyed if, before such an investigation, some indication were not given of the vast areas where government and religion have formed an untroubled alliance.

The tangible benefits to religious bodies from such practices as tax exemption for churches, draft-exemption for seminarians and clergymen, chaplaincies in the military and tax money for sectarian social agencies are evident. But the intangible benefits deriving from the juridical acceptance of the importance of the spiritual order are far more valuable (and a far greater breach of church–state separation!) than any possible list of material or financial aid. The fact that American law has committed itself to the recognition of the transcendent importance of each citizen following his own conscience indicates the profoundly religious orientation of our legal institutions.

Throughout our history, advocates of two polarized viewpoints have tried to Christianize or secularize American institutions. Some Christian groups have attempted to have the Congress of the United States commit the nation to a specifically Christian ideal; at the same time other groups have resisted every affirmation similar to that of Justice William O. Douglas in the 1952 *Zorach* opinion: "We are a religious people whose institutions presuppose a Supreme Being."[5] The fact is that the American state has never been, and is not now, in its constitutional, statutory or decisional law, a purely secular state.

The intangible but very important benefits to religion that come from the state's recognition of religion as a necessary, indeed almost an indispensable, influence for the preservation of the common good is without doubt the most important asset which religion in America has ever obtained or could secure. Court decisions and new legislation may therefore terminate specific religious practices or refuse financial aid to civic functions when they are intermingled with religion; but so long as the American state remains possessed of a lofty respect for the importance and value of the spiritual order, legal rulings will at best have a limited application.

No legislator or jurist today would reiterate in a literal way the assertion made by the United States Supreme Court in 1892 and repeated with approval by Justice George Sutherland in 1931: "We are a Christian people."[6] But there is widespread agreement with the second part of this statement of the Supreme Court wherein it is asserted that Americans accord to "one another the equal right of religious freedom" and acknowledge "with reverence the duty of obedience to the will of God."

The profoundly religious and theistic presuppositions of the American state appear to be so deeply ingrained in American public policy that it is doubtful if Congressional or Supreme Court endorsements of a neutral or secular state can, in the absence of a complete reversal of public opinion, change the fundamental direction of church–state attitudes in America. But new and influential voices today are urging as never before that the American state can and must be not merely neutral, but avowedly secular in its attitude toward all religious groups. The entire future not only of American church–state relations but of this nation's public and private morality will depend on the extent to which American lawmakers are influenced by those individuals who feel that the total separation of government from religion is a desirable development.

FRIENDLY ALLIANCES BETWEEN CHURCH AND STATE

What then are the tangible alliances made by the American state with religious groups which cannot be considered other than as intended to benefit and promote religion? Four such alliances will be investigated, while several other less widespread although hardly less significant fields of church–state co-operation will be mentioned. Tax exemption for churches and similar institutions, draft immunity for divinity students and clergymen, government salaries for chaplains and tax support for church-related social welfare agencies have their roots to a large extent in the truly extraordinary respect and esteem accorded by American institutions to the person of the minister of religion. Tax exemption is probably intended to be and is, as former Dean Willard L. Sperry of the Harvard Divinity School stated, "the most important governmental recognition of religion in America."[7]

Tax Exemption for Religious Institutions

On April 16, 1962, the United States Supreme Court refused review to a unanimous ruling of the Supreme Court of Rhode Island which had sustained tax exemption for religious bodies. The nation's highest tribunal, Justice Hugo L. Black dissenting, said that no "substantial Federal question" was involved in the December 13, 1961, decision of the Rhode Island court affirming the constitutionality of tax exemption for church and other properties.[8]

Although a denial of review by the Supreme Court does not necessarily imply approval of the decision, it seems permissible to state that the exemption from property and other taxes granted in every state of the union to church-related groups does not contravene the "establishment" clause of the First Amendment. In spite, therefore, of certain rigorous statements in favor of church–state separation in recent decisions of the United States Supreme Court, this same tribunal has validated tax exemption statutes by which religious groups receive enormous financial and moral benefits. Only Justice Hugo L. Black (Justice Felix Frankfurter, being hospitalized, did not participate in the 6–1 decision) apparently saw the clear contradiction between his majority opinion in the *Everson*[9] case and the allowance of tax exemption to churches in Rhode Island and elsewhere. Since the Supreme Court has now asserted that there is no "substantial Federal question" in the tax exemption ruling of the Supreme Court of Rhode Island it will be helpful to analyze the relief requested without success by the Rhode Island plaintiff.

A clear-cut factual case presented the Supreme Court of Rhode Island with an unavoidable challenge to the constitutionality of exemption from property taxes granted to churches in the city of Cranston. The plaintiff, the General Finance Corp., owned property in Cranston which, assessed in 1959 at $24,780, was taxed at $842.52. If exemptions from Cranston's property tax had not been given to religious and other bodies in that city, the plaintiff's taxes would have been concededly diminished by $30.42.

Although the record in the Rhode Island case does not disclose exactly what the plaintiff was required to pay *precisely* because of

tax exemption granted to specifically religious organizations, it may
be assumed that the sum would have been a substantial part of the
$30.42 complained of. The question presented, therefore, was
whether the protesting taxpayer was being required to support religion in violation of the Rhode Island Constitution, which states
that "no man shall be compelled to frequent or *to support* any
religious worship, *place* or ministry whatever. . . ." [Emphasis
supplied.] The Federal question involved raised the issue whether
the tax exemption granted in Cranston ran contrary to the United
States Supreme Court's interpretation of the First Amendment in
its 1947 *Everson* decision where the Court stated that neither "a
State nor the Federal Government . . . can pass laws which . . . aid
all religions."

The opinion of the Supreme Court of Rhode Island repeats the
arguments in favor of tax exemption employed by the several other
state tribunals which have universally sustained even the broadest
exemptions granted to religious bodies. The Rhode Island court
held, in essence, that no preferential aid is given by the challenged
statute to religious organizations, since all nonprofit groups benefit
equally under its provisions. The Rhode Island tribunal asserted
that the legislature is vested with the broadest power to grant tax
exemption and that it need not withhold this benefit from qualified
religious groups.

No entirely satisfactory rationale for tax exemption has ever been
stated in any American judicial decision. It may be that the only
possible ultimate justification is a public policy consciously encouraging religion as a valuable aid to good citizenship. Courts and commentators quite understandably are reluctant to reach such ulti-
mates and, if they must give a plausible reason for tax immunity
for religious bodies, tend to urge one of the three following justifications:

1. Tax exemption for churches and related institutions has
always existed in American law; in fact, it can be traced back to
Constantine or even to the Talmud, according to which rabbis
were given certain tax exemptions.

2. Churches by means of the educational programs which they
sponsor participate in the work of the state and thereby relieve it
of some of its burdens.

3. No court decision in American jurisprudence has ever ruled
that tax exemption to religious groups is a discrimination against
nonbelievers.

However popular and widely accepted these reasons may be, the fact is that American courts have never carefully scrutinized the implications of the complex structure of tax-exemption benefits conferred upon religious bodies in America. The American judiciary has not even raised the hard questions, much less resolved them. The extent of the benefits granted to religion by tax exemption are almost beyond calculation; some indication of the amount of direct subsidy available to churches can be seen in the exemption of church-operated cemeteries, the revenues from which not infrequently supply one of the main sources of financing for many parishes. If the trend toward the establishment of an *absolute* separation of church and state is to continue, it would seem logical to predict that the constitutionality of tax exemption may be challenged. By an inexplicable paradox, however, such does not appear to be the case. Except for the voices of some extremists and the urgings of some sincerely troubled religionists, tax exemption for religious purposes seems today to be as securely guaranteed as at any time in American history.

The most vehement critic of tax exemption ever to hold high public office was President Ulysses S. Grant. In a message to Congress in 1875, he urged the withdrawal of tax exemption from church bodies but weakened his case considerably by allowing tax exemption for "the last resting-place of the dead, and possibly, with proper restrictions, church edifices."[10] This suggestion, apparently one of the nation's most direct and potentially influential frontal assaults on tax exemption, nonetheless conceded the advisability of the *principle* of tax exemption—at least in two important instances.

Leo Pfeffer, whose studies on church–state matters have been characterized by John C. Bennett, Dean of Union Theological Seminary, as embracing "the point of view of extreme separationism"[11] asserts that "the opinions in the *Everson* and *McCollum* cases lead to the conclusion that tax exemption for churches violates the First Amendment as interpreted by these decisions."[12] Pfeffer concedes, however, that the language of the 1952 *Zorach* decision stating that "the First Amendment . . . does not say that in every and all respects there shall be a separation of church and state" may have created "an opening in the wall between church and state sufficiently large for tax exemption to creep through."[13]

Both Canon Stokes and Leo Pfeffer feel that Catholics are more affirmative in their approbation of tax exemption than are Protestant or Jewish groups. Pfeffer states that "the great majority of religious groups do not oppose tax exemption. Either, like the Catholic Church, they affirmatively defend it, or, like Jewish and many Protestant organizations, they accept the exemption and maintain a prudent silence."[14] Canon Stokes feels that any opposition to tax exemption "is denounced with vigor by the authorities of the Roman Catholic Church."[15] Although no Catholic sources are noted by either author, it may be that, if Catholics appear to be more certain of the wisdom and fairness of tax exemption than some other religious groups, such an attitude derives from the Catholic commitment to the proposition that the state has some duty to cooperate with religion or at least not to impede its progress.

The Supreme Court of California, ruling in 1956 in favor of the constitutionality of tax exemption for nonpublic and church-related schools of less than collegiate rank, probably summed up current public opinion and contemporary American law when it wrote: "The United States Supreme Court, in discussing the prohibition of laws respecting the establishment of religion, recently stated that the standard of constitutionality is the separation of church and state, and that the problem, like many others in constitutional law, is one of degree. (*Zorach v. Clauson,* 343 U.S. 306, 314.) The principle of separation of church and state is not impaired by granting tax exemptions to religious groups generally, and it seems clear that the First Amendment was not intended to prohibit such exemptions." On December 3, 1956, the United States Supreme Court, Justices Black and Frankfurter dissenting, dismissed an appeal in this California case "for want of a substantial Federal question."[16]

Sincere anxiety that church groups may be unjustly accepting the benefits of tax exemption to the detriment of agnostics or other nonbelievers has led to some rethinking on a subject which apparently some religionists fear to discuss. On April 9, 1947, *The Christian Century,* in a strong editorial entitled "Churches Should Pay Taxes," reiterated the position of the former editor of the *Century,* Dr. Charles Clayton Morrison, to the effect that churches should not receive or accept the indirect subsidy of tax exemption from the state. A position similar to this was taken by Rev. Dr. Eugene Carson Blake, past President of the National Council of Churches of Christ in the United States of America, when he urged, in the

August 3, 1959, issue of *Christianity Today*, a Protestant fort-
nightly, that churches pay some taxes on their real estate. Dr. Ed-
win T. Dahlberg, then President of the National Council of
Churches, supported Dr. Blake's recommendation that churches
start to pay 1 per cent of the amount they would pay if their property were assessed, increasing this contribution by 1 per cent a year
to a ceiling of 10 per cent.

While the sincerity and generosity of the advocates of partial
renunciation of tax exemption is clear and commendable, this
complex question cannot be resolved by settling on an arbitrary
figure of 1 per cent taxation on real property while leaving 90 per
cent of the same property tax-exempt. Federal law permits taxpayers to deduct up to 30 per cent of adjusted gross income for
direct gifts to churches or other religious causes. Would not any
re-examination of tax exemption for religious purposes be required
to make an over-all study and evaluation of the innumerable ways
by which state and Federal income, property, estate and inheritance
taxes assist religious groups? No sectarian or secular organization
has ever proposed such a study; yet it is clear that no equitable
redistribution of tax benefits and tax burdens would be possible
without a thorough knowledge of the intricacies of state and
Federal patterns of taxation.

It is interesting to note the paucity of literature and the almost
total nonexistence of litigation concerning tax exemption which
Canon Stokes has termed the "greatest single help given by the
State to the Church in this country."[17] The only type of controversy
about tax exemption that has arisen in recent times centers on the
extent to which religious organizations may avail themselves of this
benefit. Income from businesses not related to the religious purposes of the tax-exempt organization has been prohibited by statutory and decisional law.[18]

Virtually no writer has called tax exemption a danger to the
independence of the churches, nor has anyone urged that the modern state can ill afford the luxury of allowing taxes to be abated on
behalf of religious organizations. John C. Bennett, in fact, has
suggested that tax exemption, which he terms "the most remarkable of all forms of aid to all religious bodies," is "good for the
state perhaps more than for the Church, to signalize in this way
the high place to religion."[19]

Dean Bennett's suggestion is developed in an article in the May–

June 1962 issue of *Religious Liberty*, a Seventh-Day Adventist journal committed to the doctrine of an *absolute* separation of church and state. In an article by Professor Daniel Walthar on "Tax Exemption and the Church" the author, after writing about possible abuses of tax exemption by the churches, concludes: "Church property *per se* must remain tax free. To lay a tax on churches would enhance the power of the State; it would enable the State to control the churches and would certainly be contrary to the basic principle of church–state separation. The State that has ever-increasing need of financial resources might jeopardize the church's ability to operate as an effective agency. Moreover, church taxation would enable only wealthy churches to subsist."

Professor Walthar's conclusions are seconded to some extent by an admitted unbeliever, Professor Robert Lekachman of Barnard College, who feels that "tax-exemption should in logic be retrieved but in practice left undisturbed." The only reason advanced for the recommendation of nondisturbance is that "social harmony and a decent respect for established practice imply that the issue of tax-exemption should not be raised."[20]

Three major conclusions can be deduced after a survey of the profoundly entrenched place which tax exemption for religious organizations has in American law:

1. Compelling reasons of tradition, conviction or a sense of the impossibility of victory seem to inhibit the ultraseparationist organization, the American Civil Liberties Union, or the even more absolutist group, Protestants and Other Americans United for the Separation of Church and State, from advocating even a diminution or a restriction on tax exemption for religious bodies. Only a few extreme church–state separationists seem to be actively committed to a struggle to abolish tax exemption for religious organizations.

2. A remarkable consensus of Protestant, Catholic and Jewish sentiment continues to exist on the question of tax exemption—with, however, a sincere, if not always articulate, desire not to accept benefits if such acceptance results in actual harm to others.

3. The remarkable convergence of opinions on the desirability of tax exemption for religious groups gives rise to the hope that similar friendly alliances between church and state can be achieved in areas where at present "ignorant armies clash by night." Furthermore, the distinction, presumably valid, between permissible

aid by abatement of taxes and forbidden aid by direct subsidy may hopefully serve a useful purpose in providing a solution for the impasse which seems to have come about with respect to public funds for nonpublic schools.

Exemption from Military Service for Seminarians, Clergymen and Conscientious Objectors

In 1940, Congress enacted and President Roosevelt signed a law regulating exemptions from military service which contained the following language: "Regular or duly ordained ministers of religion, and students who are preparing for the ministry in theological or divinity schools, recognized as such for more than one year prior to the date of the enactment of this Act, shall be exempt from training and service but not from registration under this Act."[21]

A more explicit way of indicating a moral and financial commitment to religion can hardly be imagined. During the entire duration of World War II, amid manpower shortages at the battlefronts and in the munitions factories, the United States Government allowed every clergyman and every student studying to be a clergyman complete exemption from participation in the war effort! A more sweeping affirmation of the importance with which the nation regards its ministers of religion could hardly be enunciated. It is doubtful if any nation involved in mankind's most devastating war maintained as firm and complete a protection of its future clerical manpower as did the United States.

The fact that draft exemption for present and prospective clergymen is taken so much for granted in America is another example of a happy coincidence between the goals of the American state and the purposes of organized religion. From the viewpoint of a strict church–state separationist, exemption from military duty for otherwise eligible seminarians and clergymen could be disputed as inconsistent with the "no-aid-to-religion" doctrine which the United States Supreme Court has enunciated in its six major church–state decisions between 1947 and 1962.

The draft immunity extended to seminarians in peace time, as opposed to a time of war, is not substantially different from the deferment granted to every full-time student in college and graduate school. For this reason it may be that no direct test of the constitutionality of complete draft exemption for actual and potential clergymen can be expected at this time.

Although reasons of public policy rather than the preservation of religious freedom may have influenced Congress in its judgment to grant exemption from military duty to conscientious objectors, it is difficult to see any reason other than one favorable to religion behind the directive of Congress during both World Wars that no minister of religion or student of divinity should be drafted.

With regard to those conscientiously opposed to war, Congress could have concluded that their coerced presence within the military would have endangered morale. But no such secular or non-religious justification for draft immunity for the clergy can be attributed to Congress.

It would appear, therefore, that once again we behold, as on the question of tax exemption, a specific, uncontroverted area wherein the American government by deliberate design bestows a preference upon organized religion with the avowed purpose of extending a benefit to religion as such.

No sectarian or secular body has ever suggested that exemption from the draft is an impermissible advantage for the personnel of the organized religions of America. Such exemption could, however, at least theoretically jeopardize the independence of the clergy. Furthermore, it extends a clear preference to religious believers over nonbelievers—and as such could be challenged as contrary to the First Amendment.

CONSCIENTIOUS OBJECTORS. Cognate to, but somewhat different from, the automatic dispensation from military service extended to clergymen and seminarians is the ever expanding immunity granted by statutory and decisional law to persons who are conscientiously opposed to war or bearing arms. A more moving and instructive lesson in America's scrupulous regard for the sacredness of conscience can hardly be seen than that of the troubled tenderness with which the nation has sought to treat conscientious objectors. Although this topic does not form precisely another friendly alliance between government and religion, the consensus obtained on this matter between religionists and secularists is so extraordinary that its significance is worthy of exploration.

American history and tradition are rich in examples of immunity bestowed upon those who are opposed to war. Madison proposed the adoption, during a discussion on the Bill of Rights, of an amendment to provide that "no person religiously scrupulous shall be compelled to bear arms."[22] The New York Constitution, adopted in 1821, reflects the sentiments of other state constitutions in this provision: ". . . all . . . inhabitants of this State, of any religious denomination whatever, as from scruples of conscience may be averse to bearing arms, shall be excused therefrom by paying to the State an equivalent in money. . . ."[23]

The nation's first conscription act, adopted on March 3, 1863, specifically exempted Quakers, but, in 1864, it was broadened to state that: "Members of religious denominations who shall by oath or affirmation declare that they are conscientiously opposed to the bearing of arms and who are prohibited from doing so by the rules and articles of faith and practice of said religious denominations shall, when drafted into the military service be considered noncombatants . . . or shall pay the sum of $300 . . . to be applied to the benefit of sick and wounded soldiers."[24] While not every feature of this Civil War Act may appear equitable, the purpose of the law, affirming a solid American tradition, was to secure the fulfillment of the great moral principle respecting the inviolability of conscience.

No conscription was necessary after the Civil War until America entered World War I in 1917. At that time Congress exempted: ". . . the members of any well-recognized religious sect or organization whose existing creed or principles forbid its members to participate in war in any form, but no person shall be exempted from service in any capacities that the President shall declare to be non-combatant."[25] It is interesting to note that the United States Supreme Court, in a case challenging the exemption of conscientious objectors accorded by the Selective Service Act of 1917 as a violation of the "establishment" clause, disposed of this question summarily as follows: "We pass without anything but statement the proposition that an establishment of a religion or an interference with the free exercise thereof repugnant to the First Amendment resulted from the exemption clauses of the act . . . because we think its unsoundness is too apparent to require us to do more."[26]

The 1940 Selective Service Act broadened the possibilities for exemption to include anyone who "by reason of religious training and belief" had conscientious scruples against "participation in war in any form." Even, therefore, without membership in a particular sect one of whose tenets was pacifism, a person could be exempted. Scruples, however, based on a "political and social philosophy re-

specting the folly and futility of war" have been held to be insuffi-
cient for exemption from participation in military service.[27]

The great struggles in Supreme Court jurisprudence over the
rights of conscience have not arisen directly because of citizens
claiming draft exemption. The great contests have sprung up from
aliens claiming citizenship even though they possessed conscientious objections to participation in war. The remarkable series of
decisions over this problem has enriched American church–state
literature in a manner possibly greater than any other line of Supreme Court opinions. In every decision from the *Schwimmer*[28]
ruling in 1929 to its reversal in the *Girouard*[29] holding in 1946, the
Supreme Court has given to the nation moral ideas and noble language from which the solutions to other church–state conundrums
may hopefully be fashioned.

When Hungarian-born Rosika Schwimmer asked for citizenship
her request was not granted because she qualified her oath of allegiance to the United States by an explicit refusal to take up arms
in defense of any country. The United States Supreme Court held
that her pacifism was an insuperable disqualification for citizenship.
Although it was not clear that Rosika Schwimmer was opposed to
bearing arms precisely because of religious scruples, neither was it
clear that her refusal to take up arms contradicted the oath of
allegiance required by the Naturalization Act of 1906.

Justice Holmes, with Justice Brandeis concurring, dissented from
Justice Butler's majority opinion, although even his dissent did not
assert that an objection to participation in war because of religious
convictions would be an excusable scruple in an applicant for citizenship. In its next case on this matter, however, the Supreme
Court was required to rule precisely on the question of whether a
definite pledge in advance to fight in any way could be exacted
from a petitioner seeking naturalization.

Professor Douglas Clyde Macintosh, a Canadian by birth, an
ordained Baptist minister and Dwight Professor of Theology at
Yale Divinity School, refused to give an unqualified answer to
Question 22 on the form for petition for naturalization. The question asked was: "If necessary, are you willing to take up arms in
defense of this country?" In response Macintosh stated: "Yes, but
I should want to be free to judge of the necessity."

Professor Macintosh, who had voluntarily served as a chaplain
with the Canadian army and saw service in Europe during World

War I, made it clear at the hearing on his petition for naturalization that he was not a pacifist. But he also felt obliged to insist that a citizen should have the right to refuse military service when his own conscience clearly told him that the war in which he was being asked to participate was morally unjustified.

In a 5–4 split the Supreme Court, Justice Sutherland writing the majority opinion, denied citizenship to Professor Macintosh with this potentially dangerous Erastian affirmation: "We are . . . (a people) whose government must go forward upon the assumption and can safely proceed on no other that unqualified allegiance to the nation and submission and obedience to the laws of the land as well as those made for war as those made for peace are not inconsistent with the will of God."[30]

This distressing assertion of the superiority of government over conscience brought forth a dissent by Chief Justice Hughes in which Justices Brandeis, Holmes and Stone concurred. The heart of the dissent reasoned as follows: "When one's belief collides with the power of the state the latter is supreme *within its sphere* and submission or punishment follows. But, in the forum of conscience, duty to a moral power higher than the state has always been maintained." [Emphasis supplied.][31] The autonomy of the state to matters only "within its sphere" is spelled out by Chief Justice Hughes when he asserts that there is no evidence that Congress intended to demand "that either citizens or applicants for citizenship shall assume by oath an obligation to regard allegiance to God as subordinate to allegiance to civil power." The Chief Justice noted that Congress has always sought to avoid conflicts with conscience and that "in no sphere of legislation has the intention to prevent such clashes been more conspicuous than in relation to the bearing of arms." Chief Justice Hughes stated furthermore that Justice Sutherland's reasoning was subversive of all real religion and presupposed that a *certain* conscience *must* be obeyed.

Fortunately what Chief Justice Hughes termed "our happy tradition" in "avoiding unnecessary clashes with the dictates of conscience" came to full flower in 1946 when the Supreme Court, concluding "that the Schwimmer, Macintosh . . . cases do not state the correct rule of law," granted citizenship to Canadian-born James L. Girouard who, for purely religious reasons, would agree in the event of war to serve as a noncombatant but not to bear arms.

Justice Douglas writing for a 5–3 majority, found that the Supreme Court could not assume that Congress had required a promise to bear arms as a prerequisite to citizenship. The Court could not assume "that Congress intended to make such an abrupt and radical departure from our tradition unless it spoke in unequivocal terms."[32] Although in its narrowest interpretation the line of cases ending in *Girouard* could be said to revolve around statutory construction, the over-all results are important in coming to an evaluation of the norms by which American law will judge the rights of those who resolutely refuse to give to Caesar those things which they deem to belong to God. Particularly significant is the following generalization written by Justice Douglas: "The struggle for religious liberty has through the centuries been an effort to accommodate the demands of the state to the conscience of the individual. The victories for freedom of thought recorded in our Bill of Rights recognize that in the domain of conscience there is a moral power higher than the state. Throughout the ages men have suffered death rather than subordinate their allegiance to God to the authority of the state. Freedom of religion guaranteed by the First Amendment is the product of that struggle."

On February 20, 1950, the Supreme Court broadened the immunities of conscientious objectors when, reversing the lower courts, it granted citizenship to Martin Ludwig Cohnstaedt,[33] a Quaker who had stated to immigration officials that he could not in conscience contribute anything which would be used directly and solely in furtherance of armed conflict. Cohnstaedt would, however, remove the wounded from battlefields if he could do so as a civilian. The absence of an opinion in the Supreme Court reversal left the new law on conscientious objectors very vague—especially on the important distinction between combatant and non-combatant duty. But the basic principle of not coercing conscience was reaffirmed and expanded.

Does the draft exemption granted to clergymen and divinity students, along with the concessions made to those with conscientious scruples about participating in war efforts, supply us with any principles which will illumine other areas of church–state relations where the aims of the two broadest agencies within our society have a less peaceful co-existence? I believe they do.

First, the unanimity of approval which has greeted the Supreme Court's concessions to the demands of the conscientious objectors indicates that the principles employed by the Court transcend all of the disputed principles which have always polarized the nation into rigorous church–state separationists and more moderate church–state co-operationists. It seems true to say that *every* theory of church–state relations in America holds as beyond dispute that the rights of the dissenting conscience should be accommodated whenever possible and even sometimes with great inconvenience.

Secondly, the major premises behind the term "the rights of conscience" seem to be shared by all Americans in such a profound and unanimous way that hopefully certain church–state impasses may receive some illumination from further explorations of the way in which respect for the rights of conscience has in the past resolved seemingly irreconcilable differences.

Thirdly, it is interesting to note that Justice Frankfurter, who had dissented in the *Girouard* case, joined the majority in the *Cohnstaedt* decision. Justice Frankfurter's shift in position here, however, does not alter his powerful dissent in the second flag-salute case[34] where he argued *against* excusing children, who were Jehovah's Witnesses, from saluting the flag. Some of the implications of the Supreme Court's decision exempting conscientious objectors from the flag-salute ceremony, as discerningly noted in Justice Frankfurter's dissent, will be discussed in a later part of this volume.

Finally, the concessions to conscience which we have discussed above have been granted ultimately only because jurists believed deeply and passionately in the merits of the claims of the spiritual order when they are in opposition to the temporal. Although the Constitution does not expressly affirm the supremacy of the spiritual over the temporal, it does so by implication in that the Supreme Court has ruled that the greatest consideration is to be extended to the citizen, religious or otherwise, whose conscience would be violated by compliance with a particular legal requirement.

Chaplains in Prisons and Military Installations

If tax exemption of religious groups is a "gloss" on the establishment clause, if draft immunity of clergymen and concessions to conscientious objectors indicate an expanding of the free exercise clause, then the existence of governmentally supported prison and military chaplains reveals an area where the guarantee of the free exercise of religion has been responsible for another seeming inconsistency in the no-aid-to-religion interpretation of the establishment clause.

As in other areas where a quiet church–state harmonization has taken place, very little is known about the origin, extent or financing of chaplains for state and Federal prisons, the justification for which is, of course, somewhat different than for chaplains in the Army or Navy.

In 1940, there were 106 full-time chaplains of all faiths for all of the state, Federal and correctional institutions of the country. By 1960, this number had increased to 170 full-time clergymen in addition to 190 part-time chaplains. A survey of the tax-financed salaries of these clergymen in the year 1959–1960 in the forty-five states reporting revealed the following facts:[35]

All states paid full-time chaplains an annual wage ranging up to $8,004 in Minnesota, $7,500 in Louisiana and $7,440 in Illinois. Chaplains' salaries in some states have recently been increased as, for example, in Massachusetts where a salary of $3,480 in 1959–1960 was advanced to $5,200 in 1961. In several states the prison chaplain shares in some of the benefits of state employees such as rights with regard to sick leave, vacation, health insurance and retirement. Jails and other short-term institutions are rarely provided with full-time chaplains although a new jail, opened in Miami in March, 1961, has a full-time chaplain and a chapel which seats a congregation of three hundred. New York City, because of its unique problems, makes use of thirty-two part-time chaplains of whom nine are Catholic, eight are Hebrew, nine are white Protestants and six are Negro Protestants. These part-time chaplains receive $2,390 annually. It is interesting to note that the 1959 report of New York City's Commissioner of Correction appeals for a "more realistic salary inducement" if there is to be "additional coverage to the inmates." Apparently the Commissioner felt that a higher salary would induce the part-time chaplains to spend more of their time in the prison ministry. All Federal penitentiaries and reformatories provide both Catholic and Protestant chaplains; Jewish chaplaincy service is provided on a part-time basis.

Although very little statutory or decisional law has accumulated about the subject of prison chaplains, provisions in two state constitutions are noteworthy. The Constitution of Michigan, although it forbids the appropriation of money for payment of any religious services in either House of the Legislature, expressly stipulates that "the Legislature may authorize the employment of a chaplain for each of the state prisons."[36] The Washington constitution specifies that its provision with regard to appropriations "shall not be so construed as to forbid the employment by the state of a chaplain for the state penitentiary, and for such of the state reformatories as in the discretion of the Legislature may seem justified."[37]

The only attack on the constitutionality of state funds for prison chapels and chaplains seems to have been the unsuccessful 1940 challenge of the New York League for the Separation of Church and State to the legality of the erection of the "Chapel of the Good Thief" on state property at the Clinton State Prison, Dannemora, New York.[38]

The work of prison chaplains has always been highly regarded by penal officials as is indicated in a revised statement on the matter adopted at the 90th Congress of Correction held in 1960. As one of the Declaration of Principles of the American Correctional Association, this professional organization of workers reaffirmed its traditional position in these words:[39] "Religion represents a rich resource in the moral and spiritual regeneration of mankind. Especially trained chaplains, religious instruction and counseling, together with adequate facilities for group worship of the inmate's own choice are essential elements in the program of a correctional institution."

In a "Manual of Correctional Standards" issued by the same organization recommendations concerning chaplains' salaries are made. After outlining the best procedures for recruiting the most competent chaplains into the field the following is stated concerning their salaries:

> In order to secure this type of chaplain it is necessary to pay a salary above that of the general level of salaries in fair-sized communities. Parti-time chaplains are ordinarily paid a fixed fee. This should not be on the minimum level but should be high enough to attract outstanding clergymen. Vacations with pay should be granted with the schedule allowed for professional staff members. . . .[40]

It has generally been assumed that a salary for a clergyman engaged at the state's request in a spiritual ministry to prisoners is more desirable both for church and state than to have a completely voluntary arrangement.

Justification for the virtually omnipresent practice of "employing" prison chaplains has not been elaborated in court decisions or law review articles. However, three justifying reasons would seem to be implicit in the practice: When the state deprives a citizen of his liberty, the state has the duty not to jeopardize the exercise of a citizen's right to religious freedom—a right which, unlike certain civic privileges, is not at all restricted by a person's imprisonment. If the state requests and receives a certain benefit from a specialist, the state should pay adequate compensation, even though the specialist is a clergyman. The rehabilitation of prisoners is of such urgent importance to the entire community that the state need not rely upon the zeal of individual church groups to evangelize their communicants when they are imprisoned; the state may take affirmative action and "use" the rehabilitating power of religion.

Comparable to the practice of all the states and the Federal government in financing the salaries of clergymen who exercise a ministry among those incarcerated for a crime is the custom which many states and cities follow of furnishing tax-supported chaplains for mental hospitals and even, in some cases, city hospitals of a general nature. Less, however, is discoverable about this area of church–state collaboration than is available concerning the ministry of religion in prisons.

In view of much psychiatric evidence that religion can frequently be of assistance to mentally disturbed persons, the employment of competent chaplains in mental hospitals can more easily be justified on a pragmatic basis than can the use of tax-supported chaplains for other types of activities. Federal hospitals and an apparently increasing number of state institutions for emotionally disturbed persons employ clergymen as chaplains. A survey made in 1940 shows that in twenty-two public general hospitals in New York City, with a total daily population of about 20,000 patients, several chaplains of all faiths received annual amounts ranging from $280 to $1,114. According to the figures available from the Department of Hospitals, in 1940 the city of New York paid out $15,888 for Protestant clergymen, $20,366 for Catholic priests, and $9,314 for Jewish chaplains.[41] Once again it appears that by custom and by a profound respect for the religious freedom of all persons who come within the guardianship of the state, many governmental units have specifically guaranteed that a minister of religion will be present to the sick and dying.

MILITARY CHAPLAINS. Although a few vigorous attempts have been made to abolish the system of publicly supported chaplains for the armed forces, the present system under which some three thousand clergymen, all commissioned officers on the Federal payroll, serve the spiritual needs of almost two million Americans, appears to be satisfactory to both sectarian and secular groups. John C. Bennett justifies the system in these words: "The military chaplaincy can be seen as an embodiment of the intentions of the American people in regard to religion. It is a form of actual aid, even financial aid, in effect, to the Churches, to all Churches on a proportional basis. It is an example of co-operation between church and state at a point where *both* have a stake in such cooperation. The Churches have a stake in providing pastoral services for their members and for all who will receive them. The state has a stake in the religious liberty of the citizen to engage in the 'free exercise' of religion in positive terms when he is in military service. A reasonable and impartial method of co-operation is called for by the situation and it is permitted by the words of the Constitution."[42]

Dean Bennett's explanation is the traditional one but the military chaplaincy has assumed such enormous consequences since World War II that a searching analysis of this phase of church–state relations is indicated. It may be that more can be observed about actual church–state affairs in America from studying military chaplaincies than can be seen in almost any other area.

The system began in 1899 when, for the first time, provision was made in Acts of Congress to secure ecclesiastical endorsement prior to the appointment of men as chaplains. With the advent of World War I, there emerged the Roman Catholic Military Ordinariate, the Chaplaincy Committee of the Jewish Welfare Board and the pan-Protestant General Commission on Chaplains. During World War I, some 2300 clergymen were commissioned as chaplains. After the war the need of a permanent organization prompted Congress to provide for a chief of chaplains with the rank of colonel.[43]

During the twenties there developed an intriguing debate in Protestant circles concerning the advisability of close cooperation between Christian ministers and the military. Considerable sentiment for a civilian chaplaincy developed but World War II came about before its advocates within the Federal Council of Churches could change the climate of opinion. The second war and its aftermath have resulted in a quasi-permanent government roster of some

3000 chaplains in seventy-two countries with an additional 300 chaplains serving as civil service employees on the staff of 176 Veterans' Administration hospitals and homes. Some 2100 of the 3000 military chaplains and 210 of the 300 Veterans' Administration chaplains are Protestant clergymen.

All chapels for all three branches of the armed forces are constructed at government expense. No complete figures are available on the cost of chapel construction. The Army alone, however, in 1956 built several chapels and related buildings at a cost of $5,-367,000. Dr. Marion Creeger, the executive secretary of the General Commission on Chaplains and Armed Forces Personnel, estimated in 1959 the annual cost to the Federal government of religion in the armed forces to be around $100,000,000.

There is some possibility of the rise of a career clergyman in the armed forces, although all religious organizations are seeking to avoid such an eventuality. Most sectarian groups urge their personnel to enter the chaplaincy for a period; Jewish units, for example, require all rabbis to serve as chaplains for a period shortly after their theological training is finished.

No evidence has been found that any clergyman has ever refused to accept the officer's remuneration which his commission includes. Despite the historical position of some few sectarian groups that they cannot in conscience accept state support, ministers of every denomination enter the chaplaincy and accept remuneration.

No criticism is thereby justified of the participants in the chaplaincy corps nor of the forms which it has assumed in the difficult generation since the end of World War II. But if we are to remain with the traditional justification for tax support of the religious ministry, then the implications of that justification should be thoroughly comprehended. As noted above by Dean Bennett, the Federal government has customarily supplied chaplains to men in the military lest otherwise their religious freedom be impinged upon.

Does the chaplaincy situation offer relevant analogies for less tranquil church–state areas? Assuming that chaplaincies are, as Dean Bennett wrote, "permitted by the words of the Constitution" does it follow that citizens, not in the military but rather at paramilitary civilian installations working on nuclear research or related problems, are receiving less than their share of implemented religious freedom from the government? If such individuals have received an occupational deferment from the military, or if their position would not exist but for the nation's war effort, then should these individuals receive less protection of their religious liberty simply because their greater intellectual ability kept them out of actual military service?

The central question comes to this. If the government has an obligation to facilitate the "free exercise" of religion by those in its military forces, must not this obligation, by reason of equal protection, be extended to others who, by a different type of state action, are also in danger of having their right to "free exercise" of religion nullified or restricted?

The strict church–state separationist would reject this analogy stating that it is the usual attempt of a religionist to construct from one deviation from the establishment clause a second deviation. The fact is, however, that a major—indeed a monumental —support is being given through military chaplains to religion in the name of the "free exercise" clause. And whenever a benefit, presumably valid, is given to one class, the fair-minded person must either state that the benefit should be withdrawn or that comparable benefits should be given to those who are similarly situated.

Tax Assistance for the Work of Sectarian Social Agencies

Although tax exemption for religious institutions, draft immunity for clergymen and publicly supported chaplains have been the subject of some church–state discussion, the close liaison between government and religion in the field of social work has hardly ever been regarded as a friction point in church–state relations. However, the extent to which tax money finances the work of sectarian social welfare agencies is most substantial. A long tradition of co-operation between voluntary sectarian agencies and public welfare officials has apparently been of such a harmonious nature that little disagreement seems to have occurred over church–state problems. There exists, to be sure, a conflict between schools of thought concerning the relative roles of public vis-à-vis private agencies, but this conflict does not center on a legal or constitutional problem.

A 1961 study by Dr. Ruth M. Werner of the amount of public financing of voluntary agencies indicates that these units, "generally sponsored by religious groups, believe that all children of their faith should be cared for by agencies representing the same faith."[44]

Something of the extent of the utilization of voluntary agencies can be seen from the following: All but four states (Arkansas, Mississippi, Nebraska and Nevada) supplement public services in connection with foster family care by the use of voluntary agencies.[45] In the forty-two states which reported for a survey issued in 1962 by the Children's Bureau of the U.S. Department of Health, Education and Welfare, 66 per cent of the children received services primarily from public agencies and 34 per cent from voluntary agencies.[46] In New York City in February, 1962, there were a total of 18,756 children under care outside their homes as charges of the Department of Welfare. Of these 17,015 or 90.7 per cent were being cared for under the auspices of voluntary agencies.[47]

The involvement of church–related social agencies in tax-financed programs may be seen from the report of the Hearings held in February, 1962, before the Committee on Ways and Means of the U.S. House of Representatives. The subject was H.R. 10032, a bill to increase the Federal participation in various social welfare programs. Official representatives of Protestant, Catholic and Jewish organizations spoke on behalf of the legislation, affirming in their testimony their deep commitment to the importance of the role of the voluntary social welfare agency in all tax-financed plans to extend greater social security to those in need. The church–state alliance in the social welfare field, so clearly endorsed in these hearings, is worthy of some attention.

Speaking on behalf of the National Council of Churches was Bradshaw Minterer, chairman of the Department of Social Welfare of the NCC and Assistant Secretary of Health, Education and Welfare from 1954 to 1956. Citing a June, 1958, statement of the general board of the National Council of Churches entitled "A Pronouncement of the Churches' Concern for Public Assistance," Mr. Minterer noted that this document, in urging Protestant social welfare agencies to continue and intensify their work, affirmed that "the people who receive public assistance benefits ordinarily have special needs in addition to money."[48] Pursuant to this affirmation, Protestants and members of the Eastern Orthodox religion have developed some 4000 church-related health and welfare agencies, virtually all of which accept substantial sums of tax money in partial return for the services they render.

Challenged by a member of Congress on the committee as to

whether the tax-financed Protestant agencies raise a church–state question, the representative of the Protestant churches of America replied without elaboration that the newly proposed program which he endorsed would not, in his estimation, result "in any clash between church and state."

Mr. Minterer issued a policy statement which is worth quoting in full because of its possible applicability to church-related schools. Speaking for the National Council of Churches he stated:[49]

We have reason to believe that our constituency is in substantial agreement regarding certain principles which should guide church-related health and welfare agencies in the acceptance of tax funds. There is general agreement that church-related agencies may accept per diem payments on a case-by-case basis for services purchased by government for individuals, under the following conditions: (A) That the policies and procedures are not interfered with beyond minimum standards . . . and providing that the agency accepts its responsibility to report fully on individual cases as may be required by government. (B) That the individual served has the right *insofar as possible* to choose the agency which is to perform the service. [Emphasis supplied.] (C) That the agency is making available to the total community in competent fashion an essential community service. (D) That the acceptance of such funds by a church-related agency should not mean that the possibility of public provision for such services is thereby ruled out. (E) That in its over-all financing, the agency should not become financially dependent upon the per diem payments by government for its continuance as an agency. (F) That this compensation is not used for religious ministrations.

Although the suggested conditions under which church–related agencies should receive tax support seem commendable, there is some truth in the comment that the church–state alliance in this field is deemed legitimate co-operation and not compromise because all church groups are involved in operating hundreds of social welfare agencies.

The Council of Jewish Federations and Welfare Funds also testified on behalf of H.R. 10032. Representing 215 Jewish social agencies operating on a budget annually exceeding $250,000,000 the Council's President and spokesman, Mr. Irving Kane, welcomed a greater financial participation by the Federal government in the work of Jewish health and welfare agencies.[50] Similarly, Mrs. Charles Hymes, President of the National Council of Jewish

Women, a group with a membership of 123,000 in 329 affiliated local units, commended the general approach of the Administration-sponsored H.R. 10032 and noted with approbation its continuation and broadening of the use of voluntary social welfare agencies.[51]

The National Conference of Catholic Charities confirmed what the Protestant and Jewish spokesmen had said about the advisability of utilizing voluntary social agencies. The Secretary of the Conference, Rt. Rev. Msgr. Raymond J. Gallagher, after presenting his views on H.R. 10032, was asked to comment on any church–state problems which he might see in connection with the use of Federal funds to assist the work of church-related social agencies. Monsignor Gallagher stated that the traditional terms of the relationship between the government and a sectarian agency "would indicate that it is carefully spelled out so that none of the money obviously is used for the promotion of religious purposes *per se*."[52] The Catholic spokesman went on to say that there "does not seem to be any great reality to the danger of losing one's autonomy" on the part of the agency nor does the state feel that, by employing the services of a voluntary agency, it is "supporting a religion."[53]

No secular or sectarian group has urged any substantial reversal of the basic national policy of employing voluntary and sectarian social agencies. The utilization of voluntary agencies has for so long been so fundamental a part of America's way of handling the unfortunate that even the most rigorous advocates of the "no-aid-to-religion" version of the First Amendment do not insist that *all* social service be performed through public agencies alone. Some, however, like Philip Jacobson, program co-ordinator of the National Community Relations Advisory Council, have pointed out that the acceptance of government funds by religiously sponsored agencies violates the separation of church and state. Mr. Jacobson does not advocate any "abrupt withdrawal" or immediate change in the universally accepted practice of taking government funds, but his belief that "a truly religious undertaking should not require the aid of the state," leads him to assert that if a voluntary social welfare agency accepts state funds it should remove "Baptist or Methodist or Catholic or Jewish from its name and stop holding itself out to the public as religious in character."[54]

Public involvements with the state which might result from the acceptance of tax money by sectarian social agencies have troubled the consciences of the religiously dedicated workers in this difficult field. The seemingly ever more impossible task of caring for the sick, the dependent, the emotionally disturbed and especially the aged without some sort of government subsidy has apparently led most social workers to the conclusion that the sectarian agencies are in effect quasi-public community agencies managed by the church as a contribution to the welfare of society.

A conscientious and realistic examination of this problem can be seen in an article, "Public Financing and Church Responsibility," by Spencer E. Braden, a social work executive, in the *Lutheran Social Welfare Quarterly*.[55] Mr. Braden reports the present dilemma of the social agencies as follows: "In most church agencies and institutions, the mere mention of public funds has stirred a theological conscience." Whenever such money has been sought or accepted, some have wrestled with fears and feelings of guilt. In the end the funds have generally been accepted, but they have been accepted with a certain uneasiness."[56]

Mr. Braden adds that the "amount of these public fund subsidies has become so great and has been allowed to become such an integral part of fiscal operational policies that its elimination would mean some very drastic changes in the patterns of operation and management."[57] He concludes that either the agency must accept public funds or "close down its agencies completely . . . and relegate the whole function to government." Neither of these alternatives "seems very palatable," Mr. Braden feels.

The four subjects which have been explored—tax exemption, draft immunity, tax-supported chaplaincies and government assistance to sectarian social agencies—indicate areas where a Protestant-Catholic-Jewish consensus has remained remarkably unchanged over a long period. The consensus has extended to nonbelievers, to strict separationists and to virtually all of America's citizens to such an extent that one could safely state that these four areas of church–state harmony are, at least for the present, beyond dispute.

Are there any common underlying factors present in these four phases of peaceful co-existence which could be transferred to areas more scarred by controversy? The possibility of such transference will reoccur through the rest of this volume; hopefully, analogies and insights can be explored, and the results might alleviate some of the neuralgic points in church–state tensions.

The American Protestant attitude toward the state, however, is too replete with complexities and inconsistencies to permit of much generalization. The customary Protestant insistence that the work of the church is demeaned and impeded by state assistance quite understandably has broken down in confrontation with the imperatives of a modern welfare state armed to the teeth because of the Communist menace.

Some other conclusions seem appropriate. The churches of America have *not* allowed the state to take over all those areas of health and welfare services in which the church has always been active; in fact, the abdication of the church to the state in the matter of the secular education of youth seems to be almost the one case in America where the non-Catholic churches have declined to insist upon the role of the voluntary agency.

An untroubled church–state concord can exist in those areas of mutual concern in which all the major religions continue to claim a vital partnership with the state. As soon as one of the major religious groups secedes from the partnership, however, church–state problems seem to arise.

The intricacy of the church–state relationships in actual practice is so complex that it seems artificial and unrealistic to try to resolve every tension in a situation delicately balanced against the legalistic and still ambiguous formulas evolved from the interpretations of the establishment and free exercise of religion clauses of the First Amendment, as elaborated by the United States Supreme Court in its six church–state cases from *Everson* (1947) to *Engel* (1962). A warning given by Justice Frankfurter has particular application in this matter: "Preoccupation by our people," wrote Frankfurter, "with the constitutionality, instead of with the wisdom, of legislation or executive action is preoccupation with a false value."[58]

Finally, no sect has ever existed in American history which on principle has rejected every benevolence of a government committed by law and tradition to extend the horizons of religious freedom. On the other hand, not a single example can be cited where the Federal or state government has ever, in return for assistance rendered, sought to influence church bodies to support the state in anything contrary to their principles.

Other Church–State Ententes

As Justice Douglas noted in his concurring opinion in the New York public school prayer case decided on June 25, 1962, the whole structure of our government is "honeycombed" with expenditures of state funds for purposes in which religion is intermingled.[59] The four areas described above may be major islands of church–state peace in America but there are countless other instances, almost down to the interstices of American life, where religion and government collaborate in a mutually harmonious and beneficial way. Among them the following are noteworthy:

It is significant that President Kennedy in September, 1961, signed into law a bill establishing a three-year, $30,000,000 program to combat juvenile delinquency. The program provides that one third of the total sum appropriated will be spent annually over a period of three years for public and private agencies' demonstration projects in delinquency control. No ban on sectarian agencies is contained in the act which will be administered by the Department of Health, Education and Welfare.

Although some commentators tend to belittle "Washington piety" and the importance of Congressional, Presidential or other official proclamations of days of prayer it is important to note, nonetheless, that President Kennedy issued a request prior to Memorial Day, 1962, that the hour of 11:00 A.M. on May 30 be set aside in each locality as a time to "unite in prayer for success in our search for a just and lasting peace."[60]

The conscientious agnostic could object that the money and, more importantly, the enormous prestige of the office of the President should not be given to an endorsement of the efficacy of prayer. But at least until the Supreme Court opinion in the New York prayer case on June 25, 1962, religious ceremonials employed in the public life of America were always the most accepted and the least controverted of the nation's religious symbols.

Other "aids" to religion exist at all levels of government. The Bible is used for the administration of oaths. NYA and WPA funds were available both to public and parochial schools during the depression period. Religious organizations are given special postal privileges. There are no limits to the deductibility of gifts and bequests to religious institutions under the Federal gift and estate tax laws.

Rigorists in church–state separation have not questioned the practice of tax-financed public libraries purchasing and displaying sectarian books and periodicals. Such aid to religions—done presumably on an across-the-board basis—can be justified, of course, on the grounds that religion as an integral and important part of our culture may not reasonably be neglected. But a more separationist view could suggest that the diversion of library funds to the purchase of religious books and periodicals is not only preferring religionists, but is depriving the entire community of the availability of other secular books and periodicals which could be otherwise purchased.

Another form of indirect state aid to religion may be seen in the custom of many public libraries accepting the gift of a religious book or sectarian periodical and then displaying it along with other tax-purchased items with whatever endorsement is given to a library-circulated piece of literature.

In 1946, it was evident to all leaders in the health and hospital fields that, because of the difficulties in hospital construction during the depression and the war, there existed an acute shortage of hospital facilities. With the unanimous endorsement of hospital experts, including the American Medical Association, Congress enacted, in 1946, the Hill-Burton Hospital Construction Act. This law provided for the expenditure of from one-third to two-thirds of the funds required to equip or build hospitals within designated areas of need. Every private, "nonprofit" group was declared eligible to receive Federal funds if its state's department of health approved of the medical standards of the particular group.

The highest court of Kentucky[61] has sustained grants to Episcopalian and Catholic hospitals, while the Supreme Court of Missouri[62] ruled against the contention of the Attorney General of that state that Missouri's constitution proscribed a Federal–state grant to a sectarian hospital.

There seems to be a substantial consensus, except among some Southern Baptists and some very rigorous church–state separationists, that the Hill-Burton formula is a desirable one. When the church–state issue was introduced into a discussion of a proposed grant on the floor of the United States Senate on October 16, 1951, by Senator Olin D. Johnston of South Carolina, Senator Herbert Lehman of New York replied: "I am astounded and distressed that the question of religious denomination has been brought into this debate. To me there does not appear to be the slightest reason to suppose that the provisions of the bill contravene the First Amendment to the Constitution."[63]

The Hill-Burton formula was not designed to assist church-related hospitals. It simply confronted realistically the fact that a hospital, fully approved *as a hospital* by the proper authorities, should not be refused Federal-state funds because the church, to which the hospital was affiliated, would be barred *as a church* from receiving any tax support.

It is significant to note that the United States Supreme Court, in late 1962, refused to review a case from Kentucky where Federal–state funds had been utilized to construct a hospital which was then leased to an order of Catholic nuns for a nominal sum. The highest court of Kentucky concluded that no constitutional problem arises if a state allows a charitable organization to conduct a publicly built hospital when the state is not financially able to carry on the maintenance of the institution which it was able to construct.[64]

One could enumerate many more "aids" to religion besides these five categories. In these and other spheres of life, an obvious harmonization of the purposes of church and state has been attained. No one has seriously contended that the autonomy of religion has thereby been subverted or even weakened, nor that the state has failed to perform all its duties to its citizens. A partnership between the moral powers of the state and the spiritual powers of the church for a common purpose is not to be condemned unless it clearly subverts or weakens the mission of one of the participating parties.

Whenever it is discovered that state funds have been financing religious activities the almost instinctive reaction of some persons is to suggest a deficiency in the faith of the religionists involved who have, it is presumed, accepted a gratuity in order to save themselves from a contribution which otherwise they would be required to make. Anyone seeking to show that such a reaction is not necessarily a proper one has the burden of arguing against a quasi-theological dogma of American life that church activities are of a private character to which the state can be indifferent.

A fixation on separationism in church–state relations has obscured the fact that the American state, in its legitimate and duty-bound mission to promote the physical and spiritual health of its people, encourages all types of nonprofit activities. Religious groups are entitled to share at least the prestige given to other nonprofit organizations.

In some ways the universal desire to be fair to all groups of Christians, and even more so to all non-Christians, has brought about a paralysis in clear thinking and action. Accompanying and deepening this paralysis is a widespread attitude which assumes that the relationship of church and state is basically a legal issue and that the primary and perhaps the only principle involved is "no-aid-to-religion." This enormous oversimplification seems to be an atmospheric fallout from the decisions of the Supreme Court on the establishment clause, and the several publicists who have popularized from these decisions only those dicta which support a doctrinaire theory of a "wall of separation."

The review above of some of the areas where church and state have been friendly partners in projects of mutual concern would not be complete without noting that the United States Supreme Court, in its entire history, has never actually declared unconstitutional even one state financial benefit granted to religion. The one possible exception to this generalization is the *McCollum* decision where the Court ruled that tax-supported public school property could not be utilized for classes in sectarian instruction. No actual disbursements of money were involved in the *McCollum* case, however, since the participating churches assumed all but the insignificant cost of heat, light, etc., which would have been spent even if released-time classes did not operate.

Yet even conceding that the *McCollum* decision may have been the one example where the Supreme Court *did* invalidate an expenditure of state money for religious purposes, the *Zorach* opinion—four years after *McCollum*—shows, in the opinion of Leo Pfeffer, "some retreat from the broad scope of the *Everson-McCollum* principle."[65] And *Zorach* did, of course, permit released-time religious education so long as it was conducted off the school premises.

In every other case before the Supreme Court, actual expenditures to religious groups—*all* of them, incidentally, involving Catholic organizations—have been sustained. In 1899, the Court upheld a grant of Federal funds for the benefit of a hospital controlled by a corporation organized by an order of Catholic nuns.[66] In 1908, the Supreme Court ruled that funds held by the Federal government as trustee for the Sioux Indians, who were the real owners of the funds, could be disbursed to Catholic schools as payment of tuition.[67] In 1930, the Court sustained a Louisiana law granting secular textbooks to children in Catholic schools;[68] in 1947, the same tribunal held that the payment out of public funds of the expense of transporting children to parochial schools did not violate the First Amendment.[69]

We conclude, therefore, that the separation of church and state has never once in Supreme Court jurisprudence proscribed an actual expenditure of state funds for legitimate secular purposes even if a religious group may thereby benefit. No friendly alliance between church and state has ever been interdicted—although the Supreme Court has warned more than once that it is prepared to do so if necessary.

Although one would wish that friendly alliances of the nature we have discussed would permeate all of American church–state relations, such unfortunately is not the case. All three major religious groups have very fundamental church–state problems; all three groups have been before the Supreme Court seeking to discover what American law will decide about their claims. In each instance, however, the decision has not been entirely satisfactory.

Protestants find their fundamental problem in the place of religion in public education; the *McCollum* opinion, modified by *Zorach* but reinforced by *Engel*, gives some solution but presents serious difficulties. Catholics confront their basic problem in the financing of parochial schools for some 6,000,000 children; the *Everson* opinion said that child-welfare benefits are permissible but left doubts about further financial aid. Jews have the problem of being required by their religion to abstain from labor on Saturday and being obliged by law to refrain from business activities on Sunday; the Supreme Court has denied that Jews and other Sabbatarians have the right, by reason of the "free exercise" of religion clause of the First Amendment, to transact business on Sunday even though they refrain from business on Saturday.[70]

Each of the three major religious groups in this country therefore has a complex problem and a profound anxiety about what the law, the Supreme Court and their coreligionists will decide in the future concerning the validity of their claims to what they conceive to be their own free exercise, under the Constitution, of the religious faith to which they have given their allegiance and their whole lives. The analysis and exploration of these three anxieties will be the subject of the next three sections of this study.

(As of December 21, 1960, the total funds allocated to church–state related hospitals under the Hill-Burton Act, as compiled from the Register of the United States Department of Health, Education and Welfare, were as follows:)

	Total number of Church-related hospitals	Per cent of total	Number who received Hill-Burton funds	Per cent of total	Total amount received
Protestant	662	41.2	236	37.2	$112,505,669
Catholic	889	55.3	370	58.4	$202,775,912
Jewish	57	3.5	28	4.4	$ 14,588,744
Total	1608	100	634	100	$329,870,325

Religion
in Public Education

THE PUBLIC SCHOOL IN AMERICAN HISTORY

Of the many values which the American public school is expected to communicate to its students none is more universally accepted than a profound reverence for democracy. Included in this value is the patriotism and Americanism which every product of the public school is assumed to possess.

Beyond these basic generalities, however, any discussion as to what values the American public school is designed to communicate leads one into a sea of contradictions, ambiguities and confusion.

The public school has meant something different in every generation. In each age it has reflected the ethos of its dominant group of the teachers. This helps to explain why John Dewey's attitudes and philosophy had such an impact on public education in the middle years of the first half of this century. His thought, and especially his book *Democracy and Education*, made explicit what was implicit in Dewey's generation within the social, economic and political developments of the nation.

If, then, the public schools in each generation are a mirror reflecting the general attitudes and morality of the society of that age, where does one begin to discuss the place which religion has had and should have in the vast network of public schools now attended by almost every fourth person in America?

It is a great deal easier to describe the place which religion and moral values have had in the public school of the past than it is to describe what place they have, or should have, in the contemporary public school. The pan-Protestant movement which created the common or public school imparted to that institution the task of creating from the nation's young people a generation of educated scholars and virtuous citizens. It seems unlikely that any nation has expected more than America has from its public schools. They have long since become more than an educational medium, assuming some of the characteristics of a sacred institution or even of a quasi religion. Yet in a profoundly religious nation the public school has become progressively secularized.

It would be helpful for purposes of discussion if we could simply classify the public school as a secular school. Justice Jackson implied this view in his dissent in the *Everson* case in these words: "Our public school . . . is organized on the premise that secular education can be isolated from all religious teaching so that the school can inculcate all needed temporal knowledge and also maintain a strict and lofty neutrality to religion."[1] Leo Pfeffer endorsed this viewpoint when he wrote, "The American public school is a secular school. . . . The Catholic Church, and probably most of the Protestant churches, as well, undoubtedly do not approve of its secularity. Yet secular it is, in curriculum, method and spirit."[2]

If the assertions of Justice Jackson and Mr. Pfeffer were completely valid, a discussion of the place of religion in the public school would be relatively uncomplicated. But, as Justice Jackson subsequently pointed out in his concurring opinion in the *McCollum* decision, there are many reasons why it is not possible "completely to isolate and cast out of secular education all that some people may reasonably regard as religious instruction." Justice Jackson continued: "One can hardly respect a system of education that would leave the student wholly ignorant of the currents of religious thought that move the world society, for a part in which he is being prepared."[3]

The thorny problem of dealing with religion in the public school has received several attempted solutions. All of them have left educators, religionists and jurists dissatisfied both as to their effectiveness and their constitutionality. The Supreme Court has on three occasions confronted two of these "solutions," released-time and a nondenominational prayer. We shall explore these opinions later, but first we shall turn to the most important problem in the public school today—*what moral and spiritual values are these state agencies mandated and/or permitted to transmit?* This is the central question in church–state relations in American education. It has, however, never been litigated—possibly because the full importance and implications of the problem have never been adequately investigated.

Before coming, however, to the various specific methods devised to integrate religion with the education offered in the public school, some preliminary observations and some surprising paradoxes regarding the public school may be worth recording:

When virtually all states in the latter half of the nineteenth century enacted laws forbidding grants of tax money to private schools, the people of America—in an act designed in part to stifle Catholic education—granted to local officials a monopoly over one of the greatest enterprises of American life. Some few matters affecting a relatively large number of citizens had indeed, prior to this time, been given over to the Federal and state governments. But never in American history was there such a complete transfer from the people to the state of such a delicate and universal function as the education of the nation's youth. This transfer, as it happened in nineteeenth century America, brought about results never intended by the participants. The reasons and background of that transfer have been explored elsewhere,[4] but it must be noted that the state monopoly on education which now obtains in America was not intended by the officials of church or state who inadvertently created it.

The victory attained by the lobbyists of the last century for the various amendments to the state constitutions forbidding aid to sectarian schools is possibly the most dramatic example in the nation's history of legislation through collective national anxiety. The anxiety grew out of the fear that the nation's unity—then recently threatened by the Civil War—would not be secure, that the Protestant nature of the country might diminish and that European languages and customs might persist and create certain cultural "pockets" within the land. The "anti-aid" amendments, in which most Protestant groups acquiesced, gave a type of monopoly on education to the state. These constitutional amendments supply one of the strongest proofs of the Protestant expectation in the last century that the government which they had created was a state basically friendly to Protestantism and all its institutions. In agreeing to the secularization of education, Protestant sects did not perceive that they were in effect surrendering to Caesar some of the things which belonged to God. Or if they did so perceive, then they felt that Caesar was on the side of God.

In view of the history behind the transfer, it is not strange that Protestants have always looked upon the public school as a unique challenge for their apostolic zeal. It is curious and a bit tragic, although not entirely surprising, to read today of Protestant officials who deplore the fact that more Protestants are not entering the teaching profession for service in the public schools.

Because Protestants in the last century deliberately chose the common school as the *one* educational institution worthy of tax support, and because they have always maintained an informal guardianship over their creation, it sometimes appears that criticism of the public school—especially by Catholics—is in effect criticism of the Protestant origin and guardianship of the nation's public schools. Although it may be unavoidable that some non-Catholics will so construe critical observations of this kind, the fundamental basis for all criticism of the public schools' approach to religion and morality does not center on the Protestant origin or orientation of these schools, but rather on the inherently intractable task assigned to them.

MORAL AND SPIRITUAL VALUES IN TAX-SUPPORTED SCHOOLS

One of the greatest anxieties of Protestant Christianity in America has been the attitude which the public school should adopt towards religion. For several reasons the Protestant churches in America have not been as successful with frequent after-school religious instruction as the Jews have been, nor have many Protestants followed the example of the Catholics in establishing their own school system. The attitude which the public school takes toward religion, therefore, is more crucial for Protestants than for other religious groups in America. It is consequently quite understandable that there has always been a tendency on the part of some Protestants to introduce into the public school truths, values and practices of Protestant Christianity. Indeed, in view of the complex cross-fertilization of Protestantism and Americanism, it would be expected that the American public school would to some extent mirror the attitudes of the Protestant churches.

It seems fair to say that until around 1900 the public school in America taught little that was really inconsistent with Protestant Christianity and that, in fact, many of the lessons from McGuffey's readers and other texts reiterated to some extent the lessons of many Protestant primers. But after 1900 the silently accepted alliance between Protestant Christianity and the American public school began to erode and even to disappear. One could theorize that the "multiple establishment" of religion in a pan-Protestant, nondenominational public school was of such a nebulous nature that its disintegration was inevitable. Or one could, with equally probative evidence, demonstrate that the onslaught of naturalism, combined with a certain fragmentation within Protestantism, would by itself have sufficed to effect the erosion of Protestant Christian values in the public schools. In any event, the fact is that at the present time many if not most Protestants are asking for the insertion of religious if not sectarian values in the schools, Jewish groups are opposing the adoption of all values even remotely sectarian, while Catholics assert that theistic values can and must be communicated in the public schools of America.

It seems likely that only time and the growth of a consensus of opinion can resolve the dilemmas of the public school with respect to religious values. It seems clear, moreover, that the law can do little to regulate a situation so inherently complex and so replete with competing and conflicting rights. Indeed, the law, both statutory and decisional, has traditionally said remarkably little about the content of the public school curriculum. There exists a small body of law at the state level concerning topics related to this subject, but not until the *McCollum* decision in 1948 did the United States Supreme Court ever make a pronouncement on the curriculum of the public school. Prior to this time, legal directives on this matter never advanced beyond vague exhortations to teach morality and patriotism while shunning sectarianism.

Some fifteen years and five church–state decisions after *McCollum*, many have come to assume that an outlook on church–state relations, so repeatedly reaffirmed by the Supreme Court, is not now open to re-examination. Indeed, suggestions that *McCollum* was decided wrongly and that at least its spirit should be reversed sometimes elicit a great deal of abuse upon the person so arguing.

But is it not reasonable for a commentator to urge that the Supreme Court, as it has done in the past, embraced a fundamental error at the beginning of the series of cases that started at *Everson* and continued through *Engel*, the antiprayer decision of June 25, 1962?

The fact remains, however, that *McCollum* must be faced and its incredibly sweeping affirmations re-examined. But before we come to that subject, we must analyze the positions of sectarian and educational groups regarding the place of religion in the public school. Three intermingled but distinct forces have been operating in connection with the discussion of what treatment the tax-supported school may extend to religion. The first is the broad endorsement of religious values and the encouragement of education in the *relevance* of religion, as recommended by the classic study of the American Council on Education. The second is the admittedly sectarian approach from which released-time religious instruction has emerged. The third is the relatively new state-sponsored codes of moral and spiritual values prescribed for public school personnel. A somewhat detailed treatment of each of these attitudes towards religion in public education may be of assistance in trying to comprehend the complexity of the intertwining of the secular and the sacred in American education.

Endorsement of Religious Values

The zeal of a dedicated Christian and his candor in seeking to communicate his faith is evident in the following statement written in 1943 by a prominent Protestant religious educator, Erwin L. Shaver:[5]

The fifty percent of our children who are not now receiving any training in religion because of parental neglect or other reasons should not be denied this most important element in their complete social history. When parental indifference or other circumstance has failed to give a child a healthy body, society has stepped in—by means of private or public agencies—to see that he has soundness of health. The same principle has been applied in giving every child his mental training, regardless of whether parents cared or could afford it. This has been done because the welfare of society is at stake. Social welfare is jeopardized as much or even more *if any child is denied his right to know and to make use of all that society has learned in the area of religion.* [Emphasis supplied.]

Mr. Shaver, in the quotation cited, is merely arguing on behalf of released time but the thrust of his argument extends beyond that. He asserts by implication that a completely secular school may be responsible for denying to a child "his right to know" about religion. Not only is the child deprived of his right to know, but the "social welfare is jeopardized" more by this denial than if the child were refused the means to maintain health or secure an education. Pressing Mr. Shaver's analogy a bit further it might also be possible to conclude from it that the state has a duty to assist the child in "his right to know" about "*all* that society has learned in the area of religion." In any event, Mr. Shaver, along with countless other educators, expresses the view that religion is a "most important element," the neglect of which will lead to the same consequences for society as will the neglect of the health or education of our youth.

Equally sincere individuals, with a more secularistic outlook, would question this statement and would urge that among the "other reasons" noted by Mr. Shaver is apathy on the part of the churches or indifference by the laity. The advocates of no-religion-in-public-education would insist that any appeal by religious bodies to the schools for assistance in reaching the "fifty percent . . . who are not now receiving religion" betrays a weakness in the sectarian groups who seek an alliance with the public school.

Admittedly there is truth on both sides of the dispute. But the religionists, regardless of whatever heroic zeal they may possess, confront in the public school an instrument which, unintentionally and inadvertently, may render very difficult and even impossible the implementation of the child's "right to know" about religion. In November, 1947, Harry Emerson Fosdick noted this point when he wrote that: "Public schools that rigorously exclude religion are not neutral; the dice are loaded against religion."[6] The same writer quotes approvingly a statement by Luther A. Weigle, former dean of the Yale Divinity School: "The ignoring of religion by the public schools inevitably conveys to the children a negative suggestion. They cannot help but notice the omission. It is bound to discredit religion in their minds. It is natural for them to conclude that religion is negligible, or unimportant, or irrelevant to the main business of life."[7]

Fosdick and Weigle seem to separate on the possibility of a common religious faith suitable for communication in the public schools. Dean Weigle sums up a frequently repeated affirmation and an even more frequently expressed aspiration when he writes:

Underlying all our differences, America has a common religious faith— common not in the sense that everybody shares it, for there are some among us who deny or ignore God; but in the sense that it is common to the three great religious groups—Protestant, Catholic and Jewish— to which the great majority of American citizens profess to belong. These citizens—Catholic, Protestant and Jew—worship the one God, Creator of all things and Father of man. They believe that His will has been revealed in the life and literature of the Hebrew people as this is recorded in the Bible, and that it is discernible in nature about us and in conscience within. They acknowledge the principle of human duty set forth in the Ten Commandments, in the Golden Rule, and in the law of love to God and fellow men. They sing hymns and psalms that transcend differences of creed. They can all unite in the Lord's Prayer: "Our Father who art in heaven . . . Thy kingdom come. Thy will be done."[8]

At its best, this "common religious faith" allows a public school teacher to convey certain attenuated truths not susceptible of very critical analysis; at its worst, the selection of those things "common to the three great religious groups" blurs all the profound differences of understanding with respect to them and thereby distorts and devaluates them.

But the truths in Dean Weigle's affirmation, while containing within themselves the seeds of falsehood, have always so impressed American public school educators that it is difficult to say how many of them would disagree with this description of America's "common religious faith." At least Protestants would be less divided on its acceptability than would Catholics, while Jews would be much more likely to raise serious objections to the statement as constituting the incipient creation of an ersatz public school religion.

The distinguished American Council on Education, after a lengthy study by a large and learned group, issued a statement[9] in April, 1947, which is possibly the strongest denunciation of secularism in education ever issued in modern times by any non-church-related group.

After rejecting secularism in remarkably vigorous terms, the report observes:

1. The problem is to find a way in public education to give recognition to the place of religion in the culture and in the convictions of our people while at the same time safeguarding the separation of church and state.

2. Teaching a common core of religious beliefs in public schools is not a satisfactory solution.

3. Teaching "moral and spiritual values" cannot be regarded as an adequate substitute for an appropriate consideration of religion in the school program.[10]

Having postulated these general principles the Committee went on to make the affirmative conclusion that: ". . . among the results which the community has a right to look for in the graduates of its schools is a positive attitude towards the values that religion represents in our culture."[11]

In another section of the report the Committee advances further and states: "For us the democratic faith means that the worth of persons and the increasing perfectability of human institutions rests on a religious conception of human destiny. We believe that the Judaeo-Christian affirmation that man is a child of God expresses an authentic insight which underlies all particular theological formulas.

"We further believe that many of those who are valiantly for the democratic cause under wholly nonreligious slogans are unconsciously trading on 'borrowed capital' that has been furnished by the religious tradition of the culture."[12]

In a later report on the same problem the Committee added, ". . . to be silent about religion may be, in effect, to make the public school an antireligious factor in the community. Silence creates the impression in the minds of the young that religion is unimportant and has nothing to contribute to the solution of the perennial and ultimate problems of human life. This negative consequence is all the more striking in a period when society is asking the public school to assume more and more responsibility for dealing with the cultural problems of growth and development."[13]

It is a simple task to point out ambiguities in this report of the American Council on Education.[14] It may be that the fundamental weakness of the report lies in the fact that it seems to assume the existence of a nonsectarian Christianity or an undenominational religion. It remains, however, one of the most thoughtfully balanced and carefully chiseled documents on an almost inherently intractable subject which has been issued by any group in recent history. It has been influential on the thinking of the churches—and especially on the attitudes of Protestant Christians who, as has been mentioned, have a deeper interest in preserving religious atmosphere in the public school than any other group. It is time now to evaluate the expectations which organized sectarian groups have for religious instruction and religious education in collaboration with the public school.

PROTESTANT-CATHOLIC-JEWISH VIEWPOINTS ON RELIGION IN PUBLIC EDUCATION

It would be expected that all religious groups in America would have done a great deal of soul-searching about what, if any, religion they could expect the public school to impart. We shall review here the positions of the three major religious groups, adding the caveat that the official statements and attitudes to be discussed cannot possibly do justice to the spectrum of opinion within all religious bodies concerning an institution so ubiquitous, so pervasive and so symbol-laden as is the public school.

Protestant Positions

The most recent and the most nearly official statement of Protestant groups in America is the study document, "Relation of Religion and Public Education," published in April, 1960, in the *International Journal of Religious Education.* This document is the end product of several events, some of which should be recalled here:[15]

In 1947, the International Council of Religious Education appointed a Committee on Religion and Public Education to which were referred four major concerns:

1. Could state-supported schools in America ever turn children against religion as has been attempted under Nazism, Fascism and Communism?
2. Are the public schools "godless" as sometimes charged?
3. Should the Protestant churches now establish parochial school systems?
4. In view of the prospects for rapid increases in numbers of children to be educated what can we expect by way of support for public schools?

This committee, with Dean Luther A. Weigle as its chairman, filed a report, adopted by the International Council of Religious Education in 1949, which took the following positions:[16]

1. A free American public school system is indispensable to the maintenance of our democratic institutions.
2. Parochial schools "are not the Protestant answer. . . . We are committed to the public schools."

Dean Weigle's committee recommended a permanent study group of the subject of religion in public education, a recommendation which eventuated in the formation, in 1953, of the Department of Religion and Public Education in the National Council of Churches. It is this latter unit which sponsored a study of several years' duration from which there came forth the study document noted above. This document, every line of which was the subject of extended debate and redrafting, may eventually be submitted for approval to the National Council of Churches. Until such time it can be taken as the most carefully considered and nearly representative available Protestant statement on religion in public education.

The study document of the National Council of Churches continues the ambivalence of the Fosdick-Weigle-American Council position—as may be seen in this declaration:[17] "The public school should recognize the function of religion in American life, and maintain a climate friendly to religion, doing its share to assure to every individual the right to choose his own beliefs."

The study document differs, however, from the Weigle position in making the following findings:

1. A "common core" of religious beliefs suitable for the public school "seems to offer little present hope."
2. The same behavioral goals may be sought by school and church but "It must be made clear that the sanctions of faith . . . are left to the teaching and nurturing ministries of the home and church."
3. Public schools may "appropriately cooperate in a reasonable arranging of school schedules to permit parents and churches to meet their respective responsibilities for specifically religious instruction."[18]

It is not certain that this document actually subscribes to a theistic commitment for the public school. It has been remarked, in fact, that it affirms as a philosophy of education for the public schools something less than what Justice Douglas asserted in the

Zorach case when he wrote the oft-quoted words that "We are a religious people whose institutions presuppose a Supreme Being."[19]

Precluding any more dilution of the document as it now stands —after extensive attenuations during the course of several tentative drafts—what can be said of the basic policies to be eventually proposed to the National Council of Churches for adoption? At least three operating principles seem clear concerning the present position of Protestants in relation to religion in the public schools: No "common core" of religious truths or values is being seriously considered. A public school should have a climate friendly to religion, but this does not authorize the communication of any truths or values peculiar to Christianity; it only prevents instruction that would contradict such values. Public schools may co-operate in, but apparently not initiate, programs of a truly religious or sectarian nature.

Although these three affirmations attempt, in an oversimplified way, to restate the most recent conclusions of the most representative group of Protestants in America they do not represent the more extreme positions of a more religious or of a more secularistic bent. Many expressions of both types can be found, but at least one other truly official statement of the National Council of Churches should be recorded. In December, 1953, the Assembly of the National Council, representative of 35,000,000 Protestant and Orthodox Christians, adopted a statement which in part stated: "On no account must an educational system which is permeated by the philosophy of secularism, something quite different from religious neutrality, be allowed to gain control of our public schools. . . . In some constitutional way, provision should be made for the *inculcation* of the principles of religion, whether within or outside the precincts of the school, but *always within the regular schedules of a pupil's working day.*"[20] [Emphasis supplied.]

It will be noted from the italicized phrases that the National Council of Churches has virtually asserted a claim to *some* part of the "working day" of the pupil after his "regular schedule" has been established by the state school. Later in the same statement it is averred that: "The solution of the problem lies in loyal support of our public schools and *increasing their awareness of God.* . . . The reverent reading of selections from the Bible in public school assemblies or classes would make an important contribution toward deepening this awareness."

One must infer from this that the National Council of Churches, which represents virtually all Protestant bodies in America, has urged that the public school can and should deliberately increase in its students an "awareness of God" employing as "an important contribution" to this end the "reverent reading of selections from the Bible." However one must admire the zeal and sincerity of the authors of this exhortation, one cannot but feel that their recommendations do *not*, as they hope, constitute a "solution to the problem," nor are they sufficiently sensitized to the religious aspirations of non-Protestant students in the public school.

Although it is very difficult to generalize about the predominant attitude of Protestants toward the place of religion or a religious orientation in the public schools, it seems permissible to conclude that Protestant Christians would not generally agree with the statement of Justice Rutledge in his dissent in the *Everson* case when, speaking of the "common school," he asserts that its "atmosphere is *wholly* secular."[21] [Emphasis supplied.] On the other hand, Protestants would not as a rule subscribe to those statements, frequently made by high-ranking Protestants, that the public school must inculcate a religious faith in the hearts of its students.

If the Protestant position seems vacillating and even contradictory, such is definitely not the case with the Jewish community in America.

Jewish Positions

In a document issued in 1957, entitled "Safeguarding Religious Liberty," the Synagogue Council of America and the National Community Relations Advisory Council published a compilation of attitudes on church–state issues approved by "major rabbinic, congregational and community relations organizations."[22] Insofar as the teaching of "spiritual values" may be understood to signify religious teaching, this must remain, as it has been, the responsibility of the home, the church and the synagogue. Insofar as it is understood to signify the teaching of morality, ethics and good citizenship, a deep commitment to such values has been successfully inculcated by our public schools in successive generations of Americans. The public schools must continue to share responsibility for fostering a commitment to those moral values, *without presenting or teaching any sectarian or theological sources or sanctions for* values."[23] [Emphasis supplied.]

If such a directive were given to a college professor, it would be considered an intolerable restriction of his academic freedom. For the teacher, however, whose students attend school by compulsion of law, it has come to be assumed that restrictions may be placed upon his teaching lest he indoctrinate members of his "captive audience." At the same time, society and the authors of the mandate quoted above expect the teacher to inculcate "a deep commitment" to "morality, ethics and good citizenship." In doing so, however, the teacher must avoid not merely the "teaching" but also the "presenting" of not only the "sectarian . . . sources or sanctions for such values" but even the "theological" sources for such ideals!

Taken literally the statement commands a nonsectarian, nontheistic and a nontheological approach to "morality, ethics and good citizenship." If such an academic requirement seems unreasonable and unrealistic, its rationale is explained in part by one of the preambles to the statement of the Jewish community which reads: "The maintenance and furtherance of religion are the responsibilities of the synagogue, the church and the home, and not of the public school system; the utilization in any manner of the time, facilities, personnel, or funds of the public school system for purposes of religious instruction should not be permitted."[24]

In a way that is consistent with this premise, the rest of "Safeguarding Religious Liberty" opposes teaching *about* religion, condemns "common core" concepts as a "vitiation" of true religion, disapproves prayers, reading of the Bible, singing of religious hymns, joint religious observances such as Easter–Passover, the taking of a religious census of pupils and all forms of released-time religious education.[25]

Perhaps even more sweeping than all the above is the conviction that: "We submit, moreover, that attempts at religious inculcation in the public schools, *even of articles of faith drawn from all religions and endorsed by representatives of all*, violate the traditional American principle of separation of church and state."[26] [Emphasis supplied.]

Such a categorical inhibition placed upon the public schools seems to be in conflict with one of the preambles to the same document where it is asseverated: "The American democratic system is founded in large part upon ethical and moral concepts derived from the great religions of mankind. The preservation and fostering of these concepts are essential to the fullest realization of the American ideal and their growth and development as major forces in American life should be the deep concern of every citizen."[27]

It would appear that a public school teacher, anxious to comply with all the standards set forth in "Safeguarding Religious Liberty," might well be at a loss to know what values may be communicated, even though he is permitted and required to "teach with full objectivity the role that religion has played in the life of mankind and in the development of society, when such teaching is intrinsic to the regular subject matter being studied."[28]

As has been pointed out in a luminous article by George H. Williams, professor of church history at the Harvard Divinity School,[29] Jews in America ". . . because of their long experience in cultural pluralism have theologically, institutionally, and emotionally a much easier and safer task than Christians in being absolutely consistent and unambiguous in their theoretical articulation and also in their practical implementation of the American principle of separation of organized religion from the state."[30]

On the other hand, Professor Williams notes that: "Catholics and Protestants repeatedly, though often inadvertently, confuse the realms of church and state because of their inherited tendency to think of political life as coming within the purview of theological ethics and religious concerns and because of the long history behind them of European Protestant and Catholic state churches."[31]

Professor Williams feels that "American Jewry has not developed an expressly Jewish political theory for the whole of a religiously mixed community."[32] He thinks, furthermore, that "the Jewish community, along with certain Protestant sectarians, like the Seventh Day Adventists, have become the most articulate, consistent and powerful exponents of what was once widespread Protestant principle at the founding of the Federal Republic."[33]

This attitude is described by Professor Williams as one which is "thoroughly committed to what the Founding Fathers repletely called man's *private* relationship with his Creator."[34] All religion in this view was "so manifestly a private matter that like the conscience it was not subject to political oversight."[35]

In seeking to assess the Jewish community's position in relation to non-Jewish uneasiness about religion in public education, Professor Williams remarks: ". . . Judaism has much greater powers of spiritual propagation independent of public schooling than Protestantism out of whose matrix American public schools were first formed and then gradually secularized in accommodation to a religiously divided culture."[36]

Further insight into the Jewish position on religion in public education can be perceived in a thoughtful article by Rabbi Arthur Gilbert, former National Director, Department of Inter-religious Cooperation, Anti-Defamation League. Writing about "Religion in the Public School—A New Approach to the Jewish Position,"[37] Rabbi Gilbert questions whether the "Jewish community has exaggerated in importance . . . the question of religion in the public schools."[38] He suggests in addition that the unsympathetic reaction of the Jewish people to the "genuine fear and anxiety in the Christian community concerning the moral and spiritual strength" of the country constitutes a "negativism" which is "irritating."

As Rabbi Gilbert puts it: "When we say 'no' to their efforts . . . without suggesting a similarly genuine concern for the problems that confront all of us or without offering any other more efficient alternative for dealing with these problems then we commit an irreparable damage. We tear away the defenses that our Christian neighbors have built up to handle their anxieties. Out spills the anger and fear that these defenses have held in check and the anger touches us. The Jews then are identified with those who are against these holy symbols. They are identified in their eyes with the Communist and secularist, with persons blind to the real problems that confront the American community."[39]

Rabbi Gilbert echoes Professor Williams in a lament that with regard to American church–state issues there "is no . . . developed Jewish philosophy and this is our crying need." The Jewish community, Rabbi Gilbert asserts, "has rested its case on secularistic and legalistic arguments" but if "we are to speak to the Christian's heart and mind, we must go beyond the law in dealing with this problem." It will not, however, be enough simply "to formulate the insight of our religious tradition within the theological framework of contemporary religious thought."[40] For, as Rabbi Gilbert puts it: ". . . on this issue the Jewish tradition is not that clear. In Israel, where we have some reasonable expectations that a Jewish viewpoint is being fulfilled in the destiny of the country, released time is a part of the official public school program. There it is not considered such a terrible violation of the proper relationship of church and state nor a denial of the religious freedom of Christians, Moslems or nonbelievers."[41]

Although reflective men like Rabbi Gilbert raise the most serious questions about Jewish church–state attitudes and strategy,[42] it would appear that this religious minority, for reasons which are not at all self-evident, is committed to a firm policy of eliminating all sectarian and theistic principles from public education.

Three observations on the Jewish attitude to religion in public education seem to be appropriate:

Widespread Jewish support to make the public school a totally secular school has joined what Leo Pfeffer has called the triple alliance of certain Protestant groups, most secular humanists and the Jewish community.[43] Together these three groups constitute a powerful force working to secularize the public schools, while at the same time making it more difficult for church-related schools to obtain even indirect aids.

Although the document cited above, "Safeguarding Religious Liberty," asserts that "the very foundation of American democracy" is "religious liberty"[44] the dimensions of that liberty never seem to reach beyond the completely private life of a citizen. For a Christian and for some other religionists this is a narrowing of religious freedom which in effect is a violation of it.

It is doubtful if Jacques Maritain[45] or Canon Stokes or even all Jewish political philosophers would agree with the principle enunciated in "Safeguarding Religious Liberty" where it is claimed that the "growth of democracy in the United States is in large measure a product of that unique principle in our basic law that puts religion outside the jurisdiction of the state."[46] Many would hold that the "growth of democracy" is not "in large measure" due to this cause, and that in fact democracy will not be maintained and extended unless its theistic roots are understood and deepened with every generation. Such understanding and deepening, many of these same persons would hold, cannot be anticipated unless the nation's schools transmit a knowledge of the sacred origin of human rights.

The desire and anxiety to broaden the bases of democracy and make more sacred the foundations of our rights are the central objectives of both Protestant and Jewish groups in their positions on the place of religion in public education; the fact that both groups have the same objective but widely differing means to achieve it simply signifies once again that the role and mission of the public school today is more complex than even the keenest observers can detect.

Catholics also entertain the same objectives for the public schools as their Protestant and Jewish neighbors; whether Catholics are advancing a third and different solution is a question on which even all Catholics would not be in agreement.

Catholic Positions

Many non-Catholics assume that the Catholic laity has less of an interest in the public school than their Protestant or Jewish counterparts. While ideologically and theoretically this may be true it is nonetheless verifiable that millions of Catholics, graduates both of public and parochial schools, have a deep affection for the public school. They may not always feel the emotional identification with it which many non-Catholics seem to feel. Nor do Catholics generally rhapsodize about the public school as the bulwark of democracy or as the greatest creation of the American people.

If, however, the feeling persists, as it seems to, that Catholics are less enthusiastic about public schools than they should be, then no explanation fair to Catholics is possible without a conscientious attempt to understand the intimate relation between religion and education in the mind of any Catholic. Those non-Catholics who fail to understand why some Catholics are reportedly less than ardent towards the public school might reflect on how they themselves would feel about voting on any appropriation proposed for a Catholic school! The analogy is far from perfect, but some of the misunderstandings which non-Catholics have toward the parochial school can be duplicated in some Catholics' attitude toward the public school.

A thoroughly considered Catholic statement with any official endorsement concerning the many-faceted problem of religion in public education is probably, in the nature of things, an impossibility. Catholics in the last century here and there litigated against Protestant practices in the public schools; but in recent decades Catholics, almost frightened by the invasion of naturalism and nontheistic humanism into the public schools, have generally not objected to anything in public education which will stress religious over nonreligious values. As a result, it may be that Catholics have tended to be less sensitive to the charge that a theistic orientation in the public school may be unfair to the nonbelieving child or to the student of the Jewish faith whose whole tradition and creed strongly emphasize that *all* religious exercises are the exclusive function of the family and the synagogue.

In addition Catholics have, as a central part of their tradition, the conviction that the natural moral law, ascertainable to the mind by reason independently of revelation, teaches the existence of God as almost a self-evident truth. Catholics consequently find it extremely difficult to appreciate the reluctance of some Protestant Christians to give to the public school a religious commitment, and the even greater reluctance of most Jewish .groups to allow even a theistic atmosphere in the public school.

The contemporary Catholic attitude towards the public school derives more from current Catholic apprehensions about creeping secularism than from any other fear or anxiety. If Catholics were frightened about communism at home and abroad in the thirties and thereafter, they are similarly alarmed in the sixties about the inroads of secularism—that is, the exclusion of religion from the public law and public philosophy of the nation. Other religious persons and groups are, of course, also concerned about secularism, but for Catholics secularism seems to constitute a far more imminent and pervasive threat than for other religious bodies in America.

To some extent, however, a problem of semantics is involved here. For example, *The Christian Century* for July 4, 1962, in discussing the June 25, 1962, prayer decision of the United States Supreme Court, wrote that: "Under our Constitution the government is and must remain secular. It is not secularistic nor is it devoted to the teaching of secularism but it is separated from any religious establishment, including establishment of religion-in-general."

In the use of the terms "secular," "secularistic" and "secularism" in this quotation, many principles of political philosophy are assumed or implied. Contemporary Catholics would probably take exception to the notion that the government is "secular" in the sense noted above, although one of the clearest principles of the Catholic tradition of political philosophy is that the state is a "perfect society" with a distinct role of its own which could be classified as "secular." The term "secular," however, produces in the modern Catholic mind a connotation of secularism which, for many Catholics, is a pejorative term.

In 1961, the annual message of the Catholic hierarchy re-emphasized the conviction that religion in the public school is a necessity in these words: "Popular education also bears a measure of responsibility for the decline and rejection of moral principles. At first, there was no intention of excluding either religion or morality from the common tax-supported school. But the diversity of our religious pattern and the rising pressure of secularism have produced the school *without religion,* and it is idle to suppose that this school could long inculcate in American youth moral convictions which would be firmly held."[47] [Emphasis supplied.] Two causes, as this statement sees it, have produced "the school without religion": (1) the diversity of our religious pattern and, (2) the rising pressure of secularism.

No specific remedies are given with respect to "the school without religion." The existence of such a school is accepted almost with resignation and with the silent understanding that for many, though not all, non-Catholics, the term "the school without religion" is too strong to apply to America's public schools. But even among those who would concede the validity of the description of public education as "the school without religion" it is not certain how many would deplore it. Many, of course, would insist that "the school without religion" is one of the greatest achievements of American history.

The Catholic attitude towards religion in public education is, as can be seen, one that is more insistent than the Protestant view concerning the inclusion of religion in some form and seemingly at the opposite end of the spectrum from the viewpoint of the Jewish community. It is, of course, precisely because the Catholic philosophy of education could not be squared with the outlook of the public school that Catholics have constructed a school system of their own. It is, in fact, the contemporary profound dissatisfaction of Catholics with "the school without religion" that has been instrumental in the near doubling of the enrollment of Catholic schools since the end of World War II.

One of the most perceptive studies of the growth of "the school without religion" is a volume by the Rev. Neil G. McCluskey, S.J., entitled *Public Schools and Moral Education.*[48] After a detailed study of the philosophies of education of Horace Mann, William Torrey Harris and John Dewey, key thinkers in the development of the American public school, Father McCluskey arrives at three major conclusions:

1. Disagreement over the function of any common moral and spiritual values program is the inevitable result of the irreconcilable differences among conflicting religions or philosophies or schemes of ultimate values, so that after many decades of experimenting, the problem of moral education in the common public school is more defiant of solution than ever—is, in fact, insoluble.[49]

2. The principle that religious freedom in a religiously divided community requires the elimination of any teaching or practice from the common school not acceptable to everyone makes it impossible to preserve any kind of traditional religion in the school.[50]

3. The value philosophies espoused by these three men (Horace Mann, William Torrey Harris and John Dewey) have led to the widespread elimination of religion from today's public schools.[51]

If, as Father McCluskey and others conclude, the "problem of moral education in the common public school . . . is insoluble" the consequences are serious. Although not all religious leaders would agree that the problem is "insoluble," most Christian bodies would admit that it is indeed exceedingly difficult.

CHAPTER THREE

Problems of Religion in Public Education

We must now deal with the development of a new and almost startling phenomenon: the activities of government and public school officials with respect to fostering religious and moral ideals in the nation's schools. One of the results of the impasse brought about by Protestant ambivalence, Catholic indefiniteness and Jewish insistence on their views concerning the presence or absence of religion in the public school has been the emergence of governmentally sponsored activity designed to advance moral standards within the public schools. Although school boards have stumbled over the same intractable issues that religious and educational leaders have encountered before them, it is nonetheless somewhat disconcerting to see state officials promoting codes of morality and even composing prayers for recitation in public schools. Perhaps we should, however, reflect that it is more surprising that government officials have not prior to this time interfered more in the schools which they finance.

The motivation of state officials in promoting moral values is presumably not to foster religion as such but rather to promote morality *via* religion. However laudable their intentions, the instinctive reactions of a religionist and an educator towards state regulation of moral standards in public schools is one of suspicion and distrust. Yet an inspection of the work which conscientious school boards are attempting to do in this area suggests that their efforts to advance public morality may in some instances be desirable. The various "guiding statements" for teachers which many school boards have issued are frequently patterned on the 1951 statement of the National Education Association entitled, "Moral and Spiritual Values in the Public Schools."[1]

It is not always clear why school boards and comparable officials desire to become involved in the question of the moral values public schools should transmit. It is interesting to note that in early April, 1962, at the oral pleadings before the United States Supreme Court in the New York prayer case Chief Justice Earl Warren inquired of counsel for the school board about this very question. What were the reasons, the Chief Justice asked, behind the school board's adoption of the nondenominational prayer? The lawyer for the school district declared that the prayer was adopted to promote "belief in the morals, ethics and virtues traditional in American life."[2] The Chief Justice pressed: "You shy away from the use of the word 'religion'." Counsel for the school board replied: "I don't want the Court to be left with the impression that the purpose was to teach religion."[3]

If the promotion of religion is not the aim of the many school boards now issuing statements on public school morality, then a reasonable facsimile of religious activity is often attempted. A "guiding statement" for the teachers of the Los Angeles schools urges the teaching of the Golden Rule, citing as justification evidence of the fact that the equivalent of the Golden Rule is a doctrine in seven different religions.[4] The San Diego statement lists the "existence of God" as the basic assumption underlying "loyalty to American ideals."[5] If religion is not openly advocated in these statements, then at least a misty middle region between sectarian and nontheistic spiritual values is being sought as the major premise for the ever more widely promulgated "official" public school statements on moral values.

The fact that there is absolutely no legal history and no legislative or judicial definition of "moral and spiritual values" is clearly a sign that the controversies and the litigation about religion and public education have hardly begun. For surely the nature and tone of moral and spiritual values communicated in a classroom every day are a thousand times more significant than the almost momentary recitation of a prayer or the brief reading of the Bible or even the presence or absence of released time. It is perhaps an encourag-

ing sign that the courts have not yet been asked to define and pro-
nounce on the really important things; it may be that widespread
acquiescence in the values presently transmitted in public education
indicates a broader consensus about the spiritual role of the public
school than the continual controversy over this subject would seem
to suggest.

On the other hand, it surely is a sign of a profound anxiety when
school boards feel required by duty or public opinion to assert that
the public schools must teach spiritual values and when, furthermore, school boards begin to "issue" such values.

What type of values may such officials "issue"? The June 25,
1962, prayer decision of the Supreme Court clearly states that it is
unconstitutional for state officials ". . . to prescribe by law any
particular form of prayer which is to be used as an official prayer
in carrying on *any program of* governmentally-sponsored religious
activity."[6] [Emphasis supplied.] Public school superintendents
therefore are clearly forbidden to prescribe a certain prayer as the
official one, but they are not actually forbidden to foster a "program of governmentally-sponsored religious activity." The central
question is whether public school officials are permitted to carry
on a program with a religious orientation if, in their judgment, this
is the *only* way to inculcate that morality indispensable for good
citizenship.

The New York Board of Regents apparently came very close to
that judgment when on November 30, 1951, in issuing their "Statement on Moral and Spiritual Training in the Schools," they opened
with these words: "Belief in and dependence upon Almighty God
was the very cornerstone upon which our Founding Fathers
builded."[7] In order to stress this spiritual heritage, the Regents recommended that, in every public school in the state, the day begin
with a brief prayer.

A statement supplementary to this 1951 declaration was issued
by the Regents on March 28, 1955. By this time many school
boards of the state had taken cognizance of the Regents' recommendations but, according to a report of the State Department of
Education, only 150 of the 900 school boards in New York state
had adopted the proposal concerning the daily recitation of a
prayer.[8] Nonetheless, the theistic orientation continued to exist
in the Regents' thinking, as can be seen in this affirmation repeated
from a previous statement: ". . . the school will fulfill its high

function of supplementing the training of the home, *ever intensi-fying in the child that love for God*, parents and for home which is the mark of true character training and the sure guarantee of a country's welfare."[9] [Emphasis supplied.]

In application of the Regents' recommendations, the New York City Board of School Superintendents in June, 1955, approved a "Guiding Statement for Supervisors and Teachers" wherein the Regents' theistic principles are furthered: "To the public school," the document declared, "as to the home and the church, the full life is, in the final analysis, the objective of all education for all children. . . . This implies . . . that *the program of the public schools must reinforce the program of the home and church in strengthening belief in God*."[10] [Emphasis supplied.]

Another theistic affirmation concludes the Superintendents' remarks concerning the moral and spiritual values: ". . . the public schools . . . teach the moral code and identify God as the ultimate source of natural and moral law. They encourage children to discover and develop their own relationship to God, referring them also to their families, church or synagogues. In their programs of moral and spiritual education the public schools maintain a climate favorable to religion without making value judgments about any particular religion."[11]

Both the Regents' and the Superintendents' positions make considerable advance over those recommended by the American Council on Education[12] and the study document of the National Council of Churches. They have advanced even further over the 1951 statement of the National Education Association, one of whose cardinal principles is: "As public institutions, the public schools of this nation must be nondenominational. They can have no part in securing acceptance of any one of the numerous systems of belief regarding a supernatural power and the relation of mankind thereto."[13]

Sectarian and civil liberties groups in New York were not slow in observing the theistic-religious tone in the Regents'-Superintendents' declarations of values. The opponents of the official statement reacted in a way which recalls these words of John Dewey: "If one inquires why the American tradition is so strong against any connection of State and Church, why *it dreads even the rudiments of religious teaching in state-maintained schools*, the immediate and superficial answer is not far to seek."[14] [Emphasis supplied.] Reflecting a "dread" of "even the rudiments of religious teaching" in public education, the United Parents Associations, the New York Board of Rabbis and the New York Civil Liberties Union expressed opposition to the proposed endorsement of moral values contending that to bring religious ideas into teaching would be a divisive factor among students and would import a vague theism offensive to both believers and nonbelievers.[15]

On October 4, 1956, a modified version of the Superintendents' original statement was adopted by the New York City Board of Education—not, however, in a way satisfactory to all the opposing groups. Catholic officials had unqualifiedly endorsed the original statement. So also had the Protestant Council of the City of New York—but with the caution that provision be made for students with nontheistic attitudes towards moral and spiritual values.

Even the most sympathetic observer could wonder whether the inculcation of moral and spiritual values was greatly intensified *after* the 1956 adoption of an official endorsement of such activity. It is, nonetheless, most significant that the highest educational officials of New York State and New York City composed, endorsed, made official and promulgated for all public schools a code of moral and spiritual values with a "pro-religious," theistic orientation.

Some policy statements on the role of religion in public education in states and cities outside of New York are interesting and significant. The Openmindedness study of the curriculum office of the Philadelphia public schools, issued in 1951, and the "Explorations in Character Development" undertaken by the Albany school district in California are examples of attempts at teaching religious values without employing sectarian sanctions. These statements as well as the well-known Kentucky program for teaching moral and spiritual values are assessed in an excellent article by Rabbi Arthur Gilbert in the January, 1957, issue of the *National Jewish Monthly*.

A statement quoted by Rabbi Gilbert about the Kentucky plan is noteworthy. This scheme, as described by one of its directors, prescribes that ". . . teachers of different religious commitments and those with none are encouraged to help boys and girls to arrive at their own right decisions based on sanctions deriving from law, justice, property rights, personal integrity, group approval and other democratically accepted ideas, not excluding the pupils' personal religious convictions. . . . The lessons learned in school offend no child's personal religious sensibility and at the same time give those

from religiously affiliated homes fresh reasons for being receptive
to the ethical precepts of the churches and synagogues." This approach to education in moral and spiritual values seeks to avoid
indoctrination in any point of view and protects the child of no
religious faith, while at the same time it attributes respect if not
reverence to the religion which each student brings with him to
the classroom. The Kentucky plan for education in moral values
has thus been praised by leading educators as probably the most
promising of this nature of all the plans now in operation.

There appear to be at least three ways of viewing the New York
case and comparable developments elsewhere—including the several state-proposed courses on communism for the public schools:

First, state-sanctioned practices promoting moral and spiritual
values can be regarded simply as another quasi encroachment in
the name of patriotism by public officials upon the curriculum of
the public school; such state action can be compared with official
regulations enacted in some thirty states between the years 1898
and 1940 requiring a daily flag-salute ceremony in all public
schools.[16]

A second viewpoint would regard governmental activity in this
area as an inevitable reaction to the religious vacuum in the public
school. Those holding this position could argue that the theistic
and religious elements often present in state-authorized codes of
moral values are the natural response of religious men to the challenge of the pervasiveness in public education of the NEA's nontheistic moral values which are ambiguously defined as "those values which, when applied in human behavior, exalt and refine life
and bring it into accord with the standards of conduct that are
approved in our democratic culture."[17]

A third attitude—and one perhaps very worthy of exploration—
could detect in government-sponsored values philosophy of modern
public education stretching itself to the limit of its logic and claiming that "preparation for life" must, according to the unitary theory
of education, include instruction and experience in moral decision-
making.

Whatever attitude one might adopt with respect to the relatively
novel activity of state groups proposing moral standards in public
education, such conduct cannot fail to be a warning to all religionists. The impasse created in the public school by the conflicting
views of religious groups has produced in the state school a silence

about religion which sincere and well-intentioned public school officials might be tempted to overcome with a religion of their own creation.

FOUR "CONSPIRACIES" AND PUBLIC EDUCATION

America's pluralist society, the Rev. John Courtney Murray, S.J., has written,[18] "honestly viewed under abdication of all false gentility, is a pattern of interacting conspiracies. There are chiefly four —Protestant, Catholic, Jewish, secularist. . . ."

These four different philosophies have assumed attitudes and postures with respect to the presence or absence, the service or disservice, of religion in the American public school. However powerful and influential these differing outlooks may have been, it is not clear that any one of them has been directly responsible for bringing about the present attitude of public education toward religion.

The ineluctable thrust of secularism was far advanced in Western civilization and American culture before Protestant Christians began urging the restoration of religion to the common schools. The public school had long since been dominated by secular humanism before the Catholic voice in America, pleading for religion in the public school, had obtained an audience. And the public school had become the secular school—except for a few para-Christian prayers and ceremonials—before the American Jew was led, as Father Murray puts it, "to align himself with the secularizing forces whose dominance, he thinks, will afford him a security he has never known."[19] Thus the secularist, now self-confident in his secure possession of the public school, might well have inherited this fortune anyway—independently of his own exertions.

In all the agonizing efforts over the course of two or three generations by the members of these four groups to control public education, the center of the stage has always been courses *on* religion, instruction *about* religon, training in character development or admittedly sectarian indoctrination by way of released time. Seldom, if ever, have any of the interested groups approached the real heart of the matter: the faith of the teachers and the ideological outlook of the textbooks.

It is, after all, hardly worthwhile to protest the presence or absence of such religious symbols as Bible-reading, nonsectarian prayers and even released time if the teacher and the textbook he employs are, consciously or otherwise, working on behalf of one of the "conspiracies."

If, in other words, Protestants desire the public school atmosphere to be "friendly" to religion, and if Catholics seek to outlaw a "philosophy of education which omits God," while the Jewish community wants secular values transmitted without their sacred foundations, why do not the three groups collaborate on the two most important factors in the atmosphere of education, the ideology of the teachers and the content of the textbooks?

To ask the question is almost to answer it. Shrill cries about teachers' loyalty oaths, censorship and book-burning need not be elaborated. The cold fact remains, however, that teachers and textbooks are almost the only things that determine the orientation of a school.

To require a prospective teacher to commit himself to creating an atmosphere "friendly" to religion or one with a theistic orientation or one with a strictly secular outlook not only offends the sensibilities and good sense of any educator, but is also open to question in the light of the *Torcaso*[20] opinion in which the United States Supreme Court declared unconstitutional a Maryland law requiring a public official to attest to his faith in God before he could qualify for a commission as a notary public.

If school boards prior to hiring teachers attempt to test their aptitude to transmit moral values, there is no legal or other body of knowledge on the point. In a case, however, decided by the Supreme Court of Florida in 1962,[21] a religious text for a teacher was involved but its constitutionality was not determined. On the application for a position as a teacher in the public schools in the Miami area there is the question "Do you believe in God?" In the brief filed on behalf of the plaintiffs by Leo Pfeffer, general counsel of the American Jewish Congress, the policy of requiring an expression of belief in God is denounced as unconstitutional. Such a requirement, the brief states, favors religion over irreligion and, more specifically, prefers theistic religions over nontheistic ones.

But the more important question behind the inquiry on the teacher's application is well stated but left open by the petitioners' brief:[22] "It is important to note that we are not challenging the right of the school authorities to dismiss or otherwise discipline a teacher who uses or abuses his office to promote atheistic doctrines. All we challenge is their right to refuse to engage an otherwise qualified teacher simply because he will not assert that he believes in God."

Granted that a religious test as a prerequisite for a public school position violates the spirit and the letter of the Constitution, there remains the problem of selecting persons capable of transmitting those moral and spiritual values desired by the school board on behalf of the citizenry. Could a school board decide that, other things being equal, a devoutly religious person is more likely to develop exemplary character in children than a less religious person? Or could a school board dismiss a teacher because, employing the prestige of his position, he taught atheism as more worthy of credence than its opposite? Or could public school officials refuse to retain a teacher who espoused that ultimate form of judicial positivism which would deny any meaningful or binding moral standards beyond those norms codified in penal and criminal statutes?

These are the church–state problems which may arise in the future; they certainly seem more important and substantial than the presence or absence of the symbols of religion without its substance.

If the selection of those teachers more likely to carry out the moral mission of the public school seems even more insoluble than the question of the place of religious values in these schools, it may be that, with respect to the selection of textbooks, there could develop a fruitful and mutually beneficial area of interreligious co-operation.

The type of co-operation possible is suggested by the excellent study done by the Anti-Defamation League entitled "The Treatment of Minorities in Secondary School Textbooks."[23] This carefully compiled survey shows that the tradition, achievements and contemporary history of Jewish and other minority groups are frequently given inadequate treatment in the forty-eight social studies textbooks most widely used in the secondary schools of the nation.

Following the technique and building upon the work of a comparable study issued in 1949 by the American Council on Education the ADL document states: "It is hoped that this report will encourage school personnel to demand . . . social studies texts that 1) Present a pluralistic—rather than a 100 percent white, Protestant, Anglo-Saxon—view of history and of the current social scene. 2) Portray minority groups not as 'out-groups'—strange, different and isolated—but sympathetically and in depth as valuable, contributing elements in our culture. 3) Deal frankly with past and current barriers to full equality in citizenship and to constructive inter-group relations, and with ongoing attempts to achieve both civil and human rights for all."[24]

Would it not be helpful if all religious groups formed a federation for the purpose of improving the treatment of religion and religious values in the textbooks employed by the nation's school children? Such a federation would be designed: first, to prevent distortions of any religious tradition by omission or misstatement; and, secondly, to condemn as academically unacceptable those textbooks which, consciously or otherwise, avoid a full and fair discussion of the religious issues clearly and centrally involved in the subject matter of their text.

The second objective may well be the more important since textbook writers, because of their deep desire to be impartial toward all religious groups as well as their understandable ambition to secure nation-wide acceptance of their text, tend to a certain fuzziness wherein no religious group is praised or censured, but where nothing too significant or even relevant is said about the great struggle of mankind in which clashing religious ideas played a crucial role.

A law suit brought by a minority group to enjoin the use of a certain textbook of a series of textbooks would have far greater merit than legal action designed to void a quasi-religious practice of a less than mandatory nature. A well-documented plaintiff's case that a textbook, studied and accepted by almost millions of students over a generation, distorts by silence, omission or otherwise the religious traditions of a particular sect has infinitely greater intrinsic merit than a suit, for example, to keep a crèche off the school lawn. In fact, a solidly constructed legal case asserting the "establishment" of one religion in particular textbooks might have very beneficial results for the academic, not to mention the religious, health of public education.

After reviewing the never really clear and seldom consistent positions of the various religious groups in regard to religion in the public school, one might conclude without unfairness to anyone that the problem of spiritual values in public education is profoundly confusing and almost hopelessly beyond solution. Certainly a religionist can with difficulty, if at all, be satisfied with the major premises and the operating principles of the educators, whose aspirations for education and society seem to be fulfilled by a commitment to a set of moral and spiritual values unrelated to any ideal higher than human truths.

The dissatisfaction of some religionists with the pervasiveness of secular humanism in public education has manifested itself in America by placing in public schools not the substance of religion, for this gradually became impossible, but the symbols of religion.

One almost inevitably associates all efforts to introduce religion into the public school with Protestant endeavor. Catholics have seldom attempted to tamper with the legal institutions which they found in effect as they developed toward self-identification in the American community. Jewish groups have only recently sought through legislative and judicial action to influence the climate of the public school. The contemporary massive struggle to set the tone and atmosphere of the public school is largely a contest between an alliance of Protestant and government officials against a coalition of secularists.

Protestant action in America, fighting a generally unsuccessful battle to retain or restore a religious atmosphere in the public schools, has been responsible for the presence of three undeniably religious, even if nonsectarian, activities in public education. These three activities are the most important religious symbols in the public school today. A hostile critic might call them remnants or relics of a once Protestant-oriented public school; a more sympathetic critic would call them reminders of the religious origin and history of the land. No religious educator could validly claim that these three practices make the public school a religious school, nor that they have in themselves the capacity to inspire a religious faith or create an intellectual curiosity about religion in any student who participates in them.

The three practices are the only major religious features of the public school today; they are released (or dismissed) time, Bible-reading and the recitation of the Lord's Prayer. A fourth but minor practice is the custom of having in the classroom a commemoration of those religious feasts and customs such as Christmas and Easter which are common in the home and church lives of the school children.

It is difficult to understand how much sound and fury could have been expended over these few religious practices. Every suggestion of their abolition—especially Bible-reading—produces a cry of anguish from those who seem to share, in Father Murray's rather strong phrase, "the still pathetically current, if somewhat moribund, Protestant idea that the public schools are really Liberal Protestant schools, wherein a nonsectarian Christianity is by law established and subsidized."[25]

If the United States Supreme Court in one sweeping opinion forbade released or dismissed time, Bible-reading and the recitation of the Lord's Prayer, it seems unlikely that the basic nature or role of the public school in our society would be substantially changed. The elimination of all these practices by force of law would, of course, erect legal principles in Supreme Court jurisprudence which might well have an impact on the school curriculum of the next generation. But the actual elimination of released time, Bible-reading and prayer recitation could not alter in any too substantial a manner the education and experiences which students would receive after all of these practices had been completely removed from their daily academic lives.

Indeed, the elimination of these symbols of religion might serve to dramatize the fact that the substance of religion has been absent from public education for many decades; everyone—naturalist and supernaturalist alike—would then be obliged to look upon public school as truly the completely secular school. The public school might then be seen as a state agency required by law to live in a permanent compromise, eschewing the great religious dilemmas of mankind, but pretending that such avoidance neither minimizes their importance nor vitiates an education in which no answers to man's gravest cosmic problems are attempted.

The ubiquity and permanency of para-Christian practices and symbols in America's public schools is almost unbelievable. It may be that the placing of tokens of religion in public education has been a device consciously or otherwise employed by religious groups, educators and parents in order to evade the troubling and stark predicament of an educational system divorced from religion.

Some idea of the force of the deep feeling that education should not be totally separated from religion can be seen in the information obtained in a 1961 survey on religious practices in the nation's public schools.[26] Reporting on findings from 2,183 returns from 4,000 questionnaires sent out to a nation-wide sampling of public school superintendents, Professor R. B. Dierenfield of Macalester College in Minnesota feels that he has compiled information on the basis of which it is possible to have some factual "knowledge of what is going on in American public schools regarding the handling of various religious influences."[27]

Although the reader is urged to study the full report on this interesting survey, the following statistics indicate something of the religious orientation of the public school:

1. Homeroom devotional exercises are conducted in 50.22 per cent of the schools.

2. Regular chapel exercises are held in 22.07 per cent of the schools.

3. Bible-reading takes place in 41.74 per cent, while Gideon Bibles are distributed in 42.74 per cent of the schools.

4. Christmas is celebrated in 87.92 per cent of the schools, with Hannukah (5.39 per cent), Easter (57.82 per cent) and Thanksgiving (76.75 per cent) also commemorated.

5. Released time operates in 29.66 per cent of the schools with every eighth school system permitting this program to operate within school buildings.

6. 77.47 per cent of the superintendents answered "yes" to a question: "Do you believe your school system is dealing in an adequate way with religion?" 22.53 per cent answered "no."

On the basis of the foregoing, Professor Dierenfield concludes that the "American public school cannot be charged with being a Godless institution."[28] This repudiation of the "charge" that the public school is "Godless" is incidentally typical of those countless rejections of this accusation in which the writers, touched with anger, seem to betray their insecurity in the position they hold in replying to the imputations of irreligion in the public school. Professor Dierenfield expresses the hope that his "data can be used in a constructive way to attack the problem of religion in the public schools."[29]

From this data it is evident that religious practices are far more frequent in the South, where there is a relatively homogeneous Protestant population, than in any other section of the country.

Although almost every third school system (29.66 per cent) cooperates in a program of released time, the number of pupils enrolled in these programs has never, according to the most accurate statistics available, exceeded 5 percent of the school population.

As Professor Dierenfield notes: "Many of the practices which are employed by school systems to deal with religious influences might be called into question in the light of legal decisions on the subject."[30] In view of this fact, and in the light of the sometimes almost paranoid affirmations that the public school is not a "Godless institution," one wonders what impact judicial decisions or even court injunctions can have upon the intermingling of religious symbols in the secular educational systems of America. One wonders, too, about the philosophy of law of those educational and religious leaders who seek to prove that the public school is not a "Godless institution" employing, as a part of their proof, religious practices "*many*" of which "might be called into question in the light of legal decisions on the subject."

However pervasive other religious practices may continue to be, it is clear that released-time religious instruction represents, in the words of an important statement of the International Council of Religious Education, "the most serious effort that the churches have yet made to bring religion closer to the center of the child's educational experience."[31] It is this educational and religious experiment, twice litigated in the United States Supreme Court,[32] to which we now turn our attention.

RELEASED-TIME RELIGIOUS EDUCATION

The released-time movement began as a Protestant experiment just before World War I. It grew out of the twin convictions that religion as such could not be inserted into the public school and that the religious symbols in these schools were pedagogically ineffective.

The first mistake made by the founders of released time was to accept or adopt an unfortunate label for their creation. The name implies and assumes that children are "released" from their legal duty and from the custody of the public school in order to receive sectarian instruction. If the pan-Protestant movement which launched "released time" in Gary, Indiana, in 1913, had labelled their plan "shared-time," the history of the movement might conceivably have been different. The current notion of "shared-time" implies that parents, schools and churches "share" the time of the child. The concept of "released time," however, almost pictured the church as an intruder into the state-sponsored school. Justice

Black, in his majority opinion in the *McCollum* decision, placed this not wholly unwarranted construction on the program when he wrote: "Pupils compelled by law to go to school for secular education are released in part from their legal duty upon the condition that they attend religious classes."[33]

Justice Jackson expressed the same difficulty during the oral pleadings in the *McCollum* case on December 8, 1947; he asked council for Mrs. McCollum: "Does the state have the right to commandeer the time of a pupil and then rebate a part of it?"[34] Justice Frankfurter followed up this question by asking another: ". . . this Court has held, in the *Pierce* case, that the child's time is the parents' and not the state's, except that the state may require certain educational standards. Why can't the parents work out a scheme whereby they will divide the time with the state and give the state what the law requires for a secular education? . . ."[35]

The second greatest mistake made by the proponents of released time was their failure to let it be known that the *basic* purpose of released time was to reunite and reintegrate religion with education. This objective, central to and underlying the entire released-time movement, has never been fully understood or at least not adequately communicated by those who see in released time only a method by which the churches can utilize the organized power and prestige of the public school for sectarian purposes.

As Justice Frankfurter put it in his dissent in *Zorach*:

The deeply divisive controversy aroused by the attempts to secure public school pupils for sectarian instruction would promptly end if the advocates of such instruction were content to have the school 'close its doors or operations'—that is, dismiss classes in their entirety without discrimination—instead of seeking to use the public schools as the instrument for security of attendance at denominational classes. The unwillingness of the promoters of this movement to dispense with such use of the public schools betrays a surprising want of confidence in the inherent power of the various faiths to draw children to ouside sectarian classes—an attitude that hardly reflects the faith of the greatest religious spirits.[36]

It may be, of course, that the integration of religion with education attempted by released time is so dubiously efficacious that in reality the only result of released time upon the school's program of *secular* education is the symbolic effect of released time being permitted. It may also be that released-time instruction, necessarily conducted in the language of the religious and the supernatural, is of such a different order from public school secular education that it cannot be said to have any true academic integration with the secular learning to which it is destined to be no more than a mere appendage.

The theory, implicit in released time, of reuniting education and religion has been declared impossible and unwise by many Protestants. To these critics of released time, there is no possible relation between the sacred and the secular; any attempted relationship will only result in the corruption of the sacred. Such an attitude is, of course, derivable from certain orthodox Protestant dogmas which scorn secular learning as a danger to the soul.

The third and possibly the greatest mistake made by the promoters of released time was to allow a particular example of released time, vulnerable on some points, to be drawn into litigation at the wrong time, requesting the wrong thing and under the wrong circumstances.

There was, of course, no way for any religious official to interfere with the *McCollum* case once it started, since the released-time movement has no national or central office. It may well be, of course, that the future will reveal that *McCollum*, as modified by *Zorach* four years later, has given a constitutional blessing to released time which has been now denied to state-sponsored nondenominational prayers and may soon be denied to the practice of Bible-reading in the public school. Whatever the future of released time, it can take credit for two Supreme Court decisions in the second of which, in the words of Professor Philip Kurland, "most of what *McCollum* had done was undone . . ."[37]

The *McCollum* decision of March 8, 1948, is and will continue to be the great divide in church–state relations for many years to come. For this writer, who observed the entire litigation in closest detail, heard the oral arguments before the Supreme Court on December 8, 1947, and followed the legal aftermath of the opinion,[38] several reflections on what the Court did in *McCollum* seem to be worth recording. But first, a review of each important phase of the case may lend some perspective. Let us then retrace what the nation's highest tribunal tried to accomplish in two decisions in which it discussed and ruled upon the most viable method yet discovered to resolve one of the greatest educational and religious dilemmas of a free society: the place of religion in relation to the tax-supported school.

It will be helpful to recreate the *McCollum* controversy under six headings: (1) The national mood immediately prior to *McCollum*. (2) The oral pleadings on December 8, 1947. (3) The briefs of the *amici curiae*. (4) The actual decision and the "content" it placed in the "establishment" clause. (5) The aftermath of the decision. (6) The meaning of *Zorach* and the future of released time.

The National Mood after the Everson Opinion

Why the Supreme Court accepted jurisdiction in the *McCollum* case was a mystery to Justice Jackson—as he indicated in his concurring opinion—and to many observers of the Court. But one is allowed to speculate.

After the Supreme Court decided in February, 1947, in a 5–4 split, that the Federal Constitution could permit the reimbursement to parents for the costs of transportation of their children to parochial schools, a national cry of protest and alarm arose against the Court's decision. The entire Protestant press, many Jewish groups and the American Civil Liberties Union, which had participated in the case, insisted that the Court was in error and that all types of appropriations would now be sought for the Roman Catholic educational system. The organization of Protestants and Other Americans United for the Separation of Church and State (POAU) was formed directly as a result of the *Everson* ruling. It appeared to some at the time that Justice Rutledge in his dissent had written the greatest understatement in Supreme Court history in his prophetic words—"this is not just a little case about bus rides."[39]

Justice Black's majority opinion in *Everson* was widely praised for its interdiction of aid "to *all* religions" but was severely criticized for having allegedly disregarded this principle in upholding the New Jersey plan for reimbursement of parents for the transportation costs of their children to Catholic schools. Justice Rutledge's prediction that the permitting of bus transportation to church-related schools could lead to the total financing of these schools was everywhere quoted as an ominous indication of the erosion of the wall of separation between church and state.

Did the national mood of anxiety enter into the Supreme Court's decision that it would hear arguments in a case involving released time in which the trial court and the Supreme Court of Illinois had held unanimously that the program of religious instruction violated no provision of the Illinois Constitution? Or did the great national disappointment over *Gobitis*,[40] later turned into exultation over *Barnette*,[41] cause the Court to wonder whether Terry McCollum might be another child like those children required in *Gobitius* to salute the flag but excused from this requirement in *Barnette*? In any event the Supreme Court accepted jurisdiction in *McCollum* and, for the first time in American history, agreed to rule on the question of religion in the public school.

The Oral Pleadings

The Champaign school board and the intervening parents based their case substantially on an appeal to history and logic in an attempt to demonstrate that Justice Black had gone beyond the evidence in his *Everson* ruling where he stated that government may not "aid *all* religions." However valid the case against Justice Black's history may be—and it came to be identified as the "Catholic interpretation" of the First Amendment—Justice Black and his associates were clearly not pleased to have their scholarship impugned. In sharp thrusts at counsel during the oral pleadings on the *McCollum* case Justice Black and others on the Court made it clear that their version of the First Amendment as proscribing aid "to *all* religions" was *not dicta* in *Everson* and was not being withdrawn.

Although it is impossible to know what, if any, contribution the oral arguments make to the ultimate result of a Supreme Court opinion, the three-hour oral pleadings conducted on December 8, 1947, in the *McCollum* case could not possibly have left the eight members of the Court (Justice Murphy was absent, being hospitalized) with any idea of the enormous significance of the issues they were being asked to adjudicate. The attorney for the Champaign officials, who took part in the trial of the case, confessed to the Supreme Court that "I am not here because of any profound legal ability on my part. I am the School Board attorney."[42] He went on to concede the inadequacies of the record which, he said, "was made by the appellant (Mrs. McCollum) . . . and was developed as her attorneys wished it developed."[43] The absence from the record of any written authorization given for released time by the Champaign school board was another factor which seemed to trouble the Court and impede the presentation of the case on behalf of released time.

Possibly one of the worst misunderstandings of what was at stake can be seen in this colloquy between Justice Black and the school board's attorney:

Justice Black: Do I understand you to take the position that if the State of Illinois wanted to contribute five million dollars a year to religion they could do so, so long as they provided the same to every faith?

Counsel: Yes . . . and the State of Illinois does contribute . . . annually . . . more than five million dollars . . . by tax exemptions.[44]

Such open repudiation of the principle made by the Supreme Court only ten months earlier in the *Everson* case to the effect that the First Amendment forbids aid "to *all* religions" was neither necessary nor lawyerlike since the Champaign released-time arrangement imposed no cost of any consequence on the school board.

Other exchanges during the course of the oral pleadings on the *McCollum* case indicated that the decision would rest on what the Court decided to do about its *dicta* in *Everson*. Counsel for those who opposed the released-time plan concluded the oral presentation of both sides with this challenge:

It seems . . . that without any hesitancy it can be said that unless this Court is now prepared to delete from the opinions in that case (*Everson*) the strong language that was used, unless it is prepared to renounce the principles set out by the majority—and, so far as that is concerned, concurred in by the minority—then the decision in this case must necessarily be in favor of the appellant.[45]

It would appear that the Court agreed with this admonition as well as with similar advice given to it in abundance in the briefs filed by the *amici curiae*.

The Briefs of Friends of the Court

In the *Everson* litigation, the ACLU, the Seventh-Day Adventists (joined with the Baptists) and the United American Mechanics of New Jersey (a fraternal patriotic organization) had filed briefs opposing the granting of free bus rides to parochial school children. In *McCollum* the number of religious organizations filing briefs in opposition to released time grew in number. The Baptists, the Seventh-Day Adventists, the American Unitarian Association, the American Ethical Union joined the ACLU in opposing released time. The Synagogue Council joined these groups with a brief self-described as unique because it claimed to "speak for American Jewry" on what was "the first instance in which practically all American Jewish organizations, religious and lay, have joined in submitting a brief."[46]

The only brief by a religious organization on behalf of the most important Protestant movement in American religious education was submitted by the Protestant Council of New York, sponsors of released time. No massively factual "Brandeis brief" explaining the "mystique" of released time was prepared. It may be that the defenders of this nation-wide movement did not seriously think that the Supreme Court would be the first tribunal in America to declare unconstitutional a plan adopted in forty-six states and participated in by some two or more million children. On the other hand, it may be that those involved in or familiar with released time were not so persuaded of its merits that they were enthusiastic enough to defend its existence at some personal sacrifice.

The opposition of several religious bodies as well as the conflicting evidence during the oral arguments about the accessibility of the Champaign schools to the local Lutheran authorities gave the Supreme Court some reason to fear that a validation of the released-time plan might bring about a war among the sects over access to the public school for the purposes of religious instruction. The nonparticipation of Catholics in the *McCollum* case was in line with the role of an interested but not involved observer—a role which had customarily been taken by Catholic groups in connection with attempts to retain or introduce religious practices in the public schools.

The Content of the McCollum Decision

Justice Reed in his dissent in *McCollum* stated that he found "it difficult to extract from the opinions (of the majority) any conclusion as to what it is in the Champaign plan that is unconstitutional."[47] Justice Black, as he was to say later in his dissent in *Zorach*, attempted to make it clear that the released-time plan was condemned because it was ". . . beyond all question a utilization of the tax-established and tax-supported public school system to aid religious groups to spread their faiths. And it falls squarely under the ban of the First Amendment . . . as we interpreted it in *Everson v. Board of Education*."⁴⁸

Justice Black, moreover, added these words: "Here not only are the state's tax-supported public school buildings used for the dissemination of religious doctrines. The State also affords sectarian groups an invaluable aid in that it helps to provide pupils for their religious classes *through use of the state's compulsory public school machinery*. This is not separation of Church and State."⁴⁹ [Emphasis supplied.]

The words italicized would seem to preclude *all* released- and dismissed-time programs. But a sentence from Justice Frankfurter's concurring opinion threw considerable doubt on what precisely had been forbidden in the Champaign plan. Justice Frankfurter, departing in *McCollum* from his almost habitual allowance of state statutes declared constitutional by the highest court of the state, reminded that other states' statutes were not involved: "We do not consider, as indeed we could not, school programs not before us which, though colloquially characterized as 'released time,' present situations differing in aspects that may well be constitutionally crucial."⁵⁰

As will be seen later in the *Zorach* opinion, six of the justices joining in the majority view in that case did not gather from Justice Black's *McCollum* opinion what Black insists he intended.

Aside from a basic lack of clarity, Justice Black's opinion reflects the unrealistic and conceptualistic manner in which the case had been argued on both sides; he seemed to be almost unaware of the profound philosophical and educational principles which by clear implication he was adopting. Indeed he seemed to miss the essence of the controversy which he was trying to decide when he stated: ". . . the First Amendment rests upon the premise that both religion and government can best work to achieve their lofty aims if each is left free from the other *within its respective sphere*."⁵¹ [Emphasis supplied.] The entire case, of course, centers around the very question of what is the "respective sphere" of education and of religion. It is hardly a helpful answer to tell the religionists who have structured, financed and promoted the released-time movement that they must achieve their "lofty aims" outside of the "sphere" of education when their basic contention is that the "sphere" of religion, to be valid and vital, *must* be integrated with the "sphere" of education and that, on the other hand, the "sphere" of education is truncated without some contact with the "sphere" of religion.

Justice Black assumes that the school is exclusively a state agency and that it may not "utilize *its* public school system to aid any or all religious faiths or sects in the dissemination of their doctrines and ideals."[52] Justice Frankfurter follows this line of thought, insisting that in the "secular school" there must be a "sharp confinement . . . to secular education." After this rather long and not always unemotional defense of absolute separation, Frankfurter concludes by reiterating a sentence which clearly seems to be an ambiguous and dangerous oversimplification: "We renew our conviction that 'we have staked the very existence of our country on the faith that complete separation between the state and religion is best for the state and best for religion.' If nowhere else, in the relation of Church and State, 'good fences make good neighbors.' "[53]

But the ambiguity in the *McCollum* decision concerning the actual extent of the Court's prohibition or the dogmatic pronouncements on the ethos of the public school was not the most important feature of that decision. The most important result of *McCollum* was the fact that this decision, for the first time in American jurisprudence, created a new liberty by which a plaintiff, with or without a substantial monetary loss to himself or any infringement of his religious freedom, can, by invoking the establishment clause, cause to have eliminated some practice wherein the state morally or financially aids religion. Prior to *McCollum*, there had been cases where the person seeking relief claimed that *because* of a violation of the establishment clause he was restricted in his religious freedom. But in *McCollum*, for the first time, the mere presence of a violation of the establishment clause created in the nonbeliever a right to enjoin the practice complained of.

In other words the Supreme Court in *McCollum* interpreted the establishment clause without reference to the free exercise of religion clause. It made the establishment clause not the means by which religious freedom is to be secured for all, but the basis through which the nonbeliever acquires a right to enjoin any aid to sectarian religion even if such aid is granted on a nondiscriminatory basis.

The Supreme Court in *McCollum* agreed that the right to be

free from what it conceived to be an establishment of religion was one of those fundamental liberties "implicit in the concept of ordered liberty," as Justice Cardozo put it in the classical language of the *Palko* decision.[54] The new right, or "liberty," which is the word in the Fourteenth Amendment to transfer the new right to the states, is deemed to be one of the fundamental rights guaranteed by the Bill of Rights and intended by the framers of the Fourteenth Amendment to be transferred to the states.

The novel liberty created by *McCollum*, however, is unlike any of the extensions of religious liberty granted, for example, to Jehovah's Witnesses. In the cases involving members of this sect, the privilege claimed and sometimes vindicated is the right to hold and act upon one's religious views, however eccentric they may appear to others. But the "liberty" created for Mrs. McCollum and others similarly situated is the privilege of protesting against any linking of state and religion from which some aid, however accidental, may result to religion.

Professor Edward S. Corwin and others wrote after the *McCollum* decision that the "liberty" concept of the Fourteenth Amendment could not be read so as to include the establishment clause unless it be shown that someone's freedom of religion was actually invaded.[55] Professor David Fellman agrees that on this point "the Court is not entirely clear."[56] Professor Wilbur G. Katz reiterates these misgivings about conferring a "liberty" upon a citizen whose religious freedom has not been infringed but who alleges a violation of the establishment clause. For Professor Katz "separation is a subordinate concept, instrumental to the maintenance of religious liberty."[57]

Since the creation in *McCollum* of the "liberty" to protest any violation of the establishment clause, it would appear that the Supreme Court has retained this concept and reiterated it on at least the following occasions:

1. Chief Justice Earl Warren, in his majority opinion sustaining the constitutionality of Sunday laws, declined to accept the suggestion that "the purpose of the 'establishment' clause is only to insure protection for the 'free exercise' of religion."[58] It would seem to follow that a violation of the establishment clause offends the Constitution even if such violation does not infringe upon the free exercise of anyone's religion.

2. Justice Black in the New York prayer case, while ruling that

the Regents' prayer was a violation of the establishment clause, repudiated more vigorously than ever before the theory that the
establishment clause is merely "instrumental to the maintenance of
religious liberty," as Professor Katz put it.

For a 6 to 1 majority Justice Black wrote: "Neither the fact that
the prayer may be denominationally neutral, nor the fact that its
observance on the part of the students is voluntary can serve to free
it from the limitations of the establishment clause, *as it might from
the free exercise* clause, of the First Amendment. . . . Although
these two clauses may, in certain instances, overlap they forbid two
quite different kinds of governmental encroachment upon religious
freedom. . . . The establishment clause, unlike the free exercise
clause, does not depend upon any showing of direct governmental
compulsion and is violated by the enactment of laws which establish an official religion *whether these laws operate directly to coerce nonobserving individuals or not.*"[59] [Emphasis supplied.]

Justice Stewart, in his dissent, notes that the majority has apparently rested its ruling on the establishment clause alone and not on
the free exercise guarantee, for he writes that "the Court does not
hold, nor could it, that New York has interfered with the free exercise of anybody's religion."[60]

Violations of the establishment clause constitute a very new feature of church–state law. Hardly a beginning has been made in
thinking through the problems connected with the "liberty" established for the first time in the *McCollum* case—the "liberty" to enjoin an "establishment" of religion independently of any personal
injury.

Although some of the asperities of *McCollum* were softened in
Zorach, the central point of *McCollum*—that is, the creation of
substantive rights within the establishment clause—did *not* disappear even if it were true that as Justice Jackson said bitterly in his
Zorach dissent, "the *McCollum* case has passed like a storm in a
teacup."[61]

The Aftermath of McCollum

Amid all the hue and cry over the *McCollum* decision, very little
was made of its creation of a novel "liberty" which still exists, regardless of what survives of the rest of the rulings in *McCollum.*

Another extraordinary element of *McCollum* that received little
if any attention was the strange irony that many Protestant groups,

after a year of vigorous denunciations of the victory and the "designs" of the Catholic Church as they thought they saw them evidenced in the *Everson* result, were themselves told by the same Court that they were in massive noncompliance with the Constitution by reason of their vast network of classes in sectarian teachings being held in tax-supported public schools. Although America is a pluralistic society no organization of non-Protestants and others was formed (as after *Everson*) to make certain that *McCollum* was obeyed!

Despite *McCollum*, however, most Protestants hoped to continue to enjoy what Leo Pfeffer has called "the best of both possible worlds—the exclusion of parochial schools from governmental aid and the inclusion of pan-Protestantism in the public schools."[62]

Justice Black was hardly exaggerating in his *Zorach* dissent when he stated: "I am aware that our *McCollum* decision on separation of church and state has been subjected to a most searching examination throughout the country. Probably few opinions from the Court in recent years have attracted more attention or stirred wider debate."[63] Black continues and, making what is possibly a reference to the position of the American Catholic bishops, states that he is aware that "others have thought the *McCollum* decision fundamentally wrong and have pledged continuous warfare against it."[64]

The "most searching examination" of the *McCollum* decision brought forward an abundance of reasons why the very first ruling in American history by the Supreme Court on the place of religion in public education had overlooked or misconstrued several factors in this complicated field. Indeed, as one reviews the adverse comments on *McCollum* by such persons as Professor Edward S. Corwin,[65] Alexander Meiklejohn,[66] Dean (now Bishop) James A. Pike,[67] Henry P. Van Dusen,[68] and Professor Arthur Sutherland[69] one is struck by the vehemence underlying the truly devastatingly critical analyses of the Court's work in *McCollum*. The Court was accused of the "utmost insouciance,"[70] of giving an "unreasoned and unreasonable" answer to the problem before it, of causing "judicial damage to the freedom of religion and to the natural rights of parents"[71] and of establishing "the religion of secularism by judicial fiat."[72]

If criticisms and public opinion adverse to *McCollum* influenced the Court to adopt its more irenic approach to *Zorach*, then the

Catholics of America may well have been more instrumental than
most other groups. It may be in fact that the Catholics, by their
overwhelming opposition to *McCollum*, rescued the Protestant-
originated program of released time from the judicial extinction
which was implicit in Justice Black's opinion in the *McCollum*
case.

If the period between *McCollum* and *Zorach* was one of national confusion with all conflicting groups citing Supreme Court
utterances favorable to their side, the years since *Zorach* have been
even more confusing. For the fact is that *McGowan, Torcaso* and
Engel—the only church–state cases from 1952 until 1963—do not
clarify the basic contradictions which *Zorach* has left concerning
the interpretation and implications of the *Everson–McCollum*
approach. These contradictions are not dissolved by the fact that
the Court in *McGowan* and *Torcaso* (but, perhaps significantly,
not in *Engel*) reasserted its endorsement of the *Everson–McCollum* rationale; the fact remains that *Zorach* is different in tone,
philosophy and result from the *Everson–McCollum* approach.

The Meaning of Zorach *and the Future of Released Time*

Justice Jackson, ending a sharply worded dissenting repudiation
of the majority view in *Zorach*, accuses his "evangelistic brethren"
of uttering "passionate dialectics" and of starting down the road
that will "mix compulsory education with compulsory godliness."
For Justice Jackson, "Today's judgment will be more interesting to
students of psychology and of the judicial processes than to students of constitutional law."[73]

The *Zorach* opinion has been found interesting to "students of
constitutional law," but also bewildering. The reconciliation or
polarization of *Zorach* vis-à-vis *Everson–McCollum* has engaged
the talents of all church–state writers in attempts at interpretation
that unconsciously betray their authors' viewpoints on where the
line of "separation" should be drawn.

No student of church–state relations has claimed to be able to
effect a perfect reconciliation of *Zorach* with *Everson–McCollum*.
Even Leo Pfeffer, whose thesis would be served by minimizing the
erosion of *McCollum* by *Zorach*, concedes that *Zorach* "shows
some retreat from the broad scope of the *Everson–McCollum* principle."[74] He insists, however, that "*despite its language* it is doubtful that the *Zorach* decision is to be interpreted as a repudiation of

the *Everson–McCollum* principle."[75] [Emphasis supplied.] Mr.
Pfeffer has also conceded that "the language used by Justice Douglas, if not the holding itself, manifested a discreet withdrawal from
the forward position taken in *Everson* and *McCollum*."[76]

Other close observers feel that *Zorach* constituted a more radical
departure from *McCollum*. Professor Paul Kauper has written that
"all students of this subject may well agree that *Zorach* for all practical purposes overruled *McCollum*."[77] John C. Bennett has asserted that *Zorach* "said quite different things (from *McCollum*)
about the problem of the relation between the state and the various religious bodies."[78] F. Ernest Johnson, one of the closest students of the church–state problem, felt that the *"Zorach* case
formulated a quite different doctrine. For the absolutistic definition of separation between church and state set forth in the former
case, the Court substituted—not explicitly, but in effect—the principle of *cooperation* between church and state. . . ."[79]

The fundamental problem in trying to piece together a church–
state philosophy from the *Everson–McCollum–Zorach* decisions
derives from the fact that all three dissenters in *Zorach* argue
strenuously that the majority of six have completely misconstrued
the thrust of the *McCollum* opinion. If the dissenters are correct—
as they seem to be—then one can agree with Professor Kauper that
McCollum is "for all practical purposes overruled." If, on the other
hand, the majority of the Justices in *Zorach* by stating "We follow
the *McCollum* case. But we cannot expand it . . ." intended to
ratify everything of substance in *McCollum*, then *Zorach* is considerably diluted.

Although it may be impossible to harmonize all of the statements
in *Zorach* with *Everson–McCollum* and with the later New York
prayer case, a thorough analysis of the law as *Zorach* spells it out is
necessary both because the *Zorach* ruling is still the church–state
law of the land and because the approach in *Zorach* indicates that
the Court had some appreciation of the complexities behind the
most viable method yet attempted to resolve some of the fundamental dilemmas surrounding the teaching of religion in the tax-
supported public school.

From Justice Douglas' opinion for the majority in the *Zorach*
decision the following conclusions seem warranted:[80]

1. The Champaign plan in the *McCollum* case involved religious
instruction in public school classrooms and the expenditure of

public funds and was "accordingly" declared unconstitutional. The New York plan involved neither of these features and is therefore permissible.

Justice Black unequivocally disagrees with this analysis of the *McCollum* holding; he writes in his *Zorach* dissent: "As we attempted to make categorically clear, the *McCollum* decision would have been the same if the religious classes had not been held in the school buildings."[81]

The law today, however, is *not* Justice Black's version of what he intended to say in *McCollum* but rather the *Zorach* principle that "public institutions can make . . . (an) adjustment of their schedules to accommodate the religious needs of the people."

2. *No* issue of "free exercise" is involved in the New York released-time plan.

3. Coercion, however, is not permitted and "*If* it were established that any one or more teachers were using their office to persuade or to force students to take the religious instruction, a wholly different case would be presented."

This warning by Justice Douglas has reference apparently to the conduct of teachers themselves, since he seems to concede by implication that in released time "the state encourages religious instruction or cooperates with religious authorities" . . . and that in so doing "it follows the best of our traditions."

4. The "wall of separation" metaphor is not used in *Zorach*; it is asserted rather that the "First Amendment does not say that in every and all respect there shall be a separation of Church and State." What is proscribed is any "concert or union or dependency one on the other."

5. *Zorach* asserts that the "nullification of this law (permitting released time) would have wide and profound effects." If the law in question were condemned on constitutional grounds, then all the following things, in Justice Douglas' opinion, would *also* be "flouting the First Amendment." The list of things which Justice Douglas cites is impressive: "Churches could not be required to pay even property taxes. Municipalities would not be permitted to render police or fire protection to religious groups. Policemen who helped parishoners into their places of worship would violate the Constitution. Prayers in our legislative halls; the appeals to the Almighty in the messages of the Chief Executive; the proclamations making Thanksgiving Day a holiday; 'so help me God' in our court-

room oaths—these and all the other references to the Almighty that run through our laws, our public rituals, our ceremonies—would be flouting the First Amendment." Justice Douglas states without qualification that "we would have to press the concept of separation of church and state *to these extremes* to condemn the present law on constitutional grounds." [Emphasis supplied.] Since *Zorach* is still good law, there is a solid argument that all the items mentioned by Justice Douglas have received a constitutional blessing and that one of them may not be declared unconstitutional so long as *Zorach* is not reversed.

A state-sponsored prayer for school children is *not* among the examples cited above. One can question, however, whether Douglas himself, in his concurring opinion in the New York prayer case, has remembered his list of "extremes." In his somewhat ambiguous opinion in *Engel*, Douglas raises some questions about the permissibility of prayers in Congress if the New York Regents' prayer is declared invalid; but an open contradiction between his views in *Engel* and in *Zorach* is not clearly apparent.

6. The *Zorach* opinion recognizes, as the *McCollum* ruling did not, that the public school cannot treat the spiritual needs of its students as if they did not exist. *McCollum* ignored the fact that in 2200 communities in 46 states released-time programs had been initiated by conscientious parents, church leaders and educational officials in an attempt to solve an urgent problem. Justice Douglas in *Zorach* vindicates the right of the public school to accommodate its schedule "to further the religious needs of all the students." To do otherwise might cause the government ". . . to throw its weight against efforts to widen the effective scope of religious influence."

Statements like these resulted in part from the fact that the promoters of released time submitted in the *Zorach* case a "Brandeis brief" on released time to which Douglas makes reference when he acknowledges that the "briefs and arguments are replete with data bearing on the merits of this type of released-time program."

The *Zorach* decision has come to be identified with a theory of "cooperation" rather than "separation" between church and state. This is probably not an entirely accurate restatement of the law in *Zorach*; this decision seeks rather to view the entire situation as one in which a violation of the First Amendment is alleged. If no infringement of religious freedom is involved, then cooperation between officials of the state and of the church is not in itself an "establishment" of religion. But such "cooperation" means that, while separation remains "complete and unequivocal" with respect both to the "free exercise" and "establishment" clauses, the state may respect "the religious nature of our people" and accommodate its "public service to their spiritual needs."

7. The most famous *dictum* of *Zorach* is, of course, the eleven-word sentence "We are a religious people whose institutions presuppose a Supreme Being." This aphorism, which has become one of the most frequently quoted phrases in modern Supreme Court jurisprudence, has been analyzed in a pamphlet issued by the Center for the Study of Democratic Institution, a unit established by the Fund for the Republic. In "Religion and American Society," a statement of principles carefully worked out by an interreligious group of scholars, the following is noted about Justice Douglas' statement:[82] "One school of thought has deduced from it that government is duty-bound to encourage, strengthen, and support the forces of religion in American life. Another, fearing that such a result is indeed the logical consequence of the *dictum*, has tended to dismiss the Douglas statement as an outburst of judicial piety. A third has accepted it simply as a statement of historical fact about the nation, with no novel or inevitable consequences. We lean toward the third interpretation. To say what Justice Douglas said, it seems to us, is only to acknowledge that American democracy as a theory of government exists within the political tradition of the West and that the political tradition of the West developed slowly out of a Judaeo–Christian view of life."

It is not possible to determine with precision what philosophy of education the majority of six adopted in *Zorach*, although the idea of the *exclusively* secular nature of the public school clearly dominates the minority views of the Court. The majority in *Zorach* seems to have attempted a middle path between the absolutism of *McCollum* where *no* provision is made for parental rights and the *Pierce* decision where, in fulsome *dicta*, parental rights in education are acknowledged. The *McCollum* decision, as Alexander Meiklejohn has pointed out,[83] actually reversed *Pierce* in part since, if students can be released for their *entire* academic careers to a church-related private school, why can they not be released for a much smaller part of their school career?

Ironically it is the *Zorach* decision which, seeking to save *McCol-*

lum and also to validate an off-the-premises released-time plan, enunciated one sentence which, more specifically than all other *dicta* of the Supreme Court, bars aid for nonpublic church-related schools. Government, Justice Douglas writes, "may not finance religious groups . . . nor blend secular or sectarian instruction . . ." It is this latter phrase which, as we shall see later, was relied upon in the decision of the Vermont Supreme Court declaring unconstitutional an arrangement in that state under which students from towns without a high school could attend a public or church-related school in a neighboring town with tuition paid to either school by the town of residence.

So much then for the struggles which the public school's greatest experiment in religious education had on two occasions before the Supreme Court. The enemies of released time who brought the cases all the way to the Supreme Court may have unwittingly contributed to this idea better legal protection than may ever be subsequently obtained for any other device to bring religious training into public education. At the same time, however, the *McCollum* and *Zorach* cases may have enunciated opinions which will eventually lead to a deepening of the secularization of the tax-supported school.

If released time has been the most viable experiment in religious education, Bible-reading in the public school has certainly been the most pervasive, the most prestige-laden and the symbol widely considered as the most precious of all the religious influences in public education. It is this subject—soon to be tested by the Supreme Court—to which we now give consideration.

BIBLE-READING IN PUBLIC SCHOOLS

It is an historical fact that virtually all of the litigation over religion in public education has been initiated by those who oppose religious practices in the public schools on the grounds of separation of church and state. Seldom, if ever, has there occurred a clearcut plaintiffs' suit insisting that voluntary religious practices *must* be allowed by the state, because otherwise the state would enter the area of religion forbidden to its cognizance and would thereby infringe upon the religious freedom of parents and school children. All of the judicially made law, therefore, on religion in public education derives from lawsuits where the record and the result reflect the atmosphere of litigation born of a minority plaintiff's grievance against a law or a practice carried out with the presumed consent of the majority.

The *McCollum* decision particularly reflects this atmosphere. The vehemence of that decision derives in part from the fact that there was no Illinois statute authorizing released time nor was there any written record of specific permission granted for such a program by the school board. The Champaign plan enrolling 850 Protestant children, 18 to 22 Catholic pupils and no Jewish students (after its first year of operation) apparently seemed to eight Justices of the Supreme Court to be almost an intrusion by the churches—and particularly the Protestant churches—into a tax-supported state agency.

Despite the devastating denunciation of the Champaign system, a plan conducted without benefit of a statute, it is quite understandable how reluctant all church groups are to seek from the legislature a statute authorizing a particular type of religious activity for the public school. Educators also are hesitant to request or even to allow the legislature to interfere with the conduct and curriculum of the schools in which the educators themselves should have as broad an autonomy as is possible.

In the twentieth century, non-Catholic religionists have had to confront the question of the advisability of their seeking legislation to authorize Bible-reading in the schools. Before we can attempt some assessment of contemporary opinion of the value and symbolic significance of Bible-reading in public education, a review of legislation and judicial opinion on this issue, the most frequently litigated church–state question in this century, will be helpful.

In the fall of 1962, the United States Supreme Court agreed to review two decisions in which a clear-cut ruling on the constitutional issues involved in Bible-reading cannot seemingly be avoided. These decisions, to be discussed later in this section, may well result in an almost sensational dramatization of the long struggle to keep the public school a nonsectarian but religious institution.

Most Americans tend to think of Bible-reading in the public schools as a relic of the days when the common schools had a certain atmosphere of Protestant Christianity. While there is some truth in this assumption, the fact is that Bible-reading and other religious practices did not become *legally* a part of the public school program until some decades after these schools had adopted their original curriculum. It appears that during the nineteenth century only one state, Massachusetts, enacted a statute requiring Bible-reading; from the passage of this law in 1826, *no* state enacted a law requiring Bible-reading in the state schools until the year 1913! In that year Pennsylvania passed the first law ordering the reading of the Bible in the schools of that state.[84]

By what church–state theory did the educators of Pennsylvania request or at least accept a direct command of the *state* that might well have usurped the power and function of the school board, the principal and each individual instructor in directing *what* values would be taught and in what manner? And by what philosophy of church–state relations and academic freedom did the public school administration and teachers of the nation acquiesce in the *state* silencing the teacher under penalty of law by requiring him to read the Bible "without comment"?

The era of the enactment of statutes authorizing Bible-reading in public schools—all but one of which have been put on the books since 1913—coincides with the period of the birth and growth of the released-time movement. Bible-reading was not, however, an innovation like released time since the nation's schools had for a long period accepted the custom of reading the Bible as a desirable practice. The House of Representatives, when it passed a resolution in 1876 condemning the use of public funds for sectarian schools, probably reflected American public opinion when it provided that its resolution should "not be construed to prohibit the reading of the Bible in any school or institution."

The United States Supreme Court has never ruled squarely on the constitutionality of Bible-reading. In 1930, the Court declined review for want of a substantial Federal question in a case in which the Supreme Court of the state of Washington had refused to direct the state superintendent of schools to institute Bible-reading in the public schools when no statute existed requiring the superintendent to order such reading.[85] The nation's highest tribunal has therefore in effect decided that the *exclusion* of the Bible does not violate any constitutional right—although this ruling was given, it should be recalled, several years before the religious guarantees of the First Amendment were transferred to the states *via* the Fourteenth Amendment. In 1952, in the *Doremus*[86] case the Supreme Court did not reach the constitutional question involved in a

Bible-reading decision in which the Supreme Court of New Jersey had unanimously sustained a Bible-reading statute.

This New Jersey litigation over the use of the Bible in public education was the first suit in the nation over this matter in over a generation. Prior to this time the majority of state courts had allowed Bible-reading to continue, and at most six states had banned Bible-reading in its entirety as a sectarian practice. In four major cases where the King James Version of the Scriptures was deemed a violation of religious freedom, Catholics were the plaintiffs.

The first of these cases occurred in Wisconsin, in 1890.[87] Although the decision was involved and relied on many points for its total result, the essential one was that the King James version *is* a sectarian book and that therefore the Catholics were correct in protesting its use in the public school. In 1910, the Supreme Court of Illinois ruled similarly—though in this suit there was involved the reading of both Old and New Testament, the recital of the Lord's Prayer, the singing of hymns of Protestant origin and the questioning of students on the meaning of passages from Scripture.[88] Over a vehement dissent the highest court of Illinois excluded all Bible-reading from the public schools.

In 1915, the Louisiana Supreme Court decided that the reading of the New Testament in the public schools constituted a preference given to Christians and a discrimination against Jews.[89] The same decision held that the imposition of the King James Version on Catholics was discriminatory. In 1929, South Dakota's highest court ruled that Catholic children need not comply with the statute which demanded that they seek to be excused from the reading of the Bible; the Court, however, apparently allowed the practice of reading the Bible to continue.[90]

The Supreme Court of New Jersey was the first appellate tribunal called upon to pass on Bible-reading subsequent to the *McCollum* decision. For a unanimous court Justice Case found that in *McCollum* "the facts are so different from ours that no discussion seems necessary."

The plaintiffs in the *Doremus* case[91] neither asserted nor implied that Bible-reading, mandatory in the public schools of New Jersey, violated the religious liberty of any persons. Neither did the plaintiffs allege that the trifling expenditure involved justified them in bringing a taxpayer's suit to enjoin the alleged unauthorized expenditure. Despite these two circumstances, the Supreme Court of

New Jersey ruled on the merits, making clear its opinion that neither *McCollum* nor the separation of church and state demand or even authorize the stripping of all religious sentiment from the state. It would be a tragic experience for the American state, the New Jersey court felt, if its people lost their religious faith. "Who can say," the court queried, "that those attributes which Thomas Jefferson in his notable document called 'unalienable Rights' may survive a loss of belief in the Creator?" Just "a brief moment with eternity," the court went on to say, at the beginning of the life of our children may supply that perspective which will be "effective to keep our people from permitting government to become a man-made robot which will crush even the Constitution itself."

When the United States Supreme Court agreed to hear the *Doremus* case, it specifically noted that jurisdiction in the case was postponed. At the oral arguments in the case, it seemed clear that the Court was apparently seeking a way to avoid a decision on the merits of the law requiring Bible-reading in the schools. Justice Jackson possibly reflected the anxiety of his associates when he remarked to counsel at the oral pleadings that "We won't have anything but religious questions if we don't watch out."[92]

The Supreme Court's curious 6–3 ruling in the *Doremus* case, handed down on March 3, 1952, just a few weeks before its April, 1952, *Zorach* decision, dismissed the complaint as not a case or controversy within the meaning of the Constitution. The Court ruled that the plaintiff had lost his standing because his child had graduated by the time the appeal reached the Supreme Court. Whether this Supreme Court opinion fits neatly into its prior holdings about the amount of legal injury required to produce a "case or controversy" is a question which will be carefully and thoroughly explored in the appeal from what is the most important case on Bible-reading in American history—the declaration by a three-judge Federal court in 1959 and again on February 1, 1962, that a Pennsylvania law requiring Bible-reading in the schools of that commonwealth is unconstitutional.[93] In view of the review of this significant ruling by the United States Supreme Court the Pennsylvania result is worthy of some detailed consideration—as are two 1962 decisions of the Supreme Court of Florida[94] and the Maryland Court of Appeals.[95]

In 1949, Pennsylvania amended its law respecting Bible-reading in the schools to provide as follows: "At least ten verses from the

Holy Bible shall be read, or caused to be read, without comment, at the opening of each public school on each school day, by the teacher in charge. . . ."[96] No definition of what books or version of the "Holy Bible" should be employed was included in the statute. No provision was inserted to excuse students desiring an exemption, and any school teacher who, for whatever reason, omitted the reading of the Bible could, after a hearing, be discharged.[97]

On September 16, 1959, a three-judge Federal court declared this law unconstitutional.[98] At the trial conducted before this special panel of judges, Dr. Luther A. Weigle, Dean Emeritus of the Yale Divinity School and an ordained Lutheran minister, testified on behalf of the constitutionality of Bible-reading while Dr. Solomon Grayzel, an ordained rabbi, a translator of the English version of the Jewish Bible and an acknowledged expert in Semitic and Hebrew studies, gave evidence to the contrary.

Dean Weigle stated that the Bible was nonsectarian in the sense that it does not favor one specific sect over another. He added, however, that the reading of the Holy Scriptures to the exclusion of the New Testament *would* be a sectarian practice. During the course of cross-examination the following passage from Dean Weigle's book, *The English New Testament*, was quoted: "The Bible is not a mere historical document to be preserved. And it is more than a classic of English literature to be cherished and admired. The Bible contains the Word of God to man. . . ." Without repudiating the belief, basic to every Christian, that the Bible is the "Word of God to man," Dean Weigle expressed the judgment that the Bible could be used in a public school for its great moral, historical and literary value.

Dr. Grayzel testified that there were portions of the New Testament that were offensive to Jewish tradition; he cited instances which, assertedly, were not only sectarian in nature but tended to bring the Jews into ridicule or scorn. While Dr. Grayzel conceded that such material from the New Testament could be explained to Jewish children in a way that would do them no harm, the reading of these sections, without explanation, could, in Dr. Grayzel's opinion, be psychologically harmful to children of the Jewish faith. In particular, Dr. Grayzel cited the gospel according to Matthew, Chapter 27, where the trial of Christ before Pilate is related. To Dr. Grayzel this scene portrays Jews as refusing to exchange Barabbas for Jesus; it also contains the words (verse 25), "Then answered all the people, and said, 'His blood be on us, and our children'." Dr. Grayzel stated that this last verse had been the cause of more anti-Jewish riots throughout the ages than anything else in history.[99]

From such totally conflicting evidence the Court came to these conclusions: (1) The Bible "is essentially a religious work . . . inasmuch as the verses of the Bible address themselves to, or are premised upon a recognition of God."[100] (2) ". . . the practice required by the statute amounts to religious instruction, or a promotion of religious education."[101] (3) This "religious instruction" clearly violates the establishment clause as construed in the *McCollum* decision. (4) "Inasmuch as the 'Holy Bible' is a Christian document, the practice aids and prefers the Christian religion."[102]

The three-judge court could have rested on these grounds but it went on to assert that the Pennsylvania law also violated the Federal Constitution because it infringed on the religious freedom of the teachers who were required to observe the statute. The court likewise felt that there was a certain compulsion operating on the children because, although there was no sanction for any noncomplying student, there was not, on the other hand, any specific exemption clause.

The court also expressed its view that the rights of parents were interfered with by compulsory Bible-reading. Wrote Judge John Biggs: "Parents may well wish that their children develop a religious sensibility. If the faith of a child is developed inconsistently with the faith of the parent and contrary to the wishes of the parent, interference with the familial right of the parent to inculcate in the child the religion the parent desires, is clear beyond doubt."[103]

While the school board was appealing the decision to the United States Supreme Court the Pennsylvania legislature amended the statute so as to provide that any child bringing a written request from his parent could be excused from participation in the daily Bible-reading exercise. The amended statute gave the Supreme Court the opportunity to vacate the appeal and remand the case to the District Court for further consideration in the light of the statutory amendment.[104]

The amendment to the statute caused no change in the attitude of the same three-judge court which, on February 1, 1962, re-affirmed its 1959 holding that compulsory Bible-reading was unconstitutional as a "promotion of religiousness."[105] This second declaration of nullity was again appealed to the United States Supreme Court and in the fall of 1962 the nation's highest tribunal agreed to pass on the legality of Bible-reading as required by the Pennsylvania statute.

On April 6, 1962, Maryland's highest court, in a 4–3 split, came to a conclusion opposite to the Pennsylvania result on daily reading of the Bible and recitation of the Lord's Prayer.[106] The dissenters followed in principle the approach taken by the Federal court in Pennsylvania. The majority came to these conclusions: (1) Where the time and expense are negligible and where provision is made for excusing a child from participation, the reading of the Bible and the recitation of the Lord's Prayer is not a violation of the First Amendment. (2) ". . . neither the First nor the Fourteenth Amendment was intended to stifle all rapport between religion and government."[107] The court supports this judgment by quoting *Zorach*: "When the state encourages religious instruction . . . it follows the best of our traditions."[108] "We think there is little doubt that a decision in this case lies somewhere between the decision in *McCollum* and that in *Zorach*."[109]

The Supreme Court of Florida has also sustained the practice of Bible-reading, attacked as unconstitutional in a suit involving religious exercises in the public schools of greater Miami.[110]

Many observers have rejoiced that the Supreme Court has agreed to decide on the constitutionality of public school Bible-reading, which in 1958 was required in thirteen states, allowed in twenty-five more and prohibited in eight. What then can one predict about the future legal position of the most litigation-scarred but possibly the most prestigious of the religious symbols in America's public schools?

If the mandate in *Everson–McCollum* that the state may not "aid all religions" is to be taken as an absolute and as meaning both purposeful and incidental "aid," then it would follow that Bible-reading may not be conducted in the tax-supported school— except perhaps on the theory that it is a great work of literature and like, for example, "Paradise Lost," may be read to the students as a classic. A total proscription of Bible-reading would follow immediately from the Supreme Court's interpretation of the establishment clause—regardless of the version of the Bible used and irrespective of whether anyone claims an infringement of his free exercise of religion.

It is important to emphasize the fact that the Supreme Court, by rejecting in *McCollum* and subsequent decisions the theory that the establishment clause is merely instrumental to the free exercise clause, has opened a Pandora's box which, if the Court follows its own logic, will lead to the eradication of all practices in which the state gives moral or financial aid to religion in any form. The Supreme Court has insisted, in other words, that the Constitution is violated if the state allows its machinery to become involved with religious activities in such a way that religion is benefited. All citizens therefore, by reason of the establishment clause, are granted freedom *from* all religion in any way sponsored by the state; such freedom *from* religion is a right independent of, and existing simultaneously with, the freedom *of* religion guaranteed by the free exercise clause.

The contention, therefore, heard so frequently that the rights of the majority should not be denied in order to respect the rights of the minority is not a valid point—*if* one accepts the thesis that the establishment clause rejects as unconstitutional *every* asserted right of a majority or a minority to any state-sponsored religious activity. The establishment clause under this interpretation imports an attitude of neutrality and noncommittalism toward religion on the part of the state. The traditional objection against such an attitude has asserted that the state—and the public school—by being uncommitted is thereby committed to the unimportance or irrelevance of being committed.

It is impossible to reconcile the literal consequence of the rigorous no-aid-to-religion interpretation of the establishment clause— subscribed to by the Supreme Court in *Everson*, *McCollum*, *McGowan*, *Torcaso* and *Engel*—with the *Zorach* opinion. The open contradiction between the holding and spirit of *Zorach* and other Supreme Court opinions before and after it suggest that the members of the country's highest court of appeal share the nation's ambiguities and even moods concerning the many-faceted problem of a religiously uncommitted government trying to protect *all* the rights of *all* the members of its four religious "conspiracies."

The uncertainties of Supreme Court opinions, however, do not justify any contumelious criticism of the Court as incompetent or, even more unfair, hostile to religion. It should be remembered that the Supreme Court in the 172 years from 1791 to 1963 has considered only eleven cases[111] involving the religious problems of publicly maintained schools and that in only three of these (*Mc-Collum, Zorach* and *Engel*) did the Court pass on the merits of religious practices in the public school. A beginning, therefore, has hardly been made; the Court consequently should not be criticized too harshly if, in the first three cases testing the thrust of the establishment clause, it has appeared to issue conflicting views. One should be grateful, and indeed astonished, that the church–state arrangement placed in the Constitution at the time of the formation of the Union has apparently been so well suited for the nation that litigation has not been necessary.

If the Supreme Court decides to apply its *Everson–McCollum–Zorach* formula to Bible-reading, the Court's views will undoubtedly reflect the national perplexity over the seldom discussed *ultimate* justifications for the separation of church and state. The perceptive statement "Religion and American Society"[112] notes that: "It is said that Thomas Jefferson favored separation of church and state so that the state might be protected from the church, whereas Roger Williams favored it so that the church might be protected from the state."

In the many legal controversies over Bible-reading echoes of the fears of both Thomas Jefferson and Roger Williams have been heard. But the feeling of Roger Williams that the separation of church and state is needed to protect the church is today the great anxiety of those who observe state activity inserting itself into every area of life and culture hitherto reserved for the church or family. It is protection against the silent but thunderous state non-committalism to religion which church groups and defenders of Bible-reading in the public school are seeking. One may argue that the protection would not be needed by a truly vibrant church or that the protection is indeed a flimsy bulwark or that a symbol rather than the substance of protection is sought in the struggle over Bible-reading in the schools.

Regardless, however, of whatever legal, constitutional or theoretical argument may be used by the Supreme Court to eliminate Bible-reading in the public schools such an act would be taken by many millions of persons as a decree of hostility to religion and as a decision based on a factitious interpretation of the Constitution. On the other hand, the outlawing of the use of the Bible by Supreme Court decision would be employed by the proponents of state aid for sectarian schools as another argument to support their position that the public school must be by law a secularistic school.

PRAYER IN PUBLIC SCHOOLS

If released time and Bible-reading appear to be too inconsequential to have provoked the litigation which has marked their destinies, a simple prayer recited by school children at the beginning of their day seems almost inherently incapable of providing the occasion for passionately debated litigation and a Supreme Court opinion eliciting a heated controversy of some national consequence. But a twenty-two word "sub-Christian," nondenominational prayer has done just that—bringing into dramatic focus some of the deeper issues in the century-old struggle by religious forces to keep some point of insertion, however tenuous, in the general culture and in the public school from which religion has been extruded.

Although the recital of the Lord's Prayer in public schools is one of the most widely employed religious practices, there is little clear-cut law pertaining to this practice. Whatever law exists is embodied in rulings on Bible-reading or hymn-singing to which the recitation of the Lord's Prayer is frequently appended. Questions about the constitutionality of reciting the Lord's Prayer follow the same pattern as with Bible-reading; its voluntary nature and the sectarian character of the prayer are the chief issues. Although the Lord's Prayer has been chosen for use in the public school because it is acceptable to all groups of Christians, persons of the Jewish faith object to it because it originates in the New Testament.

It is ironical that, historically, the Supreme Court's first case on prayer in the public school did not involve the "Our Father," a prayer which has been used for decades and which is now recited daily by millions of school children in many if not most of the states. Since, however, the June 25, 1962, decision of the Supreme Court banning a state-composed prayer may have serious consequences for the practice of reciting the Lord's Prayer, a rather thorough analysis of that 6-to-1 ruling will be useful.

When the Board of Regents of the State of New York on November 30, 1951, unanimously adopted a statement recommending that a nondenominational prayer be recited at the opening of each school day, they could hardly have anticipated that their act would, a decade later, be described by the United States Supreme Court as "inconsistent with both the purposes of the establishment clause and the establishment clause itself."[113] Nor could the Regents have expected that the prayer which they recommended would be declared unconstitutional largely, but not exclusively, because the Regents *composed* it.

The prayer itself was simple to the point of being innocuous; it read: "Almighty God, we acknowledge our dependence upon Thee, and we beg Thy blessings upon us, our parents, our teachers and our country." Despite the national furor after the June 25, 1962, Supreme Court opinion, nothing concerning the author of the prayer or the method of composition has become known. It seems clear that the prayer as promulgated was in a form calculated to offend the least number of persons. It is not trinitarian or Christian or even Scriptural except possibly for the words "Thee" and "Thy." It would appear that the Regents, having come to the conclusion that some religious or devotional exercise should be recommended for the public schools of New York, adopted the prayer that is now banned in lieu of Bible-reading or the Lord's Prayer to both of which there would be substantial objection in New York state.

One wonders whether the Supreme Court might have felt less hostility to the prayer if it had *not* been "composed by governmental officials" but rather by and with the approval of an interreligious body of clergy and laymen. The prayer is clearly theistic and to that extent prefers one religion over another. In justification of this preference the Regents made reference to the spiritual heritage of the nation and the undeniable reality of a theistic commitment underlying the legal and moral institutions of the country.

While everyone must concede that the Supreme Court has pointed out an objectionable feature in the prayer in that its author is a state official, the tone and spirit of Justice Black's opinion for the majority reflects, like his *McCollum* opinion, an insensibility to the problem to which the Regents addressed themselves. In the 1951 Regents' statement on moral and spiritual values, of which the recommended prayer was but a small part, a group created by the New York constitution attempted to assist teachers, parents and school children in articulating, for one of the nation's most pluralistic student bodies, the ethos of the nation and of its public school. As public schools are organized today no state-wide interreligious group or organization of parents or educators could, in the nature of things, speak to or for the public schools on any matter of important policy. This function in New York state is by law and custom vested in the Regents.

One can wonder about the advisability or effectiveness of adding a recommended prayer to a statement on the moral aspirations of the public school; Chief Judge Charles Desmond of the New York Court of Appeals remarked on this point, as he concluded his opinion sustaining the prayer: "The motives and purposes of the Regents and of the local board are noble. The *success of the practice is problematical* but there is no problem of constitutionality."[114] [Emphasis supplied.]

In his opinion invalidating the prayer, Justice Black wrote: "The history of man is inseparable from the history of religion."[115] How then is this inseparability to be taught to students in public schools? It is a fair assumption that many educators, religionists and parents feel that the complete concentration on secular learning has obscured the inseparability of religion and life and has thereby distorted both the secular and the sacred aspects of the learning and culture which the public school seeks to transmit. The Regents' affirmations on spiritual values and their recommendations with respect to the communication of these values formed a studied attempt to provide some guidelines for public school personnel who share the anxieties of parents and others over the secular bias of the public school.

In view of the possible long-range effects of the antiprayer decision of the Supreme Court, it will be instructive to analyze what the four courts who reviewed the Regents' prayer felt about its validity.

The first ruling on the Regents' prayer was a 35,000-word opinion by New York Supreme Court Justice Bernard S. Meyer issued on August 24, 1959.[116] Rejecting the claims brought in a suit against a Long Island school board by five parents and taxpayers, comprising members of the Jewish faith, the Society for Ethical Culture, the Unitarian Church and one nonbeliever, Justice Meyer wrote that he could find nothing in the ratification of the Fourteenth Amendment in 1868 which would indicate in any way that the adopting states agreed to the exclusion of the Bible or of prayer from the public schools. In an opinion which carefully and at length seeks to evaluate the ultimate meaning of the *Everson–McCollum–Zorach* opinions, Justice Meyer concluded that believing parents have a right to have their religious desires recognized in the public school—at least to the extent that the desires of nonbelievers should not be granted priority. Every individual, the Judge reasoned, "has a constitutional right personally to be free from religion but that right is a shield, not a sword, and may not be used to compel others to adopt the same attitude."[117] The state cannot "subordinate the spiritual needs of believers to the psychological needs of nonbelievers."

He sustained the prayer as constitutional but only if the "parents of each child are advised of the adoption of the resolution calling for the saying of prayer, of the wordings of the prayer and of the procedure to be followed when it is said, and requested to indicate whether the child shall or shall not participate in the exercise."[118] The decision of the trial court finding the prayer to be not sectarian and not religious instruction as such was affirmed by the Appellate Division where Justice Beldock reinforced the lower court by stating: "The contention that acknowledgements of and references to Almighty God are acceptable and desirable in all other phases of our public life but not in our public schools is, in my judgment, an attempt to stretch far beyond its breaking point the principles of separation of Church and State and to obscure one's vision to the universally accepted tradition that ours is a nation founded and nurtured by belief in God."[119]

New York's highest court, over the dissents of Judges Dye and Fuld, sustained the lower courts and found, in the words of Chief Judge Desmond, that the prayer "is not 'religious education' nor is it the practice of or establishment of religion in any reasonable meaning of those phrases."[120] Concurring Judge Froessel noted that: (1) The challenged recitation follows the pledge of allegiance which itself refers to God. (2) School children in New York are permitted to sing "America," the fourth stanza of which is a prayer, invoking the protection of "God . . . the Author of Liberty." (3) The preamble to the New York State Constitution, taught in the public schools, reads: "We the people of the State of New York, grateful to Almighty God for our freedom . . ." (4) "To say that such references . . . unrelated to any particular religion or church, may be sanctioned by public officials everywhere but in the public school defies understanding."[121]

Judge Dye's dissent anticipated Justice Black's objections to the prayer although less vehemently. For Judge Dye the Regents' prayer is "a form of State-sponsored religious education" since, according to the Regents, its purpose was "teaching our children, as set forth in the Declaration of Independence, that Almighty God is the Creator."[122] This, in Judge Dye's judgment, violates the

establishment clause as well as his own individual views which
he states as follows: "The inculcation of religion is a matter for
the family and the Church. In sponsoring a religious program, the
State enters a field which *it has been thought best* to leave to the
Church alone."[123] [Emphasis supplied.] It is not at all clear by
whom or when or why such a policy was "thought best" but if one
accepts it as a fact that it *has* been "thought best" it follows that
the public school (which Judge Dye equates with "the State")
cannot allow itself to collaborate with the family and the church
even in those areas where *each* of those three agencies claim a prior
right to be heard.

The Regents' prayer, in Judge Dye's opinion, is forbidden because "the State may not invade an area where the constitutionality
protected freedom is absolute. . . ."[124] Although this conclusion
logically follows from Judge Dye's concept of the public school the
idea that the state may not "invade" the area of religion strikes the
religionist as almost a mockery of contemporary practices with
regard to the role of the state in education.

The state has for many decades extruded religion from the domain of education, a field which, until very recently in Western
civilization, has been an area where religion has been at least a partner with the state in a substantial and meaningful way. It is therefore ironic that Judge Dye and the United States Supreme Court
should rule that public education, having long since expelled religion as irrelevant or at least unnecessary, is now "invading" the
area of religion by taking from it a non-denominational prayer for
use in a classroom.

Public education, having seen the series of miscalculations that
led to the purely secular school, where neither the secular nor the
sacred can be satisfactorily taught, is now prevented by the Supreme
Court, in the name of the establishment clause, from trying to seek
some way out of the unreality of an academic institution where,
because the sacred, the sectarian, the supernatural and even the
spiritual are excluded, the secular takes on an importance and
significance far beyond its true value.

If the state must now, in Supreme Court thinking, avoid "en-
croachments" on religion, then it is time for the Court not to
waste its energy on what the Court itself feels is a "relatively
insignificant" encroachment but to re-examine its opinions from
Everson to *Engel* in which the Supreme Court has ordered that the

state and its public school "deny" the area of religion by denying every asserted claim of religion to have some stake in the formation of the atmosphere of the public school. Is not this whole approach an approval of a massive "encroachment" by the state on the area of religion?

The Supreme Court Opinion

Many students of the *Engel* decision will agree with Justice Potter Stewart, who, in his dissent, said that Justice Black's historical review of certain quarrels of the sixteenth or eighteenth centuries "throws no light for me on the issue before us in this case."[125] For Stewart, as for millions of Americans who tried to understand why the Supreme Court should outlaw a prayer for school children, the review by Justice Black of English and early American church–state tensions seemed irrelevant to the issue at hand. Even Justice Douglas, in his concurring opinion, concedes that he cannot "say that to authorize this prayer is to establish a religion in the strictly historic meaning of those words."[126]

If then the alleged encroachment is, in Justice Black's words, "relatively insignificant," why the vehemence of the Court and the nation-wide frenzy which prompted several Senators and all but one of the nation's Governors to seek an amendment to the Constitution? When such a basic misunderstanding occurs over any Supreme Court ruling, it seems logical to conclude that there is an inarticulated assumption which the Court or the public has made and which has led to a profound lack of intercommunication. Hopefully, an analysis of the following three factors may bring some understanding: (1) Justice Black's rulings and Justice Douglas' concurring opinion; (2) The implications of the anti-prayer decision; and (3) The present state of opinion on the prayer decision as it affects church–state relations.

JUSTICE BLACK'S RULINGS AND REASONS. The opinion agreed to by six of the members of the Supreme Court in *Engel* is a triumph of some consequence for Justice Black, for it is the vindication, both in principle and practice, of his philosophy of the establishment clause. From *Everson* to *Engel* Justice Black has insistently repeated that the establishment clause is *not* merely a means to make operative the free exercise clause but that the ban on an establishment of religion is violated "by the enactment of laws which establish an official religion whether those laws operate directly to coerce nonobserving individuals or not."[127]

The almost religious fervor with which Justice Black has espoused the separation principle *as a good in itself* was manifested in the extemporaneous remarks which he added when stating the *Engel* opinion from the bench. Said Justice Black: "The prayer of each man from his soul must be his and his alone. That is the genius of the First Amendment. . . . If there is any one thing clear in the First Amendment it is that the right of the people to pray in their own way is not to be controlled by the election returns."[128]

Only two decisions in Supreme Court history have made the establishment clause of the First Amendment *in itself* the reason for the invalidation of a religious practice: the *McCollum* and *Engel* rulings. In *McCollum*, however, it is arguable that the free exercise clause was also a part of the decision since the asserted rights of Mrs. McCollum and her son were involved. In *Engel*, on the other hand, it appears that for the first time the establishment clause, independently of the free exercise clause, is the one and only reason for the outlawing of the Regents' prayer. The application to the states of the notion that *any* governmental aid to religion, even if no one's religious freedom is thereby restricted, means, of course, that the right of each person to be protected against such aid is an immunity "so rooted in the traditions and conscience of our people as to be ranked as fundamental," in the famous phrase of Justice Cardozo in *Palko*.[129] To read all of this into the Fourteenth Amendment is not a simple task, especially in view of the fact that, as Justice Black puts it, ". . . as late as the time of the Revolutionary War, there were established churches in at least eight of the thirteen former colonies and established religions in four of the other five." And, of course, at the time of the ratification of the First Amendment some states still retained established churches while others maintained established religions.

Although the implications of this new theory on the establishment clause, now decisionally operative in Supreme Court jurisprudence, have not yet been fully explored by constitutional experts it would appear likely that many voices will be added to that of Professor Mark DeWolfe Howe, who has rejected the idea that the establishment clause should be transmitted to the states by way of the Fourteenth Amendment.[130] Justice Black has, however, outlined restrictions implicit in the establishment clause and has insisted that such restrictions are binding on the states. The restrictions on state activity in the field of religion found by Justice Black in the establishment clause and made obligatory on the states in the *Engel* decision seem to come to at least these: (1) The state may not use "its public school system to encourage recitation" of a prayer composed by public officials.[131] (2) It is a violation of the wall of separation between church and state for government officials "to compose official prayers for any group of the American people to recite as part of a religious program carried on by government." (3) ". . . neither the power nor the prestige of the Federal government" may "be used to control, support or influence the kinds of prayer the American people can say. . . ." (4) ". . . government in this country, be it state or federal, is without power to prescribe by law any particular form of prayer which is to be used as an official prayer in carrying on any program of governmentally sponsored religious activity." (5) ". . . each separate government in this country should stay out of the business of writing or sanctioning official prayers and leave that purely religious function to the people themselves and to those the people choose to look to for religious guidance."

The governmental intrusion into religion is clear in the first four points and its interdiction in such a manner may be applauded. But the fifth point raises important issues which we shall explore in the next section of this discussion. Prior to that discussion, a study of certain elements in Justice Douglas' concurring opinion may shed some light on what the Court intended in its ban of the Regents' prayer.

Although Justice Black tried to make it clear beyond question that the essential evil of the outlawed prayer was its governmental origins, Justice Black asserts that the "point for decision is whether the Government can constitutionally finance a religious exercise."[132] Assuming that this is the real issue requiring a decision (which is a dubious if not a false assumption), Justice Douglas proceeds to the following conclusions:

1. The case involves "no element of compulsion or coercion" since there is a regulation of the school board which provides that "neither teachers nor any school authority shall comment on participation or nonparticipation . . . nor suggest or request any posture or language be used or dress be worn or be not used or not worn."

2. The *McCollum* ruling does not decide this case since in

McCollum the "influence of the teaching staff was . . . brought to bear on the student body, to support the instilling of religious principles." But in the prayer case, "school facilities are used to say the prayer and the teaching staff is employed to lead the pupils in it. There is, however, no effort at indoctrination and no attempt at exposition."

3. "The question presented by this case is therefore . . . whether New York oversteps the bounds when it *finances* a religious exercise." [Emphasis supplied.]

4. "In New York the teacher who leads in prayer is . . . a public official on the public payroll performing a religious exercise in a governmental institution."

5. ". . . once government finances a religious exercise it inserts a divisive influence into our communities."

6. "My problem today would be uncomplicated but for *Everson* which seems in retrospect to be out of line with the First Amendment. Its result is appealing, as it allows aid to be given to needy children. Yet by the same token public funds could be used to satisfy other needs of children in *parochial* schools—lunches, books, and tuition being obvious examples." [Emphasis supplied.]

It is not clear why or how Justice Douglas placed so much emphasis on the question of alleged "financing" of the prayer by New York state. In all of the judicial opinions below and in Justice Black's view for the majority the question of financing was disregarded as so minimal as to be inconsequential. By stating that the issue centers on New York's financing a religious practice, Justice Douglas would seem to be rejecting Justice Black's principal contention—that the establishment clause precludes the prayer regardless of the violation of anyone's religious freedom or of a state expenditure. It is, in Justice Black's language, "the power and the prestige" of government which must never be extended to religion.

On the basis of Justice Douglas' dubiously valid supposition that the key question involves the financing of a prayer, he may be logical in raising his misgivings over the *Everson* result. But only to a point because the same outcome would have resulted in *Everson* even if the church–state issue had never been argued because *Everson* turned on the child-welfare benefit theory employed by the Supreme Court in its 1930 *Cochran* textbook decision, cited with approval in *Everson*.

It would seem more logical for Justice Douglas to raise misgivings over his own opinion for the majority in *Zorach*. It is the spirit and tone of *Zorach* which is wanting in *Engel*. It may well be that the absence of a reference in Justice Black's opinion to *any* previous church–state decision derives from a disagreement among the justices as to which, if any, of these decisions *Engel* was reversing or qualifying. Certainly Justice Black would hardly be expected to agree with Justice Douglas that his (Black's) majority view in *Everson* was incorrectly decided but that his opinion in *Engel* is accurate. Unless, of course, Justice Black himself shares Justice Douglas' misgivings over the result in *Everson*!

THE IMPLICATIONS OF *Engel*. It has been noted above that in the fifth point of Justice Black's opinion he ordered that the state "should stay out of the business of writing *or sanctioning* official prayers and leave that purely religious function *to the people themselves and* to those the people choose to look to for religious guidance." [Emphasis supplied.] Among the questions which the Court no doubt sought to avoid but which are inescapable in the enormously complex field of religion in education are these:

1. Is the government "sanctioning" as "official" practices such as Bible-reading in the public school if, by a statute, the state permits such activity on a voluntary basis?

2. In the dichotomy between the government and the people assumed by Justice Black in point (5) above, would it make any difference if the people by a referendum had requested the government to "sanction" the use of a particular prayer for voluntary use in the public school? And would this result be changed if "the people themselves *and* those the people choose . . . for religious guidance" had jointly requested government officials to "sanction" a particular prayer in the public school?

In Justice Black's philosophy it seems clear that neither the people with or without their religious leaders could be successful in requesting government officials to "sanction" a prayer. Justice Black in fact seems throughout his opinion to have a particular fear that the "ballot box" or "a new political administration" might be involved in the seeking of new and different prayers. There is, of course, truth and wisdom in the philosophy of keeping the government immune from the collective desires of religionists even if—and perhaps especially if—they are in a majority.

But to endorse this principle in the abstract is not to agree that "government" and "the people themselves" are forbidden to work out some reasonable working arrangement between a state divorced from an official religion and a citizenry whom the Supreme Court itself described as a "religious people" with "spiritual needs" for the fulfillment of which the state can make a reasonable accommodation.

3. Does the *Engel* decision add the prestige of the Supreme Court to the pervasive notion that the public school is a state institution so necessarily detached and divorced from the nonsecular that in effect its atmosphere disestablishes the religious nature of the American people and establishes a philosophy of education which teaches that the secular is the only subject to which the public school may direct its attention?

These questions may be considered as attempts to read into the antiprayer decision more than the Court intended or implied. But the tone of the majority and concurring opinions in *Engel* is so lacking in empathy for the problem which the Regents and the parents-intervenors confronted in the secularized public school, that the *Engel* decision has, like the *McCollum* opinion, a certain air of unreality about it. One could almost state that the majority opinion is unrealistic; it is a discourse on the history and dimensions of the establishment clause followed by an application of historical principles to the institution of the public school.

In *McCollum*, Justice Black banned from public education "a program of religious instruction carried on by separate religious sects." In *Zorach*, a dissenting Black stated that the best church–state policy can be obtained "by wholly isolating the state from the religious sphere and compelling it to be completely neutral." In *Engel*, he has once again expressed in vigorous terms his profoundly held conviction that the public school *is* the state and that therefore it must be kept firmly and totally on the *state* side of the wall separating church and state.

If *Engel* is pushed to the limit of its logic, it would direct that *all* values "sponsored" by the public school (which is the *alter ego* of the state) *must* be secular. According to *Engel*, the establishment clause forbids government "endorsement" of any values that are non-secular.

Although the concept that the public school is never permitted to endorse nonsecular ideas appalls one at first, the realization grows after a time that Justice Black has stated in his antiprayer decision exactly what the naturalist and the secular humanist have been saying for some two generations. Justice Black adds a constitutional emphasis, but it comes out the same: any religion in the public school would destroy both the public school and religion.

One of the most noteworthy of all the comments on the prayer decision appeared in the July 13, 1962, issue of *Commonweal*, a weekly edited by Catholic laymen, where an editorial included this paragraph:

What is therefore most objectionable about the decision is its lack of subtlety and sensibility. It follows one line of constitutional thought out to its remotest extreme. What it does not recognize is that a viable Church–State decision must take into account more than just one line. It must take into account national tradition and common practice as well. It must show itself alert to the rights of minorities but also to the rights and beliefs of the majority. What made the 1954 segregation decision particularly notable was its rich-textured awareness of the interplay between constitutional rights and social realities. By comparison the prayer decision is crude, legalistic and naive.

The ultimate objection to Justice Black's opinion may well come from the assumptions which lie behind it. Justice Black bans the Regents' prayer as a "governmental encroachment" on religion but does not and probably could not see that the *real* "governmental encroachment" on religion is the assumption by the government that education belongs to it and that the churches may not "encroach" on this governmental monopoly. This assumption, of course, is the very heart of the matter and Justice Black's opinion, in ignoring it, reveals the convictions which characterize those for whom the state-controlled secular school constitutes no infringement, no "encroachment" on the domain of religion or of the churches. Justice Black has in the antiprayer decision once again asserted (with an emotional vehemence which perhaps betrays the insecurity of his presuppositions) that the public school is a state-owned and state-controlled institution in which any attempt to inculcate a commitment to more than secular values will be construed as an "encroachment" by religion on the domain of the state. While reasserting the indispensability of this "encroachment" of government upon religion, Justice Black tells religionists that, by keeping them completely out of the educational lives of the nation's youth, he is making secure "an expression of principle on the part of the founders of our Constitution that religion is too personal, too sacred, too holy, to permit its 'unhallowed perversion' by a civil magistrate."

PRESENT STATE OF OPINION ON THE PRAYER DECISION AS IT AFFECTS CHURCH–STATE RELATIONS. All opinion, both popular and learned, on Supreme Court opinions is an inherently treacherous commodity. The United States, more than any other nation in the world, has become accustomed to the practice by which we take our most fundamental public policy questions and give them for solution not to Congress or to the administration in the White House but, in the form of a quasi-feigned lawsuit, to the Supreme Court of the United States. Reaction to the result almost inevitably follows the partisan—or in church–state cases the sectarian—lines which had been formed long before the suit and which usually are hardened by the controversy surrounding the case in the Supreme Court.

Sectarian lines on church–state issues have been formulated rather firmly ever since the Supreme Court first entered this area in the *Everson* case in 1947. No startling surprises occurred in the reactions of the various religious groups to the prayer decision. The danger inherent in permitting a governmentally written prayer was seen by everyone and, in some instances, this factor seems to have changed predictable opposition to the prayer opinion into one of acquiescence or even approval. Many, but not all, of those who disapproved of the *McCollum* opinion were also opposed to the prayer ruling.

Some of the controversy over the prayer decision could have been prevented and can now be calmed by a study of footnote 21 in Justice Black's opinion—a crucially important addition to the decision which was not printed with the text of the opinion in the *New York Times* on June 26, 1962, and which has virtually never been made available to the reading public. This important footnote reads:

There is of course nothing in the decision reached here that is inconsistent with the fact that school children and others are officially encouraged

1. to express love for our country by *reciting* historical documents such as the Declaration of Independence which contain references to the Deity,

2. or by singing officially *espoused* anthems which include the *composer's* professions of faith in a Supreme Being,

3. or with the fact that there are many manifestations in our public life of belief in God.

Such patriotic or ceremonial occasions bear no true resemblance to the unquestioned religious exercise that the State of New York has sponsored in this instance. [Emphasis and numbering supplied.]

If the substance of this footnote had been spelled out and explained in the text of the opinion, the meaning of the prayer decision would have been clearer and more intelligible to everyone. School children may, according to the footnote, *recite* the Declaration of Independence but only in order to encourage them "to express love for our country" and not because the public school seeks to endorse that part of the Declaration in which government officials "composed" or "sanctioned" an affirmation of their faith in the Creator.

Although an officially "sponsored" prayer is banned in the *Engel* decision, permission is granted for children to sing officially "espoused" anthems "which include the *composer's* profession of faith in a Supreme Being." It will take some subtlety to know whether children may sing the Star-Spangled Banner, a song adopted in 1931 by an Act of Congress as the National Anthem, the third stanza of which contains an unequivocal invocation of God. A further ruling of the Supreme Court may be required for the nation to know whether this anthem is "espoused" or "sanctioned" and whether it manifests the *"composer's* profession of faith in a Supreme Being" or the faith of the members of the Congress of the United States.

Although one can be as skeptical as he desires to be about what Justice Black calls the "many manifestations in our public life of belief in God," it is nonetheless disconcerting for the Supreme Court to categorize these manifestations as "patriotic or ceremonial occasions" bearing "no true resemblance to the unquestioned religious exercise" contained in the recitation of the Regents' prayer. Such distinctions—and indeed all of the three qualifications on *Engel* contained in footnote 21—lend substance to the widespread feeling that the Supreme Court has, in *Engel*, added one technically correct and commendable point to church–state law—the proscription of state-*composed* prayers in public schools—but that this point was made with such ponderously irrelevant opinions and qualifying footnotes that *Engel* will but generate further confusion and controversy over the place of the inherently unimportant symbols of religion in the public school.

As Max Lerner noted in a comment on the decision in the June 27, 1962, New York *Post*: "I find too much absolutism in both Justice Black's and Justice Douglas' opinions. . . . They are both fearful that state intrusion into religion will cause religious discord in the society, yet the irony is that their decision has produced the most intense religious discord since the issue of Catholicism was raised in the 1960 campaign."

Despite the fact that footnote 21 asserts that "there is *of course nothing*" in the *Engel* decision to upset the three sets of practices mentioned in the footnote, concurring Justice Douglas and dissenting Justice Stewart both feel that footnote 21 does *not* save the practices specified from the thrust of the ruling. Justice Douglas states: "What New York does on the opening of its public schools is what we do when we open court. . . . What New York does . . . is what each House of Congress does at the opening of each day's business." The concurring opinion goes on to say that in all these cases "the principle is the same, no matter how briefly the prayer is said, for in each of the instances given the person praying is a public official on the public payroll performing a religious exercise in a governmental institution."

Justice Stewart, writing in a similar vein, apparently fails to see how footnote 21 saves the many examples of public prayer he mentions and the "countless similar examples" to which he alludes. Justice Black wrote in his qualifying footnote that the "many manifestations in our public life of belief in God . . . bear no true resemblance" to the Regents' prayer, but Justice Stewart seems totally unpersuaded by such a distinction and states: "I do not believe that this court, or the Congress or the President has by the actions or practices I have mentioned established an 'official religion' in violation of the Constitution."

Even those well-informed commentators who, knowing the content of footnote 21, tried to quiet the nearly hysterical and sometimes politically motivated criticisms of the Court, expressed concern at the tone and note of unrealism which characterized the *Engel* decision. Reinhold Niebuhr, for example, commented that "to exclude the Regents' prayer is to insist that the schools be absolutely secular in every respect, which is not what the First Amendment intended."

It is impossible to evaluate the residue of public opinion which was left after the explosion of comments on the prayer decision. It seems clear that the basic source of the profound misunderstanding which engulfed the nation in controversy centered on the expectations which citizens have of the public school. The ordinary parent whose child is taken from its home for thirty hours a week expects that such a substantial part of the child's life will be spent in an atmosphere not inconsistent with and hopefully better than that at home. Religious parents are not unreasonable when they feel that there should be some continuity in the school with the prayer or spiritual training which the child receives at home. Parents cannot be expected to, and do not, release their children to the state and thereby forget about their own ideas of moral education and the training of character.

If the prayer decision achieved nothing else, it clearly provided an opportunity for religious leaders and the entire nation to review once again the complexities surrounding the century-old controversy regarding the place of religious values in the public school. Whether any Supreme Court decision can in any substantial way help or hinder a solution to that enigma is problematical. But the anti-prayer decision of June 25, 1962, may have rendered the problem more insolvable than ever before.

As we prepare to undertake the discussion of the Catholic reaction to the long and involved history of religion and the public school, are there any over-all conclusions on which all parties to the struggle over the orientation or ideology of the public school might agree? Perhaps there are at least a few:

1. It can be expected that there will be no permanent peace between church groups, religious parents and public education as long as the public school insists adamantly on teaching *only* the secular to the exclusion of the sacred, sectarian and the supernatural.

2. Wrote Dr. F. Ernest Johnson, Professor Emeritus of Teachers College, Columbia: "I have never heard anyone refute the statement that, if a general education program in the public school covers practically everything else that is vital, yet excludes religion entirely, it tends to create the impression that religion is peripheral to education."[133]

3. No peaceful co-existence seems possible between advocates of a religious orientation of the public school and the defenders of a secular school devoid of attention to religion as such. Harmoniza-

tions of these polarized views attempted in released time, Bible-reading, the recitation of a prayer or similar activities have been adjudged unconstitutional or been deemed ineffective.

A profoundly held belief that the ethos of the common or public school would be inconsistent with the faith of Catholic parents and Catholic children led the Catholic Church a century ago to initiate the construction of its own system of religiously oriented schools. It is this system, now enrolling every eighth child in America, to which we now turn our attention.

CHAPTER FOUR

The Church–Related School

A NAME FOR THE NONPUBLIC SCHOOL

The first and possibly the most important problem which must be confronted in any discussion of the nonpublic school in America is the name by which such a school should be designated. The term "public school" has been for so long a prestige-laden title for an institution so closely identified in the American mind with every virtue and glory that the term "nonpublic school" has by its very name a negative connotation. This term implies that such a school does not fulfill a public function, is not blessed by public authorities and is not responsible or accountable to the public at large.

The term "private" school contains even more negative implications. A "private" school suggests an exclusiveness, based perhaps on snobbery or wealth. The "private school" designation, when applied to Catholic primary and secondary schools, is particularly inappropriate because these schools are not "private" in either of these senses of the word.

Even more unfortunate is the title "parochial" school. The terms "Catholic school" or "church-related school" or "sectarian school" not only share in the negative connotations of every "nonpublic" school but furthermore imply that their principal function is to serve as an extension of Sunday school.

If it could be concluded from the history and from the legal decisions controlling the contemporary orientation of the public school that this institution is really a "secular" school, the problem of semantics might be eased. There is in fact high authority for renaming the public school a "secular" school since, in the words of Justice Douglas in his *Zorach* opinion, "Government may not . . . blend secular and sectarian education. . . ." But the widely held feeling that the public school teaches spiritual if not sacred values in addition to secular truth renders it at least psychologically impossible for the ordinary American to classify the public school as a purely "secular" institution.

The problem of semantics surrounding the nonpublic school is made more complex by the fact that the term "private school" more and more means simply the Catholic elementary and secondary school which accounts for over 90 per cent of all students attending nonpublic schools in America. The dominant position of Catholic schools in the nonpublic school category makes it even more difficult to speak in any meaningful way about the position of the private school in American education. The endemic, almost universal feeling in the country that the public school is *the* American school has received a new stimulus with the emergence of Catholic schools as the most numerous of the "private" schools of America.

Because of this and other factors, it is difficult to assess the strength of the feeling behind the passive resistance which many American educators express with regard to the private school. Very few will express regret over the Supreme Court decision in the Oregon school case, but on the other hand very few will manifest a positive sentiment that private schools contribute in a significant way to the development of education in America. Actually, however, it is impossible to evaluate educational thinking on the "private" school because of the opaque nature of that title; for many educators the notion of "private" schools has a significance entirely different from that of "Catholic" schools.

Those who would withdraw the freedom to exist recognized for the private school in the *Pierce* case seem to be few. But others, speaking in a more moderate tone, should logically join educators like Professor John L. Childs of Teachers College, Columbia University, who in 1949 urged a reconsideration of the Oregon school decision and proposed that all children should spend at least half of their school lives in a public school.[1] Max Lerner has argued that the Supreme Court in the Oregon decision took the first step in breaking down the separation of church and state when it "decided that a religious group could not be compelled to send its children to the public schools, and it could run its own schools at its own expense."[2] Even Paul Blanshard and the POAU have never subscribed to this interpretation of the separation principle.

Other educators have less bluntly but with no less conviction expressed regret that the public school has a competitor. A "threat to our democratic unity" was seen in private schools by the former President of Harvard University, James B. Conant, when he wrote in 1953: ". . . the greater the proportion of our youth who fail to attend our public schools and who receive their education elsewhere, the greater the threat to our democratic unity. . . . I cannot help regretting that private schools have been established in the last twenty years in certain urban areas where a generation ago a public high school served *all* of the youth of a town or city."[3]

Another distinguished educator, John S. Brubacher, former professor of education at Yale University, has stated that private education is undemocratic; in 1950, he wrote:[4] "To learn to free communication and to submit to majority rule wherever possible is, perhaps, one of the greatest arguments for the universal public school. By getting children of various races, national backgrounds, religious faiths, political convictions, and economic circumstances together in the same school where they can rub cultural elbows we have one of the best assurances for keeping open the highways of social intercommunication. But let a group establish a private or independent school on whatever grounds—to teach a particular point of view, political, economic, or religious; to exclude children whose social backgrounds are unacceptable; or what have you—and a difficult barrier is erected to the interpenetration of diverse ideas." During the controversy in 1961 over Federal aid and private schools, Reinhold Niebuhr wrote in the March 30, 1961, issue of the *New Leader* that "A religiously pluralistic and semi-secular society cannot afford to imperil the unity of a people through a pluralistic school system."

However misunderstood private schools may be, and however profound the misgivings of many concerning their contribution to American society, the basic juridical question as to their right to exist seems not to be an issue which will be reopened in the foreseeable future. It may be, however, that if pressure to finance private schools grows more intense, a legal controversy over the basic right of a private school to exist could arise.

One explanation for the reluctance or the refusal of many educators to be enthusiastic for the private school may be found in the inherently illogical position which they have assumed towards this institution. The private school, they feel, may be recognized as equivalent in accreditation and in every other legal requirement binding on the public school but nonetheless can be legally barred from tax support. The private school is thus, in the minds of many, truly a school for the purposes of compulsory education laws but only a private institution or a church agency for the purposes of tax support.

A person's attitude toward church-related schools will depend on how he conceives such schools. One of the most distorted views of such a school was portrayed in a statement of the American Civil Liberties Union submitted to the House Subcommittee on Education in 1961 in connection with Federal aid to education. The ACLU, in opposing aid for what it called "Church-controlled" schools, defined them in this manner:[5] "They are devoted in considerable degree to religious instruction, or indoctrination. They are created for the precise purpose of communicating a body of religious teaching. They are meant to nurture and fortify the faith of children already linked with the religious group. They have additional functions, to be sure; they engage in secular educational work, organized play, and the like. But they exist primarily to assure that children of school age will receive religious instruction and will be shielded from competing ideologies and values. . . . A religious school (does not) cease to be a religious activity because at times its premises may be used for the secular teaching which, by State law, is exacted as the price of keeping children away from the educational institutions the public has provided for them."

It seems clear that no substantial consensus about the role and the advisability of encouraging nonpublic schools can be attained until first some agreement is reached on the very nature and purpose of the church-related private school.

The Juridical Status of the Church-Related School

Having seen, by way of preview, some of the semantic problems involved in the selection of an appropriate name for the nonpublic school, and having sampled the currents of apprehension and even hostility which characterize contemporary American opinion on the private school, it is time to examine in detail not the private or nonpublic school as such but the Catholic, Lutheran, Seventh-Day Adventist, Jewish and other church-related schools of the nation. Particular attention will, of course, be directed towards the Catholic school and its claim to a juridical status deserving of some public support for its contributions to the secular education of its student body.

Anyone writing on this subject should give the closest attention to a friendly warning to Catholics issued in 1952 by a noted Jewish sociologist, Will Herberg, who is himself an advocate of state aid for Catholic schools. Mr. Herberg warned: "American Catholics must come to realize the deep suspicion with which their every move is regarded by a large segment of the American people, and admit, at least to themselves, that there is considerable historical justification for such suspicion. . . . The Catholic Church in America would also be well advised to moderate its demands in the field of education, to curb exhibitions of ecclesiastical power in politics, and in general to do what it can do to avoid inflaming the non-Catholic mind, today in an extremely nervous state."[6]

It is a frightening experience to try to explain the position of one's own religious group in America knowing that one's "every move" is regarded with "deep suspicion" by a "large segment" of one's fellow citizens. No religious body other than Catholics is so regarded in America. If there is any one principal ground for the "deep suspicion," it seems clear that it is the Catholic position with regard to Catholic schools.

It may be that the Catholic attitude towards education is so radically different from that of the alliance of Protestantism, secular humanism and Judaism which controls the public school that it is simply not possible to expect non-Catholics to understand, much less to have sympathy for, a philosophy of education which stands as a direct challenge to the outlook of the public school.

A further difficulty involved in trying to assist non-Catholics toward an understanding of the anxieties of Catholics over education comes from the historical fact that no Catholic group in any modern nation has ever experienced the predicament which American Catholics now confront. In Belgium, Holland, England and comparable nations the question of the orientation of the tax-supported school was debated and worked out by Catholics in collaboration with Protestant groups who were just as determined as the Catholics to have schools that reflected their own religious outlook.

In America, however, Catholics constitute the only substantial religious group which, having abandoned hope of a public school where religion would be a vital factor, is seeking to have the right to a partially tax-financed school wherein the Catholic outlook would be integrated with secular education. Catholics are virtually alone in making this request. They are without Protestant or Jewish allies and are opposed by influential and determined groups whose secularism forms a powerful force against the Catholic "case." As a result, Catholics employ lines of reasoning, interlocking arguments and presumably persuasive logic to support their claim, but frequently they seem to be on a frequency different from their opponents whose whole approach to the matter seems fundamentally alien.

A further impediment between Catholics and their opponents on the matter of public funds for Catholic schools is the newness of the issue. Prior to the serious possibility of enactment of Federal aid to education in the late 1940s, Catholics had not for several decades sought any financial aid for their schools at the state level. As a result when Catholics, after World War II, began to talk about their claim to Federal aid for their schools they had no experience or background on which to draw. Furthermore, they were just becoming familiar with the arguments about distributive justice, parental rights and a pluralistic nation when the Supreme Court in *Everson* and *McCollum* in 1947 and 1948 supplied to the opponents of aid to church-related schools the suggestion that these institutions were really churches and not schools and therefore were not entitled to tax support.

An even greater difficulty present in the debate over state aid for Catholic schools arises from the fact that both Catholics and their opponents in the clash over Federal aid to education seem to be operating from positions of fear. Catholics fear that if Federal aid became a reality for public schools *only*, their own schools may decline in prestige and resources. The foes of funds for Catholic schools fear that any financial aid to Catholic education will give a further impetus to that already incredibly extensive challenge to public education—not to mention the possibility of the growth of non-Catholic private schools if state aid were available.

With these preliminaries stated, let us turn to an exploration of the juridical status of the nonpublic school in America. Particular attention will be directed to all discoverable legal and moral bases which would support the Catholic contention that any fully accredited school should be entitled to some share of the public school fund to which all citizens contribute.

It is interesting to speculate whether the juridical status of the nonpublic school would be significantly different if the *Pierce*[7] case had never been accepted or decided by the United States Supreme Court. As is well known, the state of Oregon, pursuant to a referendum in which the voters of that state decided, by a margin of 115,000 to 103,000, to close all private schools, enacted a law in 1922 obliging *all* children to attend a *public* school between the ages of eight and sixteen. In the famous lawsuit that resulted, a Catholic group, the Society of Sisters, and a nonsectarian private military academy obtained a judgment against Oregon's Governor Pierce from the Supreme Court, which unanimously declared that private schools could not be eliminated even by a popular referendum. The decision turned technically on the property rights of the petitioning schools and had nothing to do with the First Amendment since this Oregon case was decided a few days before the *Gitlow*[8] ruling in which, for the first time, a guarantee of the Bill of Rights was transferred to the states by means of the Fourteenth Amendment.

Although one could state plausible reasons why the juridical status of the private school would be the same today even without the *Pierce* decision with its oft-cited *dicta* about parental rights, Catholics today are particularly grateful that the *Pierce* case is on the books and that at least the basic juridical right of a Catholic school to exist is beyond dispute. Indeed, it is a curious phenomenon that the gratitude of Catholics for the Oregon case has always been shared by liberals and secularists, some of whom would have several logical reasons to regret the existence of the *Pierce* decision and should theoretically urge that it be reversed.

The decision that declared Oregon's outlawing of private schools unconstitutional has always been favorably received. Protestant Episcopal, Seventh-Day Adventist, Catholic and Jewish groups intervened in the case as friends of the court urging an overturning of the will of the people of Oregon as expressed in a referendum. *The New York Times* applauded the decision and described the Oregon law as inspired by the most partisan and vicious motives ever recorded in American history. The ruling of the Supreme Court elicited comment in 490 newspapers in 44 states, all over-whelmingly favorable to the decision. In the *New Republic* of June 17, 1925, contributing editor, later Justice Felix Frankfurter, wel-comed the invalidation of the "notorious" Oregon statute as a "service to liberalism" because the Supreme Court had put at an end "the effort to regiment the mental life of Americans through public school instruction." The Court, he wrote, has "stifled the recrudescence of intolerance."

In the entire record in the *Pierce* case and in the copious litera-ture about it, there is no mention that private schools, if they are to be allowed to exist, and to be registered and regulated by the state, may eventually ask for tax support. Justice McReynolds made it clear that the private schools—which, by his opinion, would con-tinue to be legal in Oregon—could be regulated like public schools. He states: "No question is raised concerning the power of the state reasonably to regulate *all* schools, to inspect, supervise and examine them, their teachers and pupils; to require that all chil-dren of proper age attend some school, that teachers shall be of good moral character and patriotic disposition, that certain studies plainly essential to good citizenship must be taught and that noth-ing be taught which is manifestly inimical to the public welfare." [Emphasis supplied.] It seems clear from this paragraph that the private schools in Oregon could be required to fulfill all of the duties and obligations of the public school.

One can wonder if the continued favorable reaction to the *Pierce* decision derives from the comfortable middle ground it makes available to the secularist who, by allowing private schools to exist, avoids the tyranny of monopoly which would come from having "*l'école unique*" while at the same time he avoids financing this less-than-ideal school which, however, is supervised by the state.

An example of this attitude is given expression in Rabbi Robert Gordis' essay, "Education for a Nation of Nations," printed in a study by the Fund for the Republic entitled "Religion and the Schools." Rabbi Gordis, professor at the Jewish Theological Semi-nary of America, argues against state aid for Catholic schools and favors "the present arrangement which grants tax exemption to parochial schools without giving them tax support." Rabbi Gordis asserts that this is a "middle way" which is "the best for America as a whole and for the various religious faiths which undergird its way of life."

Apparently approval of the *Pierce* decision plus tax exemption equals a "middle way." Since tax exemption would come to church-related schools inasmuch as they are nonprofit institutions independently of their church affiliation, Rabbi Gordis is reductively stating that the right of private schools to *exist* is a "middle way." Many other opponents of state aid to church-related schools also have the illusion that their approval of the *Pierce* result relieves them of any further problems in connection with the schools which the *Pierce* decision stated could not constitutionally be outlawed.

There is more than a little logic in the proposition that the state should be willing to assist financially every school, attendance at which may fulfill the state's law regarding compulsory schooling. If the state can regulate *all* schools in the manner indicated in the quotation above from Justice McReynolds, it seems anomalous that those fully accredited and state-regulated schools which happen to be "private" bear all the public burdens but receive none of the public funds. Catholics and others have been reminded on innumerable occasions that it does not offend due process for the state to regulate that which it finances. But is there not some truth in the obverse of this principle? Can the state act in a manner consistent with fairness if it refused to finance an institution that is carrying out a function required of all citizens in a way which the state supervises as if this institution were state-operated?

This is a hard question which was never raised in the Oregon controversy, but which was inevitably and unavoidably latent in the *Pierce* decision. In famous and far-reaching words, it stated: "The fundamental theory of liberty upon which all governments in this Union repose excludes any general power to standardize its children by forcing them to accept instruction from public teachers only."[9] The term "public teachers" is certainly unusual and ambiguous as is the important word "standardize." Some light, but not as much as some commentators assert, comes in the even more famous sentence that follows this one: "The child is not the mere creature of the state; those who nurture him and direct his destiny have the right, coupled with the high duty, to recognize and prepare him for additional obligations." Added to these two *dicta* is the only other phrase about parental rights in the decision: "The Act of 1922 unreasonably interferes with the liberty of parents and guardians to direct the upbringing and education of children under their control."[10]

If the *Pierce* decision is, as many have asserted, the Magna Carta of the nonpublic school in American law, it must be said that *Pierce* is not an entirely satisfactory Bill of Rights for the private school. The truth is that the Supreme Court in *Pierce* settled very little about the basic juridical structure of the nonpublic school or its status in America. The Court held that such schools are engaged "in a kind of undertaking not inherently harmful, but long regarded as useful and meritorious." As a result, the right to conduct such schools "may not be abridged by legislation which has no reasonable relation to some purpose within the competency of the state."[11]

Although not even the most extreme separationists have raised the point, there is some doubt whether the *Pierce* decision could withstand the test of the *absolute* separation of church and state. Justice McReynolds states clearly that the permission granted by the Supreme Court to large groups of children to attend nonpublic or church-related schools will bring to these children and to the private schools they attend several blessings of the state. Among the several benefits of state supervision mentioned by Justice McReynolds the most important is undoubtedly the state's legal machinery to enforce its compulsory education law. By this legal device, the state *compels* children to attend a school where religion is taught as an inherent part of the curriculum. The state's truant officers, as well as several other features of the state's educational law, are available and indeed *must* be employed by the private school.

In view of the undeniable right and duty of the state to supervise private schools it is curious to note in a 1947 study of the National Education Association the following comment: "Supervision of private schools is far from complete in all features of the program; nor is it widespread in any one feature. In general, it may be said that supervision is conspicuous by its absence rather than by its presence."[12] In a comparable document in 1956, the NEA commented that the effectiveness of the "enforcement" of the statutes regulating private schools was "a matter of conjecture."[13] One wonders whether state educational officials, apparently careless or reluctant about regulating nonpublic schools, feel that it would be unfair to insist that these institutions comply with all their statutory duties when they are barred from receiving state aid to carry out those duties required of them by law.

The basic church-state issue in connection with the role of the private school centers on the fact that, once the nonpublic school is legally authorized, it has, by that very act of establishment, a right and a duty to some state recognition and assistance. It has a higher legal status than the mere non-profit voluntary organization because of the requirement that those who elect to use this institution *must* attend it for a designated period under penalty of violating the state's truancy laws.

To say that even the application of the state's compulsory education laws to the private school violates the Supreme Court's proscription of aid "to all religions" is to seek to press the Court's words to their ultimate meaning. On the other hand, to read into the *Pierce* decision some constitutionally protected right under the First Amendment's free exercise of religion clause is to be extreme in the other direction. The historical fact is that neither the servitors nor the opponents of private schools have discovered in or drawn from *Pierce* all that could buttress their case. Justice Rutledge, in his dissent in the *Everson* case, states that, in his opinion, the *Pierce* decision came about because of the fact that "education which includes religious training and teaching, *and its support*, have been matters of private right and function not public, by the very terms of the First Amendment."[14] [Emphasis supplied.] Following this line of reasoning, Justice Rutledge concludes that "children are not sent to public schools under the *Pierce* doctrine . . . for the reason that their atmosphere is *wholly secular*."[15] [Emphasis supplied.] Assuming the truth of these two assertions as necessary conclusions from *Pierce*, Justice Rutledge accuses the majority in the *Everson* case of misconceiving the status of the private school and giving to it a form of aid which logically could lead to total financing of private schools.

The ambiguities in the *Pierce* decision are the same as those which have existed in the American mind over a long period with regard to the status, legal recognition and financial assistance which should be extended to the private school. It is probably unthinkable for most persons today that the Oregon case could have been decided otherwise or that it should be qualified or reversed. But a strong case can be made for the proposition that it is unfair and unwise to force *all* children to attend school and then require those parents who refuse to allow their children to go to a school that is "wholly secular" to finance the education of their children entirely from their own resources. Is it too much to say that the nation should either reverse *Pierce* or give financing to the private school?

Although the case for aid to private schools may appear to some observers as clear and unequivocal, the fact seems to be that this case or claim has not yet constituted a challenge to the American mind. The nineteenth century "solution" to the school problem contemplated a "little red school house" in every hamlet of the land, free from any particular sectarian version of Protestant Christianity, but imbued with the spirit of religion and Americanism. Such a "solution" rendered private church-related schools unnecessary, with the result that formidable legal barriers were erected against their growth and development.

Let us review briefly these legal barriers to the financing of private schools.

THE STATES' DENIAL OF AID TO PRIVATE SCHOOLS

The acceptance and continued approbation of the *Pierce* decision is in part due, of course, to the fact that long before 1925 virtually all of the states had closed the doors of their treasuries to claims by nonpublic schools. It was not felt at the time of the *Pierce* decision, nor is it widely thought today, that the Oregon referendum, which resulted in a vote against the very existence of private schools, was to some extent the logical result of America's public policy for almost a century. During the period from the establishment of the common school in 1837 in Massachusetts, with a course of studies and an atmosphere reflecting the ethical views of Horace Mann, until the time of the *Pierce* decision, virtually every state had by constitutional amendment or otherwise excluded all private schools from a share in the public school fund. Massachusetts was one of the last of the states to strengthen its prohibition of every possibility of such aid when in 1917 the citizens of the Bay State, by a vote of 206,329 to 130,357, added an "anti-aid" amendment to the Massachusetts Constitution excluding all sectarian schools from any share of the common school fund.

The state of Ohio seems to be the only place where in the twentieth century there has been a significant public debate over proposed legislation to aid church-related schools. Beginning in the year 1933, three efforts were made in succeeding sessions of the state legislature to secure appropriations for private schools. The proponents of such aid reasoned that it was not barred by the Ohio Constitution, art. 6, sec. 2, of which reads: "The General Assembly shall make such provisions, by taxation or otherwise, as, with the interest arising from the school trust fund, will secure a thorough and efficient system of common schools throughout the state; but no religious or other sect or sects shall ever have any exclusive right to or control of any part of the school funds of this state."

Despite passage by the state senate, the proposals to aid private schools were defeated in the house, whose members came from more rural districts. All of the controversy in Ohio, which lasted from 1933 to 1937, was unsuccessful in obtaining aid for the 16 per cent of the state's children who attended parochial schools.[16]

Several conclusions impress one after a careful consideration of the history of America's policy of making private schools mere voluntary associations. This history, as related in the definitive study on the matter by Richard J. Gabel, *Public Funds for Church and Private Schools*,[17] suggests some observations.

The strength of the constitutional or statutory language in the laws forbidding aid to sectarian schools indicates that the framers of these laws must have feared the possibility of a serious threat by Protestants who were discontent with the public school or by Catholics who had started their own school system. While the anti-Catholicism motivating the movement to enact "anti-aid" laws is an undeniable fact, these laws also reflect the presence of a widespread apprehension that the nonsectarian common school "compromise" might be rejected by some Protestant groups.

The opposition which Catholics must have expressed to the enactment of laws guaranteeing a monopoly on educational funds to the public schools seems to be inadequately recorded. Either Catholic opposition was not given a hearing in the public press, or it was unorganized or muted because of a feeling that it would have been futile to make a claim for aid for Catholic schools. If some Catholics today, although persuaded of the justice of their claim for federal aid for their schools, are inclined not to press that claim, they should consider the formidable legal and constitutional state barriers against aid to private schools which *might* have been rendered less harsh if Catholic opposition had been more vigorous.

The *volte-face* of nineteenth-century Protestants in surrendering to the state the traditional Christian churches' concern for education is certainly a most striking example of the extent to which the American state was considered by the Protestant community to be a government entirely in accordance with its own aims and purposes. One could almost say that there was in America in the nineteenth century a union of church and state, of the pan-Protestant Church and the nonsectarian state.

The legal restrictions placed on state aid for church-related schools compromised one of the greatest of the principles of American democracy, namely, that education should be *free* to all. It is not a sufficient answer to this charge to say that the state school is free, since the citizens of all states believed in and could have adopted the provision in Kentucky's Constitution to the effect that no one should be required to attend a public school if such attendance violates his conscience.[18] The twin ideas, born a century ago, that education should be *compulsory* and *free* for all was eroded in a substantial way by the legal reduction of the private school to a status inherently less prestigious than the public school.

The "anti-aid" provisions enacted in almost all of the states constitute not merely the most formidable barrier to assistance at the state level for church-related schools, but could be an important obstacle if Federal aid to education is ever enacted and the Federal grants, though designated in part for private schools, are nonetheless handed over completely to the states. In such event a Federal policy superseding the states' proscription of aid to church-related schools would be necessary.

The firm policy adopted at the state level in the last century endorsing the public school and removing the possibility that the nonpublic school could claim public funds was subject to only a few exceptions. One could mention the widely scattered instances where, in isolated and now often discontinued arrangements, Catholic schools were public institutions or, more commonly, where Protestant academies were financed as if they were public schools. But the tide against such agreements has run so strongly over so long a period that it is safe to say that today, with some few possible exceptions, no church-related schools in America receive any substantial financial state aid.

A suit, however, involving tuition benefits to pupils in Catholic high schools in Vermont, decided on January 3, 1961, by the Vermont Supreme Court and refused review by the United States Supreme Court on May 15, 1962, is legally significant.[19] The rulings and opinions in this case summarize a century of anti-private school agitation, to which has been added in Vermont the *Everson– McCollum* rationale.

Under a Vermont statute enacted in 1915, but which, in its original form, goes back to the year 1869, Vermont law recognizes the right of parents to participate in the selection of a school for their children. In a law which could hardly be enacted in today's educational climate the legislature of Vermont provided that, "Each town district shall maintain a high school or furnish secondary instruction, as hereinafter provided, for its advanced pupils at a high school or academy, *to be selected by the parents or guardian of the pupil*, within or without the state. The board of school directors may both maintain a high school and furnish secondary instruction elsewhere as herein provided as in the judgment of the board may best serve the interest of the pupils."[20] [Emphasis supplied.]

A clearer recognition of parents' rights in education could hardly be desired. The parents may not merely select the school in the absence of a public high school, but may even sometimes exercise this right when the town does furnish a public high school!

Tuition is regulated as follows: "Each town school district shall pay tuition per pupil per school year as billed, but not in excess of $325.00 unless authorized by a vote of the town school district. . . ."[21]

Under this arrangement the town of South Burlington, which had no high school, paid in 1958–1959 the sum of $19,687.50 directly to the Rice Memorial High School in Burlington for the education of many South Burlington students at this Catholic school. The sum of $2,025 was paid in the same year to Mount St. Mary's Academy in Burlington, a school also owned by the Diocese of Burlington.

In other townships of Vermont comparable arrangements were followed. In 1960, out of 257 public school systems in Vermont, 167 provided public school instruction at the elementary level only. This situation reflects the national pattern where, in 1960, out of a total of 42,429 public school systems, 21,646 did not provide secondary education.

Many private high schools and academies have benefited by the tuition plan authorized by Vermont law. These schools still operate under the plan invalidated as to Catholic schools but not challenged as to "post-Protestant" schools which are presumably still eligible for tuition payments so long as no course in religion is required. And, in fact, such schools are not required by statute even to be nonprofit institutions.

On February 4, 1958, a South Burlington taxpayer, C. Raymond Swart, challenged the constitutionality of the Vermont tuition plan. On February 19, 1960, Judge William C. Hill, after a trial without a jury, invalidated the statute in an opinion which deserves the closest scrutiny.

Vermont law is silent on the question of state funds for sectarian schools except for this stipulation, ". . . no man ought to, or of right can be compelled to . . . erect or support any place of worship . . . contrary to the dictates of his conscience."[22] Although this provision is very different from the sixteen words about religion in the First Amendment to the Federal Constitution, Judge Hill asserted that "counsel for all parties have seemingly agreed and the court adopts the theory that the constitutional provisions under review are similar and that violation of one is violation of the other."[23]

Judge Hill consequently, finding no relevant cases in Vermont law, went to the *Everson* decision in which, he concedes, that the "question of tuition payments was not discussed by the Court." But Judge Hill argues from *Everson* nonetheless, that grants for tuition to church-related schools are unconstitutional because of Judge Hill's understanding that in *Everson* "it is stated that no contribution of tax-raised funds may be made to the support of an institution which teaches the tenets and faith of any church." *Everson* did not *actually* say this but the Vermont judge's paraphrase suggests that it would be wise at this time to analyze closely *exactly* what *Everson* decided and what is left undecided.

In the famous *dicta* of that decision, which some strict separationists like to term "definitive," Justice Black combined several obviosities with some inherently ambiguous statements which were *not* relevant to the school bus problem before the Court in *Everson*. In what is possibly the best known paragraph in all the church–state jurisprudence of the United States Supreme Court, Justice Black wrote: "The 'establishment of religion' clause of the First Amendment means at least this: Neither a state nor the

Federal Government can set up a church. Neither can pass laws
which aid one religion, aid all religions, or prefer one religion over
another. Neither can force nor influence a person to go to or to
remain away from church against his will or force him to profess a
belief or disbelief in any religion. No person can be punished for
entertaining or professing religious beliefs or disbeliefs, for church
attendance or nonattendance. No tax in any amount, large or small,
can be levied to support any religious activities or institutions,
whatever they may be called, or whatever form they may adopt
to teach or practice religion. Neither a state nor the Federal Government can, openly or secretly, participate in the affairs of any
religious organizations or groups and *vice versa*. In the words of
Jefferson, the clause against establishment of religion by law was
intended to erect 'a wall of separation between church and
state.' . . ."[24]

The enormous confusion latent in this paragraph comes from its
indiscriminate intermingling of unrelated and unanalyzed concepts.
For example, in one and the same sentence we are told that the
state may not "force . . . a person to go to or remain away from
church against his will . . ." and that the state may not even "influence" a person in this same regard. No one will object to the
"force" but it is impossible to understand what exact practices
would be forbidden as an example of the state extending "influence" for or against religion. Furthermore, the assertion that the
state may not even "influence" a person with respect to religion is
made by Justice Black in disregard of American tradition and in a
manner which assumes that proof is not necessary.

The points made by Justice Black relevant to the Vermont
problem and to the entire question of aid to nonpublic schools
center around the following two issues:

First, when Justice Black stated that neither the Federal Government nor a state can pass laws which ". . . aid all religions" did
he hereby rule out financial aid for the church-related school? To
see in these three words such an implication would mean that the
church-related school is not really a school at all but a glorified
catechism class or, on a broader interpretation, that any state aid
which even incidentally renders the practice of religion more convenient is constitutionally forbidden.

Secondly, did Justice Black mean to ban all aid to sectarian
schools when he wrote that "no tax . . . can be levied to support

any religious activities or institutions whatever they may be called, or whatever form they may adopt to teach or practice religion"? Again to draw from this *dictum* the conclusion that the church-related school is barred from state aid *as a school* necessarily implies these presuppositions: (1) The sectarian school is established *merely* to conduct "religious activities," and (2) the sectarian school is simply and exclusively one of the church's "institutions to teach or practice religion."

To conclude therefore that Justice Black and the Supreme Court in *Everson* ruled out all aid for the *secular* aspects of sectarian schools is simply going beyond the evidence contained in that opinion. In fact, such a conclusion is in conflict with the basic idea underlying the decision, the concept that it is "obviously not the purpose of the First Amendment" to cut off church schools from services which are "separate and . . . indisputably marked off from the religious function . . ."[25]

Neither the advocates nor the opponents of aid to sectarian schools can prove their case from the *Everson* decision. There is evidence to support both sides and the question is not rendered more simple by the *dicta* in *Zorach,* apparently in conflict with the philosophy of *Everson.*

Vermont Judge Hill, however, decided that *Everson* solved his problems and, while stating that it was "indeed difficult to upset such a long-standing practice" and that this practice was not being "upset lightly," ruled that secular education is not a public welfare benefit "when religion becomes an integral part of the curriculum."

It is not certain how resourceful or active state legal officials in Vermont were in carrying out their assigned task of defending the constitutionality of the challenged statute. In any event the Supreme Court of Vermont ruled on Judge Hill's decision and, while affirming it, referred to the case as presenting "sensitive and solemn issues."[26]

The court spoke with understanding of the parent who "shares the expense of maintaining the public school system yet in loyalty to his child and his belief seeks religious training for the child elsewhere," but found that the school board of South Burlington, "while acting within the literal provisions of the statute, have exceeded the limits of the United States Constitution." From the opinion it is not entirely clear where the parental-right statute also violates the Vermont constitution. The court seemed to rely

principally on the following *dicta* taken from the *Zorach* decision:
"Government may not finance religious groups nor undertake religious instruction *nor blend secular and sectarian education* nor
use secular instruction to force one or some religion on any person."
[Emphasis supplied.]

Assuming that this statement represents the controlling law, the
Vermont court found that the "fusion of secular and sectarian education . . . undertaken in religious denominational high schools
that are an integral part of the Roman Catholic Church . . ." is
something in which by command of the First Amendment "the
state shall not participate."

The court added that the government may not pay tuition to
high schools when "the Church is the source of their control and
the principal source of their support," and continued, "this com-
bination of factors renders the service of the Church and its
ministry inseparate from its educational function." It recognized
that a Catholic school "is a high and dedicated undertaking . . .
and deserves the respect of all creeds" but ruled that "however
worthy the object" and "however compelling" the "equitable
considerations" the arrangement violates "constitutional barriers."

The Vermont decision, while paying lip service to the "faithful
parent" and acknowledging the "severity of this mandate" (its
decision) and the "heavy burdens" it will impose, is nonetheless
an opinion that is unsatisfactory because it does not really analyze
the problem before it nor seek any way in which to reconcile the
desires of religious parents with the First Amendment.

The decision, furthermore, is not clear as to the manner in which
Catholic or other parents might be able to exercise the option
granted to them by the lawmakers of Vermont who have never
subscribed to the philosophy of a public school monopoly. What
if Catholics or others established schools that were *not* "an integral part" of a church and did not have a church as "the source of
their control and the principal source of their support?" Does the
court mean that "the service of the Church and its ministry" are
"inseparate" or "inseparable" from its educational function? At
what point does the "fusion of secular and sectarian instruction"
in a school cause the school to turn into a virtual seminary where
the pupils are only working "in the pursuit of their religious
beliefs"?

Some of the arguments presented by the parents in the Vermont case were not taken up in the court's opinion although Justice Holden in his opening paragraph states that the "cause has been well argued and thoughtfully presented." The court seemed content, however, not to go into the deeper implications of its decision and appeared satisfied to affirm the findings of the trial judge on the nature of a Catholic school. Nor did the Supreme Court of Vermont adequately deal with the fact that non-Catholic children attended the Catholic school in question but did not take the course on religion. The court did, however, go out of its way to state that the tuition plan would *not* be saved if the state grants of tuition were paid directly to the parents or to the student rather than to the church-related school.

On May 15, 1961, as noted above, the United States Supreme Court declined to review the decision of Vermont's highest tribunal. Such is the latest in a century-old series of statutory and decisional laws exalting the public school and rejecting the "considerations of equity and fairness" which are so manifest in the claim of the religious parent who cannot in conscience send his child to a school forbidden by law to "blend secular and sectarian education."

In view of the apparent impossibility of the church-related school obtaining any tax support for its educational purposes as such, it is not surprising that the private schools, given a *Magna Carta* in the *Pierce* decision, have turned their attention to health benefits, public welfare aids and all those ever more numerous fringe services which are given by the state to school children. It is this expanding, controversial and complex area which now merits our careful attention.

CHAPTER FIVE

Benefits to Pupils
in Private Schools

AUXILIARY BENEFITS TO PUPILS IN
PRIVATE SCHOOLS

Although the possibility of substantial state financing for the educational program of private and especially church-related schools appears to be remote, the ways in which the students in these schools benefit indirectly from state assistance are numerous. The phenomenon of such indirect aids is not surprising in view of the innate sense of fairness which Americans possess and of the simple fact that everyone finds it distressing to deny to a child any advantage which he would have obtained if his parents had not sent him to a church-related school. The fact of sheer size is also relevant here since, as Protestant theologian Jaroslav Pelikan notes in the August 1962 *Atlantic*, the Catholic Church in America conducts "the most comprehensive educational system in Christian history."

There would be fewer intercredal abrasions and intra-community tensions if an over-all formula could be devised by which state benefits allowable to private school pupils could be automatically identified. It sometimes appears that both Catholics and non-Catholics have almost deliberately chosen to concentrate their requests and their opposition on items which, like bus transportation, touch sensitive nerve endings in both parties. And once an item such as this becomes the center of a dispute, a syndrome of controversy grows up from which neither party desires to retreat without a total victory.

It may be that the Constitution of Puerto Rico has language which clarifies what the advocates of fringe benefits but opponents of state aid to Catholic schools are trying to articulate. The people of Puerto Rico wrote and adopted a Constitution, with the approval of the United States Congress, which provides in Section 5 of its Bill of Rights that: "No public property or public funds shall be used for the support of schools or educational institutions other than those of the state. Nothing contained in this provision shall prevent the state from furnishing to any child non-educational services established by law for the protection or welfare of children."

Are bus rides "non-educational services established . . . for the protection or welfare of children?" The United States Supreme Court split 5 to 4 on that question and the nation's communities seem to be not less divided on the issue.

Elements of irrationality almost beyond analysis arise whenever bus rides to parochial schools become an issue in local affairs. It may be that some of these irrational elements can be more easily dissected if we relate the true story of a Catholic high school in a medium size city in which 22 per cent of the population is Catholic. The story is factual with a few fictional additions in order to conceal identification. The story, as will be evident, has a moral both for Catholics and non-Catholics.

In the early 1950s, one of the most respected teaching orders in the Catholic Church announced that it would open a high school for girls in the city which we shall call Bay View. The religious order had acquired two adjoining estates with 52 acres of land assessed at $83,500 and taxed in the year of purchase for $6,180.00. The announcement of the new Catholic high school to be designed to accommodate up to 400 girls caused the sudden disappearance of a dispute of some three years standing in the city between those who wanted a second high school in the northern section of the city and those who felt it would be wiser and more economical to add a wing to the present high school. With the advent of a new private secondary school to accommodate 400, the board of education and the city in general concluded that the present high school had adequate space for the foreseeable future.

The city incurred several expenses in connection with the construction of the new Catholic high school. The school building was to be located two miles beyond the public high school in a

residential area. The city, on the advice of specially employed con-
sulting engineers, obtained a large appropriation to extend a new
water main to the site of the new school. Several hydrants and a
completely new sewage system were also required in order to comply with state laws regulating school buildings. A new piece of
ladder equipment was purchased by the fire department because
the school would be the only four-story building in the area. Side-
walks were constructed just outside the sisters' property and the
trees surrounding the 52 acres were chemically sprayed for the
first time.

After the new high school was opened the city continued to
extend several of its services. A school teacher paid by the city was
assigned to visit and teach at the homes of girls from Catholic
High who were temporarily unable to attend school. The public
library bookmobile arranged to stop at three different times each
week at Catholic High as it did at all the other schools within the
city. Special teachers paid by the city to give driving instructions
came to Catholic High after the parents of some of the students
requested this service so that their car insurance rates might be
reduced.

The health services offered by the state, county, and city gradually became available at Catholic High. X-ray trucks stopped for
chest examinations, state-employed doctors paid calls, medical
officials visited to make sure that all the students and the nuns had
received polio and other vaccines.

Other public services seemed to grow as Catholic High became
an accepted part of the community. A police car and a policewoman
directed traffic outside the school each morning and afternoon.
Initial difficulties about refuse collection for the school, located in
a residential area, were gradually worked out.

The academic attainments of Catholic High were praised in the
local newspaper when the school obtained a loan under the 1958
National Defense Education Act to purchase further equipment
and Russian language tapes for its modern speech laboratory. Two
of the nuns obtained financial grants, also under the NDEA program, for summer study in languages at a nationally famous
university.

Several years after the establishment of Catholic High, everyone
in Bay View City would spontaneously say that it had demon-

strated remarkable growth and development, and that the city was proud of and aided by its presence. No church–state problem had ever arisen in connection with Catholic High; in fact, most of the people in Bay View probably had never really heard of such a problem except in connection with the dispute over Federal aid to education.

Bay View's publicly owned transit system had made available to all school children as long as anyone could remember a five-cent ticket in lieu of a fifteen-cent token. All students used the special-rate tickets to go to school and also to attend school functions, including basketball games. Because the transit system was losing money each year and because some of the bus routes accommodating students going to the public high school were no longer sufficiently utilized by nonstudents, the officials of the transit system and the city proposed to the city council that student tickets be eliminated and that specially designated school buses be supplied for students living beyond a certain distance from the high school.

It was also proposed that, since the girls going to Catholic High had always taken the public bus which went near their school, the newly designated school bus continue from the public high school to Catholic High, or at least that the girls going to Catholic High could ride the school bus without charge to its destination at the public high school.

The interreligious explosion that resulted from this simple recommendation rocked the city of Bay View in a manner beyond the comprehension of its most knowledgeable citizens. The six Protestant ministers published an open letter stating that the members of their congregation had a duty as patriotic Americans to attend the public meeting of the city council and register their protest against *any* student from *any* Catholic school riding free on *any* school bus. The Jewish rabbi announced his concurrence in this viewpoint and the local newspaper began to serialize all the opinions in the *Everson* case. A Catholic pastor, after an infelicitous remark reflecting the shocked indignation of most of the Catholic community, complied with the Catholic Bishop's request that Catholic officials make no statements on the bus question but that the Bishop's attorney be allowed to handle the situation.

The part-time executive director of the chapter of the ACLU in the next large city threatened court action if the Catholics of Bay

View "seek to violate the civil liberties of their fellow citizens." The American Jewish Congress announced that it would join in such action and called upon the city council to observe "the great American tradition of the separation of Church and State."

Situations comparable to this story have occurred in some or all of the states which have litigated bus rides for parochial school children since the 1947 *Everson* ruling. These states, which include New Mexico, Washington, Missouri, Connecticut, Maine, Wisconsin and Alaska, have witnessed the strange phenomenon that somehow bus transportation for Catholic school children has become the symbol which brings relations between Catholics and non-Catholics to the boiling point. A partial explanation of the explicit opposition enunciated by virtually all Protestant organizations (but *not* by individual Protestant leaders) to bus transportation may possibly be found in the *Everson* decision which, to some Protestant Christians, was the "camel's nose" of Catholic aggression seeking tax funds for Catholic schools.

Even if *Everson* did not exist, however, there is still evidence to suggest that school buses are so intimately involved with school programming that the violent disagreements over this matter at the state level are not likely to diminish. Reinhold Niebuhr has written of the explosive effect of school bus controversy on Catholic–Protestant relations in these terms: "The acrimonious relations between Catholics and Protestants in this country are scandalous. If two forms of the Christian faith, though they recognize a common Lord, cannot achieve a little more charity in their relations to each other, they have no right to speak to the world or claim to have any balm for the world's hatreds and mistrusts. The mistrust between Catholics and Protestants has become almost as profound as that between the West and Communism."[1]

Today some twenty-two states authorize bus rides for private school children. The United States Supreme Court, since *Everson*, has thrice refused to discuss bus rides, declining the opportunity in 1951 in a case from the state of Washington, in 1960 in a decision from Connecticut, and in 1962 in a ruling from the Supreme Court of Alaska. Although the casual comment about *Everson*, made by Justice Douglas in his concurring opinion in *Engel*, may induce the American Civil Liberties Union, or a similarly disposed group, to try to have the Supreme Court reconsider bus rides, there is currently no lawsuit available for that purpose.

BUS RIDES: THE BASIC AMBIGUITY OF *EVERSON*

One way that has been suggested to remove bus rides from church–state controversy makes a great deal of sense: place the function of transporting children to and from school in a nonschool agency to be financed by noneducational funds. Under such an arrangement transportation of pupils is placed, as it should be, in the category of auxiliary noneducational services. Where this is done the problems of students getting to and from school are as inconspicuous as they were in Bay View prior to the church–state eruption over school buses.

In many instances, however, it is simply impossible to change the pattern of educational financing in a state, especially when there would be opposition from those for whom bus rides for students are an aid indistinguishable from a direct subsidy to the school attended. These individuals, furthermore, might be unyielding in their opposition to bus rides for private schools even if financed by noneducational funds.

The central difficulty about bus rides for nonpublic schools centers, however, not so much in the method by which public financing is attempted but in the basic ambiguity of the law as enunciated in *Everson*. The contention that there is an intrinsic contradiction between the reasoning and the result in *Everson* is supported, of course, by the four dissenting justices in that case; the inherent contradiction of *Everson* is also evident in the fact that judges and polemicists on both sides of the bus-ride struggle can find in all the opinions some strikingly probative sentences to support their thesis.

Everson stands for at least three principles:

1. There is no establishment of religion if a state law permits transportation of pupils to private schools;

2. The state, however, may constitutionally enact a law which would "provide transportation only to children attending public schools";

3. But the "benefits of public welfare legislation" may not be denied to individual citizens "because of their faith or the lack of it."

The question left open here is the crucial one: can a law authorizing bus rides for private school children be granted in such a way that this service is *not* "public welfare legislation"? Or, putting it another way, can a law permitting bus transportation for nonpublic school children provide something different from what Justice Black calls, somewhat unclearly, "general State law benefits."

The reimbursement directly to parents for fares paid on public buses made the *Everson* fact decision relatively easy for the Supreme Court; Justice Black could say, "The State contributes no money to the schools. It does not support them. Its legislation, as applied, does no more than provide a general program to help parents get their children, regardless of their religion, safely and expeditiously to and from accredited schools."

The Supreme Court, having supplied in *Everson* the test of "public welfare legislation" as the norm of constitutionality, failed to supply an adequate definition of this term. The Court has, as a result, left state legislatures and tribunals without adequate guidelines to differentiate between a bus law which is constitutional because it is "public welfare legislation" and one which is unconstitutional because, even though it may be described in its preamble as "public welfare legislation" is nonetheless a fatally defective sample of this type of legislation.

It is because "public welfare legislation"—the key concept in the *Everson* decision—was left undefined or found to be undefinable that communities like Bay View have had church–state conflicts. It may be profitable to review the major struggles over bus rides since the Supreme Court in 1947, intending no doubt to "solve" the problem forever, enunciated basic if general principles so intermingled with absolutes about church–state separation that *Everson* has tended to confuse rather than clarify the law on auxiliary benefits to private school children.

STATE OF WASHINGTON. In 1941, the Legislature of the state of Washington provided that children attending private schools along or near the route to the public school should be entitled to the same type of transportation supplied for public school pupils. In 1943, the Supreme Court of the state of Washington, in a 5 to 4 decision, ruled against the school bus law, relying on the provision in Washington's constitution that the entire revenue from the state tax for common schools must be exclusively applied to the support of the common schools.[2] A vigorous dissent argued that the legislation in question specifically related to public health and safety and that therefore it was designed to assist *all* children irrespective of the schools they attended.

The State Legislature agreed with the dissent and, in its very next session, re-enacted the invalidated statute so as to make the new law unmistakably public welfare legislation. The statute now read: "*All children attending school* . . . shall be entitled to use the transportation facilities provided by the school district. . . ."

Although the Attorney General of the state advised that this new law was constitutional, some school directors acted contrary to his advice. An incident involving the denial of transportation to four children of the Visser family who attended the Protestant Christian Reformed grammar school led eventually to a test case on the amended statute which, as noted above, provided in the broadest terms for transportation of "*all* children attending school."

The Supreme Court of Washington, after discussing *Everson* at some length in its opinion, reaffirmed its previous decision and, in a 6–2 split, voted that the law providing school bus transportation for *all* children was violative of Washington's Constitution.[3] The Washington court relied heavily on the second principle of *Everson*; namely, that the state is not *required* to provide transportation to those attending private schools. The Washington tribunal appears, however, to have neglected the third principle of *Everson* —the mandate that the benefits of public welfare legislation *must* be distributed without reference to religion. And if the amended Washington statute is *not* public welfare legislation then it is difficult to see how such legislation can be written. The Washington State decision appears therefore to be in conflict with *Everson* and to deny to the 24,000 students in private schools in that state the benefits of specifically designated public welfare legislation solely because of their religious faith.

CONNECTICUT. In those states where bus rides flare into public discussions and provoke court decisions the observer or historian must try to analyze the emotions involved and the pressures exerted, by the not always satisfactory method of reading judicial opinions and newspaper clippings. The Connecticut struggle over bus rides, however, has been recorded and evaluated in all its major phases in an excellent volume by Dr. Theodore Powell entitled "The School Bus Law: A Case Study in Education, Religion and Politics."[4] It is difficult to praise this study enough, not merely because of its unique contribution but also for the irenic tone and approach which characterizes its treatment of an issue which divided the people of Connecticut along religious lines in an unprecedented manner.

In 1956, 78,923 Connecticut children attended nonpublic schools while 381,543 were enrolled in public schools. No clear pattern had ever existed in the state concerning the distribution of public services to the 17.1 per cent of the children in private schools—most of them in Catholic institutions. In order to clarify the confusing state of the law and the differing practices on child-benefit services, there was introduced into the Connecticut Senate on January 24, 1957, a bill which proposed that each town could, by local option, furnish bus transportation to private school children.

The events between the date of filing of the bill to its enactment on May 29, 1957 (after the Speaker broke a 133–133 tie), and its signing by Governor Abraham Ribicoff are revealing. Mr. Powell's study concludes that opposition to the bus-ride bill ultimately enacted was "entirely Protestant" although "not all Protestants were opposed."[5] No Jewish group in Connecticut took a stand on the bus bill nor did any group dedicated to advancing the interests of public education. The Hartford Chapter of the American Civil Liberties Union was represented in opposition to the bill by a Congregational minister who also represented the Congregational churches of Connecticut.

The local option bill which passed brought forth dire predictions that town referenda would divide communities in a deplorable manner. Only seventeen towns, however, of the fifty with parochial schools would be eligible for such a referendum, inasmuch as these municipalities provide bus transportation for public school pupils only. It is impossible to estimate what damage, if any, has been done to the towns which have had such elections.

In the town of Windsor, Connecticut, for example, bus rides for private school children were approved in April, 1961, by a vote of 2589 to 2178—a difference of only 411 ballots. The initiative to obtain a referendum and the work to secure a successful result seems to have been almost entirely of Catholic origin. But who can say with any proof that such activity and such a result is more divisive than the undeniable feeling of injustice which Catholic parents have when they must finance bus rides for their own children while their neighbor's children ride to public schools in tax-supported vehicles?

One of the weaknesses of Dr. Powell's study of the Connecticut situation is a failure to state in a very satisfactory manner exactly why he thinks, as he does, that the interreligious conflict over bus rides was an undesirable element in Connecticut's public life. Mr. Powell tends to reprimand clergymen for using their office to advance or oppose the bus bill. But what is lacking is a realization that, if bus rides for private schools involve, as *Everson* stated, public welfare legislation, then such a topic—like Medicare and other social security measures—is an appropriate subject for comment by religious leaders who have the right and sometimes the duty to give their views on moral–legal matters.

The Supreme Court of Connecticut, in a 4 to 1 ruling issued on June 13, 1960, sustained the constitutionality of the law permitting bus transportation for all school children.[6] The majority opinion followed *Everson* very closely, while the one dissenter brought up the inherent contradictions in *Everson* as well as the stern language of Connecticut's constitution which prescribes that "No person shall by law be compelled to join or support any congregation, church or religious association." The dissenter clearly identified the dilemma ignored by Justice Black: can legislation which is undeniably designed to advance the public welfare bring such assistance to the parents of pupils in church-related schools that the assistance helps the parents and *thereby the school* to an extent that is constitutionally impermissible? Justice Black may have thought he answered this problem when he wrote: "It is undoubtedly true that children are helped to get to church schools. There is even a possibility that some of the children might not be sent to the church schools if the parents were compelled to pay their children's bus fares out of their own pockets. . . ." But Justice Black's admission that he is virtually encouraging attendance at parochial schools is defended on the grounds that police and fire protection already do the same thing.

It is arguable that Justice Black's blessing on public welfare benefits for the parents of Catholic school pupils comes ultimately from his support of the *Pierce* decision. In any event, it is clear that the reasoning in *Everson*, which relied on the Supreme Court's *Cochran* decision in 1930 upholding a law giving secular textbooks to private school children in Louisiana, does allow aid to a parochial

school even though such aid is given to the parents. Leo Pfeffer
points out Justice Black's undeniable concessions to parochial
schools in these words: "When the *Everson* decision is coupled
with the *Cochran* decision, they lead logically to the conclusion
that the state may, notwithstanding the First Amendment, finance
practically every aspect of parochial education, with the exception
of such comparatively minor items as the proportionate salaries of
teachers while they teach the catechism . . ."[7]

It is because the dissenting judge in the Connecticut case and
other jurists see the door opened to the financing of parochial
schools that they are reluctant to adopt the thesis that the label
"public welfare legislation" removes all church–state problems from
grants of bus rides to parochial schools. Such thinking seems to
have entered the reasoning of the Supreme Court of New Mexico
which in 1951 ruled, despite *Everson*, against bus rides for private
schools in that state.[8]

As one reads the several opinions of state courts on bus legislation the impression cannot be avoided that the ultimate issue
involved is not *Everson*, the child welfare doctrine or the state
constitution but rather the all-important question which *Pierce*
left undecided—what is the real juridical status of the private,
church-related school? As a writer put it in 1947 in the *Harvard
Law Review*, the "underlying issue . . . is brutally simple: are
parochial schools to be encouraged or not?"[9]

The denial of review by the United States Supreme Court of the
Connecticut bus law decision was followed by a similar denial of
review of an opposite result reached by the Supreme Court of
Alaska. While the two denials of review do not necessarily involve
an open contradiction in policy, the two refusals do seem to indicate that the *Cochran–Everson* reasoning and results still constitute
good law, despite *McCollum, Torcaso* and the expansion given to
the establishment clause in these and related cases. *Everson*, with
its built-in obscurities, seems destined to plague state legislatures
and courts for some time to come. A review of a conflict over bus
rides in Maine may reveal more of the legal and sectarian cross-
currents which this issue always provokes.

MAINE. Although the Maine legislature prior to 1960 had twice
rejected bills to authorize the expenditure of public money for bus
rides for private school children, several cities and towns of Maine

supplied this service to students in private—largely parochial—schools. Of the total 196,000 school population of Maine in 1960, not less than 26,500 of these attended Catholic elementary and secondary schools. In 1958, a total of 3,866 students from private schools received free bus transportation. Only seven cities had such large Catholic student bodies that special buses or additional equipment were required. In the other eighteen communities where parochial school pupils obtained transportation they rode on the same buses as students going to public schools.

It was not legally clear that a city in Maine could, in the absence of state legislation, spend money for transportation to private schools. In order to secure a ruling on the matter the city officials of Augusta, on December 10, 1956, conducted a plebiscite on the question: "Shall the city of Augusta appropriate funds for transportation of parochial school students?" The people said "yes" by a vote of 3,915 to 2,470.

Pursuant to this directive, the City Council of Augusta on June 17, 1957, enacted an ordinance authorizing transportation for private school students on terms comparable to that supplied to public school pupils. Because of a serious doubt concerning the authority of a city to appropriate funds for this purpose in the absence of state-enabling legislation, the Augusta City Council appropriated a token sum of $250 from the contingent fund. There followed the institution of a lawsuit finally resolved by the Supreme Court of Maine on May 25, 1959.[10]

Twelve taxpayer-plaintiffs, joined by a Congregational minister of Augusta, sought to enjoin the ordinance of June 17, 1957, on the grounds that (1) it is beyond the delegated power of the Augusta City Council, and (2) it violates the Constitutions of Maine and of the United States.

The Maine Supreme Court unanimously agreed that neither the Maine nor the United States Constitution forbids free bus transportation to children attending private schools. But the court, in a 4–2 split, held that state legislation would be required before city officials could appropriate funds for transportation for private school children. The court affirmed that "we are satisfied that a properly worded enabling act . . . would meet constitutional requirements."

The Maine decision centered on the technical point of whether Maine's educational statutes reserved to the state the power to authorize cities and towns to provide transportation to both public and private schools. A majority of four of the justices enumerated persuasive reasons for its position that "the Legislature . . . intended that no municipality should regulate by ordinance or order any subjects which would effect or influence general education unless permitted to do so by an express delegation of power."

The Maine legislature was not in session at the time of this May decision, but on the following January 28 it rejected, for the third time, a proposal to allow individual communities to use public funds according to local option to provide transportation for private school pupils.

The Maine Council of Churches claimed a victory in the January 28 vote and attributed it in part to its campaign against bus rides. Rev. Shirley Goodwin, rector of Trinity Episcopal Church of Portland and president of the Maine Council of Churches, was joined by virtually all Protestant clergymen in his allegation that the Catholic Church, in accepting public transportation of its pupils, is "publicly admitting it is no longer willing to support its school system."

In the 1960 political campaign, both the Democratic and Republican platforms contained commitments to enact private school bus ride legislation. Such a pledge was a radical change for the Republican party since, in the voting on January 26, 1960, sixty-nine Republicans in the House voted against bus rides with twenty-three Republicans favoring them, while in the Senate seventeen Republicans voted against with only four in favor. Democrats in both chambers had been overwhelmingly in favor of bus rides (46–9 in the House, 11–4 in the Senate).

In May, 1961, Maine's legislature finally enacted a local option authorization law for bus transportation to private schools. Cities affected proceeded to conduct referenda as, for example, in Waterville where in December 1961 city voters approved 5,395 to 1,500 a plan to provide tax-paid bus rides for private school pupils. Shortly after the Legislature enacted the new law, however, a group self-named the Maine Citizens for Public Schools began to collect the 41,722 signatures that would be required to obtain a state-wide referendum on bus rides for private schools. This body, with Rev. M. Harry Randall, a Baptist minister, as executive secretary, worked diligently for several months but by the fall of 1961 had failed by 574 signatures to obtain the necessary 41,722 (10 per cent of the

total vote for governor in 1960) required to force a referendum—
an event which would automatically suspend the operation of the
bus law which became effective in December, 1961.

Although official Protestant groups have in every state opposed
bus rides for private schools there does not appear to be another
modern instance where Protestant bodies, at least unofficially, have
been more actively involved in anti-bus lobbying than in Maine.
Is there any principle or agreement or even compromise which can
dissolve the head-on Catholic–Protestant dissension over bus rides?
Or if the dissension cannot be lessened, can it be agreed that any
resort to political means will be governed by certain mutually
agreed-on standards?

To ask these questions is not, of course, to suggest that anything
reprehensible was done in Maine. The Catholic Bishop, Most Rev.
Daniel J. Feeney, spoke on the issue only once during the entire
controversy, and then only to express his hope for the enactment
of a state-wide bus law. Similarly, many Protestants were observers
rather than participants.

But the Catholic–Protestant confrontation over bus rides in
Maine and in every state where the issue arises gives proof—if
such be needed—that the legal formula of "public welfare legislation" is not a solvent harmonizing all the clashing interest. In fact,
this formula and the *Everson* ruling in general have a simplicity
which is deceptive; on first inspection they seem to furnish a legal
yardstick of some value but upon re-examination they appear more
and more to be simply irrelevant to the central issue: to what
extent should the law encourage private schools?

Perhaps Reinhold Niebuhr identified the source of the Catholic–
Protestant collision over anything that encourages parochial schools,
when he wrote: ". . . Protestants are inclined to be unyielding on
problems of the public school because they suspect the hierarchy,
at least, of being inimical to the whole idea of the public school
system, which Protestants, as well as our secular democrats, regard
as one of the foundation stones of our democracy."[11] Accepting
this diagnosis literally, it would appear that a Catholic–Protestant
entente on bus rides will not be easily obtained. And, even more
disastrous, such an "unyielding" attitude on a matter which has, at
least to some extent, become a legal–political issue may cause the
issue to become an even more explosive political problem.

WISCONSIN. It is difficult to conceive of a clearer repudiation of *Everson* than the June 5, 1962, 4–2 decision of the Supreme Court of Wisconsin declaring unconstitutional a bus law enacted in 1961.[12] Under this law children going to private schools would be granted free transportation to the public school which they were entitled to attend; from this point they would be required to get to their own schools by their own devices. The point, of course, in granting such a restricted privilege was to avoid a clash over Wisconsin's traditionally rigid separation of church and state. It could hardly be argued that an aid was given to a *private* school if *all* children were brought to a point most convenient for the children attending the *public* school. Unless one desired to say that the moment a child contracts out of the public school *anything* concerning his educational life is no longer the function of the state.

This seems to be the philosophy adopted by the Supreme Court of Wisconsin, at least with regard to children in church-related schools. In this respect, the test case on Wisconsin's 1961 bus law did contain a serious factual issue in that there are only ten private schools in all of Wisconsin *not* operated by religious groups and none of these ten could benefit under the law allowing transportation to the door of the public school.

The majority of the Wisconsin court flatly stated that bus transportation, even to the public school, would be a benefit to the sectarian school forbidden by the Wisconsin and Federal constitutions. The alleged benefit would derive from the fact that, if bus transportation were supplied to parochial schools, these institutions would be relieved of a part of the transportation costs which they now pay and thus, theoretically at least, parochial schools might benefit by having an increased enrollment.

Interestingly, however, the Supreme Court of Wisconsin appears to have approved of a practice employed in some sections of Wisconsin by which parochial school children attend certain courses in public schools without paying any fee or tuition; the court said that school bus transportation was not a state educational objective in the sense that such courses were. It would be a curious result if "shared-time" were permissible in Wisconsin but bus transportation to nonpublic schools were not.

It seems unlikely that the issue of bus transportation for the 277,686 nonpublic school pupils in Wisconsin will disappear as a result of the decision of Wisconsin's highest court. The bus issue did not fade away after a proposed constitutional amendment to permit such transportation was defeated in a 1946 referendum by a vote of 545,475 to 437,817. In a state that is 35 per cent Catholic with a total of 23.34 per cent of the state's 975,455 pupils enrolled in Catholic schools, a Catholic–Protestant struggle over bus rides appears predictable. The Wisconsin Council of Churches can hardly be expected to change its adamant position, nor does it seem likely that the resentment of Catholics over the inherently emotional subject of bus rides for *all* school children will abate.

Although the Wisconsin decision turns primarily on the state constitution rather than on the *Everson* opinion it would appear that the reasoning of *Everson* concerning "public welfare legislation" turned out once again in Wisconsin to be too vague. The Wisconsin legislature in its school bus law clearly intended a public welfare benefit for all children. The law that was passed on December 19, 1961, by a 61–32 vote of the state assembly, cleared by the state Senate on January 10, 1962, in an 18–10 vote, and signed by Governor Gaylord Nelson, provided that *all* school pupils be given a specific, identical benefit. The equality of the benefit intended for *all* children was so carefully spelled out that the law specified that, even if the bus passes the door of a private school on its way to the public school, children attending this private school could *not* be permitted to leave the bus at the door of their school.

It seems difficult to deny that the Wisconsin Supreme Court has rejected the *Everson* mandate that "the benefits of public welfare legislation" may not be denied to citizens "because of their faith or lack of it." What is equally distressing is the fact that the compromise law enacted in Wisconsin by a substantial margin still failed to win the approval of official Protestant spokesmen. Even if some of these spokesmen conceded the public welfare aspect of the bus law they still opposed it on the ground that it would be a "wedge" for other legislation.

ALASKA. If *Everson* turned out in several states to be an ineffective formula for the adjudication of legislation on bus transportation for nonpublic schools, the holding in *Everson* was rendered almost totally useless in this matter by the following interpretation of it in a 2–1 decision on June 29, 1961, of the Supreme Court of Alaska: "In the final analysis the Supreme Court in the *Everson* case did nothing more than accept the state court's interpretation

of the New Jersey constitution and then hold that the use of the
state's general fund to pay for the transportation in question was
not a violation of the First and Fourteenth Amendments of the
Federal Constitution."[13] Under this view of *Everson* it is arguable
that in some states it is impossible to write "public welfare legislation" if the Supreme Court of the state decides to hold that
nothing may be given to private school children which might
conceivably aid the schools they attend.

The Supreme Court of Alaska, following this reading of *Everson*,
overturned the trial court and declared void a carefully drafted bus
law enacted after *Everson* and in compliance with its directives
concerning "public welfare legislation." The law noted in its preamble that its intent was "to protect the *health and safety* of *all*
school children in Alaska and to achieve the objectives of the
compulsory education laws of Alaska."[14] [Emphasis supplied.] The
authors of this law, delegates to the Alaska Constitutional Convention of 1955, questioned in 1961 concerning the intent of the
convention in proposing the law answered, 21 to 4, that the convention did *not* intend to stop the state from furnishing bus
transportation to nonpublic school children.

Circumstances of climate unique to Alaska were one of the
forces compelling the legislature to provide for transportation for
all school children. The voiding of the bus law by the Supreme
Court of Alaska means that private school pupils may be exposed
to the danger of walking to and from school in sub-zero weather
and, during the winter months, in total darkness.

OTHER STATES. The *Everson* decision has unfortunately not resolved the legal tangle surrounding bus rides to private schools in
other states. The Supreme Court of Missouri in 1953 ruled against
transportation of pupils to private schools.[15] Litigation over a custom in parts of Oklahoma of allowing parochial school children
to ride on the public school buses was in process in late 1962.

Bus transportation legislation to be proposed in Minnesota has
caused several organizations devoted to public education to organize
in that state in preparation for the anticipated request for buses
for private schools. In other populous states such as Pennsylvania
the need for greater safety in the transportation of private school
pupils is so evident that it is a cause of concern to such persons as
Dean John C. Bennett, who feels that public bus transportation is
a reasonable benefit to grant to nonpublic schools. It does not

appear, however, that the demonstrated need on the basis of child safety will bring about bus transportation for parochial schools without a Catholic–Protestant donnybrook.

Defenders of civil liberties will, of course, join Protestant and other groups in opposing bus rides for children in parochial schools. The American Civil Liberties Union filed a brief on the losing side in the *Everson* case but has never since retreated from its opposition to any plan which gives transportation to private school pupils —even if these students receive, as proposed in Wisconsin, only that which public school pupils would obtain.

One of the bewildering and frustrating features of the continuing bus-ride debate is the dogmatism with which both sides claim that the *Everson* opinion supports their case. The opponents of bus rides can count the states of New Mexico, Missouri, Washington, Alaska and Wisconsin which, after *Everson*, have invalidated bus-ride legislation. Advocates of the constitutionality of transportation to nonpublic schools can cite Connecticut and Maine as states which, in the years following *Everson*, have sustained public transportation to private schools. Legislation in other states untested by litigation can be claimed by either side—depending on whether Wisconsin or Connecticut decisional law is deemed to be superior.

The *Everson* decision was based to some extent on the "child-benefit theory." It may be that some of the ambiguities which state courts have found in *Everson* came not merely from the vagueness of the "public welfare legislation" but also from the indefiniteness of the child-benefit theory employed by the Supreme Court in its 1930 ruling in the *Cochran* case that Louisiana could constitutionally grant secular textbooks to children in sectarian schools. In view of the intimate interconnection between the law on secular textbooks for private schools, the child-benefit theory and bus transportation, it is relevant now to analyze in some detail the law concerning textbooks for private schools in Louisiana, Mississippi, Oregon and Rhode Island. After this analysis it will be appropriate to offer some generalizations about the present status of *Everson* and the child-benefit theory.

PUPIL-BENEFIT THEORY, SECULAR TEXTBOOKS AND SHARED-TIME

Many strict church–state separationists see in the so-called "child-benefit" theory nothing but an evasion of the no-aid-to-religion prohibition of the Federal and most state constitutions. To these critics *every* part of the educational process is designed to be a benefit to the child and hence it is chimerical to distinguish between benefits to the school and benefits to the child. These opponents of the "child-benefit" theory are even more certain of their position if this legal doctrine is called the "pupil-benefit" theory —as Professor Harry Jones has done in a series of lectures wherein he argues for the validity of the theory.[16]

The pupil-benefit concept assumes that a child by attending a parochial school does not render himself ineligible to receive those benefits which the state confers on *all pupils*. Little dispute arises as to the noneducational benefits which the state distributes to all *children* but as soon as these children become *pupils* the state must, according to the opponents of the theory sustained in the *Cochran* and *Everson* decisions, withhold all aid which would assist them *as pupils*. Bus rides cause habitual controversy because it is uncertain whether youngsters on the way to and from school should be classified as *children* or *pupils*.

Despite the fact that the United States Supreme Court unanimously sustained a Louisiana statute granting secular textbooks to *all* students in that state, the pupil-benefit theory has not been widely accepted. It may be that the rationale of the Supreme Court's opinion in *Cochran* was not sufficiently clear or explicit in the way in which it handled the objections to the Louisiana law. The opponents of textbooks in that state had lost in the Louisiana Supreme Court by a 3 to 2 vote over a powerful dissent.

The United States Supreme Court was not required to hear and decide the case but did so and, in affirming, relied heavily on the reasoning of the majority opinion of Louisiana's highest court. That tribunal had said, in a passage quoted with approval by the United States Supreme Court, that: "The appropriations were made for the specific purpose of purchasing school books for the use of the school children of the state, free of cost to them. It was for their benefit and the resulting benefit to the state that the appropriations were made."[17]

Both the Louisiana tribunal and the Supreme Court agreed that under the textbook statute the "school children and the state alone are the beneficiaries," and that the schools "obtain nothing from them, nor are they relieved of a single obligation, because of them." One could object that pupils and sectarian schools, relieved of the necessity of purchasing secular textbooks, thereby have more money to expend on other items with the result that the state is aiding a religion. Such reasoning is valid *if* one agrees that, the moment a *child* becomes a *pupil* in a *sectarian* school, the state cannot thereafter assist him to be a better *pupil* in the secular subjects which he, along with all other children–pupils, is legally required to learn.

John C. Bennett confesses to a change of mind on the matter of the validity of free textbooks to nonpublic school children. He writes: "I once thought that the provision of transportation was more readily defensible than the provision of school books, but the following considerations cause me to change that view: (1) School books which are the same as those used in the public schools do not aid religious education. (2) The cost is equivalent to the cost of such books if children went to the public schools which they have every right to do, whereas in the case of buses not only extra seats but extra routes may be involved. (3) The use of these books in both systems of schools is in the interest of the unity of the community."[18]

Despite the persuasiveness of these three points only the Supreme Court of Mississippi has sustained a textbook law. The Supreme Court of Oregon, as we shall see, has rejected such a law while the other two states authorizing such a practice, New Mexico and West Virginia, have not litigated the issue.

The Mississippi high court saw no basic difficulties in a law granting secular books to all school children and in 1941 sustained the law's validity in this well-reasoned paragraph: "If the pupil may fulfill its duty to the state by attending a parochial school, it is difficult to see why the state may not fulfill its duty to the pupil by encouraging it 'by all suitable means.' The state is under a duty to ignore the child's creed, but not its need. It cannot control what one child may think, but it can and must do all it can to teach the child how to think. The state which allows the pupil to subscribe to any religious creed should not because of his exercise of this right, proscribe him from benefits common to all. . . . The narrow construction contended for by complaints would compel the pupil to surrender use of his books when and because he elected to transfer from a public school to a qualified parochial school. Such would constitute a denial of equal privileges on sectarian grounds."[19]

OREGON—TEXTBOOKS AND PRIVATE SCHOOLS. In 1941, the legislature of Oregon, for reasons that are not entirely clear, amended its law to provide for the free use by private school pupils of the *same* textbooks prescribed by law for public school students. This equalization was justified in part by the fact that in the year 1931 Oregon, for the first time, provided for the free use of textbooks by all pupils attending public elementary schools. It appears also that the legislature, noting the identity of the curriculum prescribed for public and private schools, felt that the use of the same textbooks in both school systems would help to insure compliance with the legally fixed curriculum.

Oregon, where in 1960 a total of 29,165 (or 6.93 per cent of the state's 420,672 school children) attended Catholic schools, permitted the use of secular textbooks from 1941 until November 15, 1961, when the Supreme Court of the state declared the law contrary to Oregon's constitution.[20] The trial court judge in the suit, initiated by plaintiff-taxpayer Dickman and the American Civil Liberties Union, felt constrained to follow the *Everson* precedent. To this judge, Ralph M. Holman, free textbooks were less objectionable than free bus transportation since, in his view, bus rides are a *direct aid* to religious education while secular textbooks can assist such education only *indirectly*. Following this reasoning, Judge Holman affirmed the constitutionality of Oregon's grant of textbooks to *all* children—not because he himself believed in its validity but only because he felt bound by the high authority of the *Everson* decision.

The Supreme Court of Oregon, with one dissent, did not feel so bound and declared that "we agree with the dissenting opinion in *Everson* . . . that there is no way of 'satisfactorily distinguishing one item of expense from another in the long process of child education.' " The court ruled not on the Federal Constitution but only that a law authorizing free textbooks for parochial school students violates Oregon's constitution, which prohibits the use of public moneys "for the benefit of any religious or theological institution." In the course, however, of coming to this decision based on state grounds the Supreme Court of Oregon rejected the *Everson* reasoning—at least as to textbooks which, the Oregon court states, are "clearly identified with the educational process."

A lone dissent by Justice Rossman raises some intriguing questions. The 1941 amendment, Rossman reasoned, was designed "to improve the quality of the denominational schools." The legislature, he urged, intended superior instruction for pupils in church-related schools rather than any financial gain to the schools they attended. The purpose of the amendment was "to bring to the avail of the pupils in denominational institutions textbooks which the legislature favored."

This dissent suggests but does not reach the question of the constitutionality of a law dispensing free textbooks to *all* school children in the case where a state deemed that a particular text *should* be utilized by *all* children for the purpose of modernizing instruction in some particular area.

The decision of the Supreme Court of Oregon was appealed to the United States Supreme Court. In October, 1962, the nation's highest tribunal declined to review the Oregon result, its refusal being based most probably on the fact that the Oregon decision involved only the constitution of that state and not the First Amendment to the Federal Constitution.[21]

The idea which, more than any other, dominated the thinking of the Supreme Court of Oregon was the notion that, since the Catholic school has a religious purpose and "permeates" the secular curriculum with religious concepts, it is therefore practically the legal equivalent of a church or a monastery. The secular education prescribed by law and deemed the legal equivalent for all purposes of the secular education in the public school becomes constitutionally "contaminated" because of the "permeation" of a religious atmosphere.

No satisfactory counterexplanation is given by the court of the fact that the public school's curriculum is "permeated" by a secular or nonsectarian atmosphere and is therefore also "religious" or "nonreligious." No education can exist without a "permeation" of some outlook on life and human existence. An education without an ideological orientation is an impossibility. In 1929, Walter Lippmann explained this truth in words which have even more relevance today than when he wrote them. Speaking of the inseparable role of religion and education, Mr. Lippmann wrote: "No church can sincerely subscribe to the theory that questions of faith do not enter into the education of children. Wherever churches are rich enough to establish their own schools, or powerful enough to control the public schools, they make short work of the 'godless' schools. Either they establish religious schools of their own . . . or they impose their views on the public schools as the fundamen-

talists have done wherever they have the necessary voting strength.
. . ."22

As long as the realities so well expressed in this quotation are
not understood, the dominant place given by law and contemporary
society to the public secular school will continue to operate against
the pupil-benefit theory or any similar idea by which the sectarian
school could be encouraged.

RHODE ISLAND—TEXTBOOKS. One of the most interesting and
possibly significant tests of the pupil-benefit theory may come forth
from events transpiring in Rhode Island in 1962. Here for the first
time Catholic officials in late 1961 requested state aid for Catholic
schools other than bus transportation.

Arguing that the 1958 National Defense Education Act authorized loans to private schools for materials and equipment in the
fields of mathematics, science and foreign languages, Catholic
authorities in Rhode Island asked public educational officials to
consider whether the state of Rhode Island could furnish "science
texts and materials, arithmetic texts and materials, and materials for
diagnostic testing." Such aids, the Catholic petition argued, should
not raise the church–state issue since the specific items sought are
for the benefit of school children and are not related to the religious function of the Catholic schools which these children attend.

The usual alignment of religious and civil liberties groups
promptly came into existence. The Protestant Rhode Island Council of Churches disapproved the request though some individual
churchmen expressed the hope that a thorough consideration would
be given to the request made on behalf of the 48,328 children
(26 per cent of the state's total number of school children) in
attendance at 103 elementary and 19 secondary Catholic schools.

A Governor's Commission, appointed in early 1962 to investigate
the matter, heard testimony from many individuals and groups.
The request for secular textbooks threatened to become a political
issue in the fall 1962 campaign but such an eventuality seemed to
disappear when both candidates announced qualified support for
the justice of the Catholic claim.

Although the opposition in Rhode Island to the Catholic request
has been firm and unyielding, all participants and observers to the
controversy have repeatedly praised the commendable spirit of fair
play and charity which has characterized the discussion over the
novel Catholic petition.

In December 1962, the Commission created by Governor John

Notte and the General Assembly unanimously recommended the enactment of a law which would provide specified secular textbooks to pupils in private schools on the same basis as these books are provided for students in public schools. The reasoning of this seven-man, multi-faith, nonpartisan body is calm, logical and reasonable. The group, first of all, has no difficulty in recommending that the state furnish intelligence and achievement tests to *all* students in *all* schools "as a part of its responsibility for accrediting schools where pupils may fulfill the compulsory education requirement."

The Rhode Island Commission came to the conclusion that there is no firmly established Rhode Island or Federal constitutional prohibition of the distribution of secular textbooks to private school pupils on the same basis as these items are distributed to public school students. Especially is this true, the Commission felt, where the books are in a field "where competence is needed for our national survival."

In February 1963 the substance of the Commission's recommendations were enacted into law in Rhode Island. The opponents of the plan must logically subscribe to the thesis that the state in the implementation of its secular goals must act in such a way that no incidental aid to religion comes about as a result of its action. It is impossible to prove any constitutional requirement for such a policy from the opinions of the United States Supreme Court; the Sunday-law cases, in fact, expressly approve of laws with a secular purpose, the enforcement of which may give some incidental aid to religion.

The Rhode Island Commission consequently is on sound legal ground when it argues that the state may carry out its aims in the field of education even if, as the Commission concedes, "the textbooks that are suggested cannot be absolutely separated from the religious spirit that permeates religious educational institutions." The Rhode Island constitution, the Commission concludes, does *not* say that the state must aid only public schools, but rather that the General Assembly "adopt *all* means which they deem necessary and proper to secure to the *people* the advantages and opportunities of education." [Emphasis supplied.]

The ultimate decision that will be made in Rhode Island will be important and may even mark the beginning of a new era for the private school in America.

Before considering the very new concept of "shared-time" (which is neither justified on the pupil-benefit theory or opposed as a direct aid to a church-related school) it may be helpful to try to draw some conclusions about the present status of *Everson* and the viability of the pupil-benefit theory.

Although the Supreme Court of the United States has twice affirmed the validity of the child-benefit theory, it cannot be said that *Everson* is a firm, irreversible precedent as *Pierce* appears to be. Nor has *Everson* in almost a generation gained much acceptance at the state level; *Cochran* in almost two generations has been even less impressive with only one state—Mississippi—following its ruling on the constitutionality of granting secular textbooks to *all* children.

It is not surprising therefore that partisans in the Federal aid controversy, when citing *Cochran* and *Everson*, can draw from these precedents and the state cases that followed them almost all the conclusions they desire. *Cochran* has been weakened—not in principle but in practice—by *Everson*, and *Everson* in turn has been weakened by the state decisions in Washington, Alaska, Vermont, Oregon, Wisconsin and elsewhere.

Amid all the controversy over the implications of the *Everson* opinion there emerged a new and promising if uncrystallized idea on the church-state scene.

SHARED-TIME. One could hardly have predicted that, amid all the virtually unanimous Protestant and Jewish opposition to Federal aid for Catholic schools, expressed so vigorously in 1961, there would emerge from Protestant initiative the truly amazing concept of "shared-time." The proposal seems to have been discussed in writing for the first time in a formal way in the September 18, 1961, issue of the Protestant journal, *Christianity and Crisis*, in an article written by Harry L. Stearns, superintendent of schools in Englewood, New Jersey. "Shared-time" means simply that *all* students in a community would come together in the public school for the religiously neutral courses while those who so desired could attend a parochial school for instruction in those subjects in which religion is an integral part.

"Shared-time" is still only an idea, though an intriguing one for all believers. The whole concept could conceivably fade away as rapidly as it arose but its implications are worthy of consideration. The very fact that many Protestant churchmen and educators have conceded that there are sociocultural subjects in the curriculum where the public school cannot do justice to differing religious viewpoints is a concession of no small consequence. Furthermore, it may be that the unprecedented national debate in 1961 over Fedaral aid for church-related schools was instrumental in persuading many non-Catholics of the validity or the inevitability of the Catholic claim to some share in Federal aid to education. Regardless of what might happen to the concept of "shared-time" its meteor-like emergence into church-state literature and the discussion over parochial schools is in itself a symptom of the profound forces operating in this area.

The January–February 1962 issue of *Religious Education* contains a 36-page symposium in which Protestant, Catholic and Jewish authors express their views on the advisability and feasibility of the shared-time proposal. The reactions of all nineteen commentators are somewhat favorable to the idea, though the whole proposal of shared-time is so sketchy that firm commitments and conclusions are almost impossible. As these writers—and the many others who have elsewhere commented on shared-time—see the plan, its advantages and difficulties might be expressed as follows:

Advantages. Clearly the parental right to educate is given a great deal of respect in the shared-time scheme. Every parent would be guaranteed the right not to have its child taught some version or interpretation of history, literature or the social sciences which would be inconsistent with the parent's or the child's religious faith and cultural tradition.

Shared-time would do a great deal to eliminate or at least ease the financial burden on Catholic and other parents who now finance their own sectarian schools. It would reduce or eliminate the pressures on public school officials to have released time, Bible-reading, the recitation of prayers and the celebration of religious festivals.

Shared-time could cause Catholics to have more interest in the public school with the result that their voting power in various communities might be a factor in the improvement of the financial condition of public schools. Finally, it might be useful in bringing together *all* the children of a community for part of their education and by this means promote a greater solidarity among all future citizens.

Difficulties. Would shared-time turn out to be really useful to *all* groups or only to Catholics? Is there a substantial number of Protestants, Jews and others sufficiently persuaded of the value of a part-time church-related school—even for those key courses where religious and theological issues are crucial? Is the "concession" of shared-time being made only for Catholics, but with the unwarranted assumption that other church groups would be interested in "sharing" a part of that time of their adherents which is not totally taken up by the state school?

If shared-time were widely adopted would it come about eventually that the public school would diminish in prestige because it would be teaching only those subjects which are not "value-laden"? Would attempts to secure the changes necessary in state law to authorize shared-time precipitate a church-state imbroglio the adverse effects of which might cancel out any possible advantages of shared-time?

Would the administrative difficulties involved in shared-time be so enormous as to render the plan simply impossible—at least in certain communities where, for example, one-fourth of all students now attend Catholic schools and all of whom would want to share the public school facilities for such things as geometry classes or mechanical drawing?

Shared-time, however successful, would still be considered as a "compromise" by Catholics, and may be so contrary to the unitary theory of education that it is objectionable from an educational point of view. If *all* Catholics in a particular community absent themselves from a particular course in history or literature in the public school in order to attend these courses in the Catholic school, would there be adequately trained personnel to teach these students in the Catholic school?

Many more advantages and difficulties inherent in shared-time could be noted, but the foregoing cover the major features of the scheme. The idea has promise and is now being experimented with in Pittsburgh and elsewhere. The widespread discussion of shared-time in the months following its proposal revealed several informally practiced versions of the plan.

No church body has officially approved shared-time. The National Council of Churches has recommended study while Catholic officials have expressed great interest and some enthusiasm. Most public school educators seem to have adopted a "wait and see" attitude. It seems accurate to predict that Protestant groups could, if they desired, obtain shared-time arrangements. In view, however, of the history and present status of released and dismissed time religious education, it seems unlikely that enough Protestant enthusiasm exists or could be aroused to create a series of part-time Protestant schools with a faculty competent to teach those subjects on which Protestant Christianity has a definite moral and spiritual position.

An unexpected endorsement of the shared-time concept came from Leo Pfeffer, general counsel of the American Jewish Congress. In a nationwide telecast with Father Neil G. McCluskey, S.J., in March, 1961, Mr. Pfeffer volunteered his sponsorship of the shared-time plan. He felt that it would ease the financial difficulties of Catholic parents and would also bring Catholic school children more in contact with their non-Catholic contemporaries. Attesting to the constitutionality and the wisdom of the shared-time scheme, Mr. Pfeffer also indicated that the administrative difficulties inherent in the plan could be worked out.

Mr. Pfeffer's endorsement was, however, short-lived. In an article entitled "Second Thoughts on Shared Time" in the June 20, 1962, issue of *Christian Century,* he retracted his support, denying its wisdom though still conceding its constitutionality. On the latter point Mr. Pfeffer argued that, if the *Zorach* decision permitted the state to release children at fixed times for sectarian instruction, then clearly there could be no barrier to "released time in reverse" wherein students are released from sectarian schools for instruction in secular subjects. Mr. Pfeffer felt, however, that pupils from parochial schools permitted to take secular subjects in public schools would almost inevitably come and remain together as a group, thus accentuating the very "segregation" which shared-time might hopefully de-emphasize.

The withdrawal of Mr. Pfeffer's blessing on shared-time can hardly help the viability of this somewhat promising notion. But the clear affirmation by a concededly rigorous church–state separationist of the constitutionality of the shared-time plan will at least mitigate the fear of a lawsuit which some public school administrators might have if they cooperated in plans to share public school facilities with private school pupils.

The most distressing feature of Mr. Pfeffer's change of mind comes in his declaration that there *is* a solution to the problem of the religious parent and the parochial school but that shared-time is *not* this solution. If, however, the "problem" exists and if there *is* a solution other than shared-time, where and what *is* the solution?

Mr. Pfeffer's rejection of shared-time reflected the thinking of the American Jewish Congress whose governing council on March 18, 1962, voted "opposition to the shared-time proposal." The Jewish community once again repudiated shared-time when, in June 1962, the National Community Relations Advisory Council, a group representing six national Jewish secular and religious organizations and sixty-two Jewish community councils, rejected shared-time because while it "may not violate the constitutional separation between Church and State, it would impair and in the end vitiate our American public school system."

All that one can conclude about shared-time is that it will be interesting to watch what, if anything, comes of the proposal. From the concessions made by Protestant and Jewish writers on the subject it would appear that Catholics and others would be within their rights to register their children in the public school and then withdraw them from particular courses where moral values are critical. If these children received equivalent instruction in these subjects in an accredited parochial school, they would presumably be entitled to their diploma from the public school.

One could argue, furthermore, from the admissions of Protestant and Jewish commentators on shared-time, that Catholics need no longer threaten to send all their children to the public schools just to show the taxpayers how much money Catholic schools save the government; Catholics could rather simply enroll their children in public schools, take all the neutral courses, utilize all the physical facilities and withdraw from the value-laden subjects.

Shared-time, by placing its prime emphasis on the undeniable right of every child to attend the public school, automatically highlights the duty of the public school and of the state in the case where a child withdraws in full or in part from the secular school. Even if the idea does not materialize into a concrete plan, its discussion may well bring into sharper focus the presuppositions of those who advocate or oppose state aid for private schools.

CHAPTER SIX

Federal Aid to Education

THE HISTORY OF FEDERAL AID

If history contains any lesson about attempts at enactment of Federal aid to education, it is that only aids for special types of education are likely to pass. An authority on the subject has written that after the first Morrill Act became law in 1862 "*all* permanent programs (of Federal aid to education) have been for the purpose of supporting specialized educational activity."[1] Several educational programs—generally of a scientific or agricultural nature—have been assisted during the last century by the Federal government but no bill authorizing general aid for all public schools or for all pupils has ever cleared both houses of the United States Congress.

The century-old drive to enact general Federal aid to education has elicited almost a thousand bills and has been the subject of countless committee hearings and acrimonious floor debates. The House has passed a general school aid bill only once—in 1872 —but the Senate has done so on eight occasions during the period from 1880 to 1961.

It is, of course, the source of the greatest concern to all Catholics that the issue of Federal aid for Catholic schools has been *one* of the complicating factors in the failure of Federal aid to be enacted. Regardless of whether or not one subscribes to the need for Federal aid, it is distressing for a member of any church to know that the requests and claims of his church and his coreligionists have become a matter of political consequence.

The emergence of the Catholic "claim" in the Federal aid controversy involves a story which began in contemporary history in 1945. In that year Senator Aiken proposed a bill for Federal aid to public schools, with, however, an unprecedented provision for equal rights and privileges for private schools.[2] Severe opposition to the bill's inclusion of church and private schools came from the National Education Association and other organizations.

As the church–state controversy became sharper in the late forties, and especially after the *Everson* and *McCollum* decisions, the Aiken proposal of parity for *all* schools faded into the background and three general positions on church-related schools became a permanent feature of the several bills filed in each Congress on behalf of Federal aid to education. The three positions in general are as follows:

1. No Federal money should go to any nonpublic school—even if state law permits such use.

2. The states should be allowed to follow their own constitutions and grant Federal money according to their own laws.

3. States should be required to designate a certain percentage of all Federal money received for the purposes of health and welfare benefits for children in nonpublic schools.

The original Aiken plan is still proposed, however, as, for example, in the bill filed in 1961 by Congressman James J. Delaney (D., N.Y.) under which the parents of all children in nonpublic schools would, upon proper application, receive a fixed amount payable to the private school which their children attend. But it seems probable that, if Federal aid is to be enacted in the near future, it will take the form of one of the three positions sketched above. The whole climate of opinion about this subject, however, is changing so rapidly that predictions can be little more than conjectures. The Federal aid question, furthermore, is so complicated by the school segregation question, the fear of Federal control, the viability and possible expansion of the formula used by the 1958 National Defense Education Act, as well as several other factors, that it would be almost impossible to determine, even after the defeat or enactment of a bill granting Federal aid to education, the true causes behind its eventual outcome.

The 1945 Aiken-Mead bill, which authorized the Federal government to make allotments of funds directly to nonpublic schools in those states which are prevented by law from subsidizing these schools, was the first bill on Federal aid of any importance to obtain the support of the National Catholic Welfare Conference. In testifying in 1945 on behalf of the Aiken-Mead proposal the director of the Department of Education of the N.C.W.C., Rt. Rev. Msgr. Frederick G. Hochwalt, enunciated the position which has ever since been consistently held by Catholic officials and spokesmen. In view of the fact that in 1945 there were 2,119 Catholic secondary schools and 8,017 Catholic elementary schools with a student population of 2,399,908 the request that these students share to some extent in Federal aid to education was not unusual.

Since 1945, the Catholic claim has been simply that *some* recognition or participation should be granted to private schools *if* Federal aid is to be enacted. Catholics have argued on the basis of the *Cochran-Everson* reasoning but have been required to go beyond this line of argument and urge not merely the constitutionality of aid to parochial schools, but also the advisability and wisdom of such a program.

Official Catholic spokesmen have never requested that parochial schools should receive the identical benefits which public schools would receive under any proposed bill. Nor have Catholic officials ever asserted that either Catholic or public schools need Federal aid; the Catholic position is that, *if* Federal aid is to become a reality, the nonpublic school must not be treated as if it did not exist.

It should be remembered that, if Catholic spokesmen seemed unyielding, their insistence was matched if not surpassed by those who would not vote for *any* bill on Federal aid in which nonpublic schools received some recognition. For example, it seems clear now that, as Roger A. Freeman, an expert on school financing, has written, "the National Education Association could have obtained enactment of a school aid bill (in 1948) if it had been willing to concede 1 or 2 per cent of the amount to private schools for auxiliary services."[3]

Although any objective critic of the Catholic role would be able to observe that Catholic insistence on the place and rights of the nonpublic school is indeed a salutary corrective to the apothesis of the public school, most observers have not appreciated this truth and have, in general, disparaged the Church for its activities in connection with Federal aid.

It is difficult to know where to commence any effort to resolve

the vast misunderstandings which have grown up about the position and role of the Catholic Church with regard to Federal aid.
In the months of January to June of 1961 the Catholic case received
a national hearing of unprecedented magnitude. Some Catholics
feel that certain individuals, firmly opposed before 1961 to any
share of Federal aid for Catholic schools, had a reasonable doubt
arise in their mind about the fairness and wisdom of their poistion.
On the other hand, some persons and groups during the course of
1961 were hardened in their opposition to the Catholic position,
and seem more determined than ever to resist every attempt at
any proposed compromise.

Opposition to the Catholic position, grounded assertedly on the
separation of church and state, is in some cases actually based on
anti-Catholicism. More important, however, the fundamental reason for the rejection of the Catholic claim is a belief in that philosophy of education which teaches that the separation of the secular
and the sacred is desirable and indeed required for the preservation
of American democratic ideals. We shall at a later time examine
this secularistic outlook on education, but first a review of some of
the major events and crises in the Federal aid dispute is appropriate.

It is clear that possibly the strongest pressures in favor of Federal
aid to education come from public school teachers and administrators. The desires of this group for Federal aid are quite understandable in view of the fact that in 1958 American teachers had average
earnings of $4,827 whereas the average salary in that year for
seventeen professions requiring graduation from college was $9,439.[4]
If the salaries of public school teachers were placed at a level com-
mensurate with their training and their responsibility, demands for
Federal aid to education might be as infrequent as requests for
Federal aid from state and local employees in any number of
state-supported institutions and endeavors.

It is also apparent that the term "Federal aid to education," if
used without an explanation, no longer has any identifiable meaning. In the omnibus bill submitted by the Kennedy Administration
early in 1961, there were included, among other things, Federal aid
for colleges and universities, aid for Federally impacted areas, an
extension of the National Defense Education Act and the proposal
for massive aid to the *public* schools of the nation. Only in this last
proposal is there any serious church-state problem yet the whole
bill concerned itself with "Federal aid to education."

Prior to 1961, the Federal government had assisted private primary and secondary school children in two major Federal programs —the National School Lunch Act adopted in 1946, and the National Defense Education Act, which became law in 1958. These two precedents are most noteworthy.

The National School Lunch Act, adopted in 1946, resulted in the expenditure of $93.6 million in fiscal 1961. This program is administered by the states but the Act specifically provides that in the twenty-eight states where public education officials are legally barred from disbursing Federal–state funds to private schools these schools may apply directly to the United States Agriculture Department for their proportionate share of the funds allocated by Federal law to provide free or reduced-cost lunches to the nation's school children. Actual surplus foods are also distributed to private schools as are funds to help pay for the cost of recess-time milk programs at nonpublic schools.

It is significant to note that the Federal government has in this instance bypassed and "subverted" the public policy of more than half the states,—inevitably raising the question whether this could be done in another area where the Federal government intended to give a benefit to *all* children and desired that this benefit be conferred while the children are in school. The benefit conferred by the School Lunch Act is not in itself directly related to education, and for that reason there has been virtually no objection to the Federal Government's deliberate rejection of the settled policy of so many states. But would the result be different if the Federal Government decided, for example, that *every* child in elementary school should have a dictionary or that *every* student in high school should have a slide rule?

The National Defense Education Act, passed in 1958 amid post-Sputnik panic, set aside 12 per cent of the $47.5 million authorized each year for *grants* to public schools for the purchase of mathematics, science or foreign language equipment or for *loans* for the same purposes by nonpublic schools. This provision for loans to private schools was added to the original act on the floor of Congress with little debate or discussion.

Under the same NDEA program, eligible students in *all* colleges may borrow substantial sums. Half of such loans are canceled for those borrowers who teach five years in a public (but not in a nonpublic) school.

The loan provisions of the NDEA constitute, at least sym-bolically, an unprecedented recognition in Federal legislation of the importance and contribution of nonpublic primary and sec-ondary schools. Once again the Federal government refused to follow that rigid proscription of any financial assistance to non-public schools which is the fundamental policy and basic law of almost every state in the union. The NDEA represents, therefore, a rejection of the policy of exalting the public school to the point of refusing every sign of encouragement to the private school. NDEA said in effect that if the cold war is to be won the mind of every eighth American child who goes to a nonpublic school must not be neglected.

While the *actual* assistance given by the NDEA to nonpublic schools is undoubtedly very small in relation to their total com-mitment it is most significant that the NDEA was the first Federal or state law in this century to give private schools of less than collegiate rank even a semblance of parity with similar public schools. The tokenlike assistance available to private schools under the NDEA, however, points up the enormous struggle which con-fronts Catholics and others who seek to persuade the nation's leaders that the traditional policy of aiding *only* public schools must now yield to a newer and more realistic approach.

FEDERAL AID IN 1961

While it would be instructive to review the entire modern history of Federal aid to education, a summary of the dramatic events in 1961 will be adequate to highlight the forces operating in this area. On February 20, 1961, President Kennedy sent an educa-tion message to Congress which contained these words: "In ac-cordance with the clear prohibition of the Constitution no elementary or secondary school funds are allocated for constructing church schools or paying church school teachers' salaries; and thus nonpublic school children are rightfully not counted in determining the funds each state will receive for its public schools." The phrase "church school" used in this message is particularly inapposite since it has never been used by Protestants or Catholics to describe the nonpublic, church-related, fully accredited school. To call such an institution a "church school" is to reduce it to a mere adjunct of the church.

The President's position on higher education was different. His message read: "Education must remain a matter of state and local concern and higher education a matter of individual choice." Many critics of the Administration's program would in subsequent months find this distinction to be groundless.

President Kennedy's statement on the asserted unconstitutionality of aid to nonpublic schools tended to clothe what some considered a purely pragmatic position with the venerability of a long and established constitutional tradition. Ironically, on the very same day that the President sent his message on education to Congress, the United States Supreme Court dismissed the appeal in the Connecticut school bus case "for want of a substantial Federal question."[5] This Connecticut decision had sustained the constitutionality of bus rides for parochial school children in that state; the Supreme Court, in refusing to review this decision (Justices Frankfurter and Douglas dissenting) in effect affirmed *Everson* and the pupil-benefit theory on which *Everson* relies.

On March 1, 1961, President Kennedy was asked at his press conference to elaborate on the Administration's denial of all aid to parochial schools. The President emphasized the strictures of the majority view in *Everson* but insisted that the Administration's position on parochial schools was not inconsistent with its proposal to aid *all* colleges, whether church-related or not.

On March 2, 1961, the Administrative Board of the National Catholic Welfare Conference issued over the name of its chairman, the Most Reverend Karl J. Alter, a statement of four points deemed to be essential on the issue of Federal aid to education. Because of the importance of this statement it should be cited in full. The declaration of the five Cardinals of the United States and the ten Bishops and Archbishops who head departments of the N.C.W.C. read as follows:

1. The question of whether or not there ought to be Federal Aid is a judgment to be based on objective, economic facts, connected with the schools of the country and consequently Catholics are free to take a position in accordance with the facts.
2. In the event that there is Federal Aid to Education we are deeply concerned that in justice Catholic school children should be given the right to participate.
3. Respecting the form of participation, we hold it to be strictly within the framework of the constitution that long-term, low-interest

loans to private institutions could be part of the Federal Aid Program. It is proposed, therefore, that an effort be made to have an amendment to this effect attached to the bill.

4. In the event that a Federal Aid Program is enacted which excludes children in private schools these children will be the victims of discriminatory legislation. There will be no alternative but to oppose such discrimination.

On March 8, at his press conference, President Kennedy was once again asked about the possibility of aid to parochial schools. He was questioned about the proposal for loans that had been made by House Majority Leader John W. McCormack and urged in point 3 of the Bishop's statement:

Q. Mr. President, you said last week, as I recall it, that there was no room for debate on this matter.
A. That's right. There is no room for debate about grants. There's obviously room for debate about loans, because it's been debated. My view, however, is that the matter of loans is, to the best of my knowledge and judgment though this has not been tested by the courts, of course, in the sense that grants have, but by reading of the constitutional judgment in the *Everson* case, my judgment has been that across-the-board loans are also unconstitutional.

Although no one pressed the President on the fact that he, as a Senator, had voted for the NDEA which provided for loans for private, nonprofit schools, the President, elsewhere in the press conference, justified the constitutionality of NDEA loans because they were for specific purposes and were tied very closely to national defense. In the course of the President's answers he made the following statement: "Loans *and even grants* to secondary education under some circumstances might be held to be constitutional." [Emphasis supplied.]

On the same day as the President's press conference the Senate opened hearings on the bills to provide Federal assistance to education. Secretary Ribicoff, one of the first witnesses, was asked to prepare, on behalf of the Administration, a brief on the constitutionality of Federal aid to church-related schools. This brief was issued on March 28 and constitutes possibly the most important document in the entire 1961 controversy over Federal aid to education. It is by no means the best or the wisest statement of the problems surrounding Federal aid, but it conceded principles which are some of the key points of the Catholic position; this brief there-fore deserves careful analysis. We shall return to it after a narra-tion of the events of 1961, made more dramatic by the presence of the first Catholic president in the White House.

Between March 28, 1961, when the HEW brief appeared, and August 30, when Federal aid was overwhelmingly defeated in the House (by a vote of 242–170), not even the best informed persons could know all of the tactics and strategies adopted by the pro-ponents and opponents of Federal aid for nonpublic schools. The major events in the complex struggle included the following: On May 25, the Senate passed, by a 49–34 vote, S. 1021, a bill provid-ing $2.5 billion in grants to the states for operation and construction of public schools and for teachers' salaries. Although no provision was made for nonpublic schools no Catholic senator voted against this bill for this reason.

On July 6, the House Education and Labor Committee reported out H.R. 7904, a bill to expand NDEA. The Committee's recom-mendations broadened the "forgiveness" of up to 50 per cent of college student loans to include all graduates who entered the teaching profession, whether in public or nonpublic schools. The bill also included a provision for $375 million in long-term, low-interest loans available to private schools for construction of class-rooms in which science, mathematics, modern foreign languages, English to foreign-born students and "physical development," would be taught.

On July 18, the Rules Committee of the House, in an 8–7 vote, tabled all three education bills under its consideration,—the public school aid bill, the extension of NDEA and a college aid proposal. The vote of Congressman Delaney (D., N.Y.) attracted the most attention, but reportedly three other Rules Committee members —Southern Democrats—would have voted to table the NDEA had it been considered separately by the Rules Committee.

The public school bill, in other words, may well have been voted down in the Rules Committee because otherwise it would have reached the floor of the House before the NDEA; in such event the public school bill might have been passed, and then several Southern and border-state Congressmen could kill the section of the NDEA which gave private schools construction loans. Such fears "were not unjustified," in the opinion of the knowledgeable "Fact Sheet on Federal Aid to Education," issued on September

13, 1961, by the highly regarded *Congressional Quarterly*. In any event the Rules Committee's vote made necessary the use of the "Calendar Wednesday" procedure.

On August 30, a compromise bill came before the House under the parliamentary device of Calendar Wednesday. This proposal dropped teachers' salaries, included a modest construction program, a one-year extension of the NDEA and a continuation of the impacted areas aid program. This compromise bill pleased virtually no one. The National Education Association called it "woefully inadequate"; some Catholics felt that it still discriminated against nonpublic schools, while some non-Catholics said that the bill made undesirable concessions to private schools. In a 242–170 roll-call vote the House, without debate, refused to consider the compromise bill. Thus Federal aid in effect died for another year and, as events developed, until another Congress.

On September 6, the House voted, 378 to 32, to extend for two years the Federally impacted areas program and the NDEA. On September 13, the Senate, 80–9, passed a similar act, and on October 3 the President signed the bill (S. 2293) with an expression of "extreme reluctance."

It is an oversimplification of these facts and events to infer from them that the religious issue defeated Federal aid in 1961. The *Congressional Quarterly*, noted above, observed: "The religious issue was a strong factor, but not necessarily the decisive one. Many observers felt that by giving it so much attention Administration leaders merely succeeded in fanning it." Although it seems unlikely that anyone could successfully untangle the very complex forces which were operative on the "Calendar Wednesday" when the House defeated Federal aid, it seems unfair to make Catholics the scapegoat for the defeat of Federal aid to education in 1961. Close observers of the scene have so written.[6]

THE ADMINISTRATION'S LEGAL POSITION

Let us return at this point to the legal justification for its position which the Administration brought forward in its brief prepared by lawyers of the Department of Health, Education and Welfare assisted by personnel from the Department of Justice. The lawyers for the Department of Health, Education and Welfare had three sets of data to reconcile: the President's announced positions, pertinent Supreme Court decisions and existing legislation. HEW could hardly conclude to the unconstitutionality of a program it was administering, such as the NDEA, nor could it qualify the President's views. As a result, the HEW brief constructed an interpretation of Supreme Court opinions which makes the religious character of an educational institution relevant, but not decisive, with respect to the constitutionality of Federal grants.

HEW's brief states the fundamental dilemma confronting the American government in these terms: "The difficult problem is posed by the dual constitutional mandate: that the state must recognize these (nonpublic) schools *as part of its educational system* for purposes of compulsory education laws, but that it cannot support them in ways that would constitute an 'establishment of religion'." [Emphasis supplied.]

The brief then continues with this observation: "The problem is accentuated by the fact that American society is one in which religion touches much of everyday life, both in the home and in the school. It is a society in which customs, practices, morals, and ceremonies have been importantly influenced by religion. Fundamental as are the principles contained in the first amendment, it is clear that they cannot always be absolutes . . ."

In the minds of HEW's lawyers, however, the thorny problem they outline has been solved by the *Everson* decision from which the conclusion is drawn that "obviously . . . direct grants to sectarian schools are prohibited." But the Administration's brief concedes that *Everson* does *not* settle the question of whether a state, in carrying out a legitimate public purpose not related to religion, can distribute its benefits in such a way that religious institutions receive what similarly situated nonreligious institutions also receive. The HEW brief then suggests the following as relevant criteria in connection with this problem:

1. How closely is the benefit related to the religious aspects of the institutions aided?

2. Of what economic significance is the benefit?

3. To what extent is the selection of the institutions receiving benefits determined by government?

4. What alternative means are available to accomplish the legislative objective without resulting in the religious benefits ordinarily proscribed?

In discussing these criteria, the brief admits that the pupil-benefit theory "may, perhaps, be extended to textbooks for the use of individual students where the books in question are common to the secular and sectarian educational systems. It might also be extended to some equipment, or possibly to facilities, designed for special purposes totally unconnected with the religious function of the schools." Although one can think of numberless items in a parochial school "totally unconnected with the religious function" of the school, the HEW brief is careful to step back from its broad concession by calling attention to the fact that the Supreme Court in *Everson* "put transportation at the outer limits of the constitutionally permissible."

Again the government's brief makes a sweeping admission when it states: "A program of financial aid to qualified students attending institutions of their choice to carry out a public policy of assisting unusually able students to develop their full potentialities, or to encourage study in subjects where there is a shortage of adequately trained persons to serve national needs, does not seem to raise a serious question." This approbation for Federal scholarships to students preparing for college concedes that, under such a program, certain religious institutions might receive substantial support.

After asserting that general grants or loans to church-related schools would be unconstitutional, the HEW brief states that "special purposes" grant loans are permissible if they are extended for purposes "unrelated to the religious aspects of sectarian education." Thus the NDEA program is approved as well as the several programs which the Federal government finances in order to assist higher education. Indeed, in an interesting footnote, the document justifies three grants made under the National Institute of Mental Health[7] to three divinity schools to develop curriculums for training clergymen in the recognition and understanding of mental illness.

The same footnote contains a demurrer on the validity of sectarian institutions being allowed to be donees and purchasers under the program for the disposal of surplus government property. Under this arrangement an estimated $423 million of Federal property was disposed of in fiscal 1961 at original cost. While no Federal records are kept of the ultimate disposition of the excess Federal buildings, vehicles, desks, etc., about 77 per cent of it goes to schools, and church-related schools have been permitted to purchase this equipment in the same manner as if they were public schools.[8]

Before touching on what the HEW brief has to say about church-related colleges some observation on its seemingly ambivalent position on aid to sectarian schools seem warranted. The Ribicoff brief reflects, as clearly as possible, the undeniable fact that America simply has not thought out what its policy should be concerning the nonpublic school. The nation's confusion on this point is made deeper by the fact that, according to the U.S. Office of Education, 91.9 per cent of the pupils in private elementary and secondary schools attend sectarian institutions.

At the height of the nation-wide controversy in 1961 over Federal aid and Catholic schools the *New Republic*, in its March 24 issue, editorialized: ". . . it is the mission of the state to discourage parochial schools. . . . we misunderstand the scheme if we think of the state as neutral. It is neutral in that it must prefer none of our many religious and cultural strains. But it is itself committed to exerting a secular, unifying, equalitarian force." Although many would reject this position—especially the point about discouraging parochial schools—the *New Republic's* attitude is probably the unspoken view of most of those who oppose even token recognition in a Federal aid program for the nonpublic schools.[8a] The *New Republic's* outlook, for example, is not clearly distinguishable from that of Methodist Bishop John Wesley Lord who, in testifying on behalf of Federal aid in March 1961, spoke as follows: "As Protestants we recognize the legitimacy of Church-related parochial . . . schools, and that they possess certain values in spite of certain disadvantages. It cannot be argued, however, that a system of private and parochial schools could meet the basic requirements of democracy . . . Such schools are designed primarily to serve denominational interests and to foster institutional control of the educational process. Certainly the values of democratic citizenship can be more fully realized by public education."[9]

Do not these two opinions assert, or at least imply, that the basic objection of those opposed to any form of Federal aid to nonpublic schools derives from the almost mystical powers which they attribute to the public schools? Even the National Council of Churches, in a solemn "policy statement" adopted by its General Board on February 22, 1961, imputes the same quasi-sacramental character to the public school. NCC's pronouncement states: "In principle Protestant and Orthodox Churches claim the right for themselves to establish and maintain schools in any community where the ethos of the public school system is or becomes basically inimical to the Christian education of our children. But we believe that to encourage such a general development would be tragic in its results to the American people." In the same statement it is asserted that the assignment of public funds to nonpublic schools "could easily lead additional religious or other groups to undertake full scale parochial or private education with reliance on public tax support. This further fragmentation of general education in the United States would destroy the public school system or at least weaken it so gravely that it could not possibly adequately meet the educational needs of all the children of our growing society."

Even if the *Everson* and other opinions made it unequivocally clear that the Federal government could subsidize the secular *educational* programs of church-related schools, the National Council of Churches—which speaks for virtually all Protestant groups in America—would still be opposed to any plan which would "encourage" a development of these schools. The same reluctance to "encourage" church-related schools is almost articulated in the brief issued by the Kennedy Administration to justify its ban on any aid of any kind to nonpublic schools. If the brief took the position that the Government seeks as its primary objective the improvement of the quality of the *secular* education received by *all* future citizens, it would have developed and elaborated on its open concession that public money may be given to sectarian schools for public purposes not related to the religious functions of these church-related institutions.

The HEW brief was answered in a forthright and forceful document issued by the Legal Department of the National Catholic Welfare Conference.[10] The NCWC statement argues vigorously for the proposition that there "exists no constitutional bar to education in church-related schools in a degree proportionate to the value of the public function it performs."[11] When Federal aid to church-related schools flares again into a national controversy, the HEW and the NCWC briefs will be valuable as statements of what Federal law and Supreme Court jurisprudence tell us about the legal and constitutional aspects of the problem. The underlying and nonlegal problem (to what extent should American society encourage the nonpublic school?) may hopefully by that time have emerged a bit more from the obscurities now surrounding it.

CHURCH-RELATED COLLEGES AND THE ADMINISTRATION

Despite serious and possibly mounting misgivings about the constitutionality of Federal grants to church-related colleges, the Kennedy Administration has not withdrawn its unequivocal endorsement of aid to *all* colleges and scholarships to *all* qualified students attending *any* accredited college. The HEW brief attempts to justify this position, employing as its main line of defense the fact that attendance at college is voluntary and not required. One is tempted to inquire whether this reasoning would crumble if a particular state, or all the states, repealed their laws compelling attendance at school on the not implausible assumption that such laws are no longer necessary.

The second justification employed to explain the total disparity between the position taken toward grade and high school education in relation to collegiate education derives from the statistic that 41 per cent of all college students today attend nonpublic institutions. Hence the public colleges and universities "could not begin to cope with the number of young men and women already in pursuit of higher education, and expansion of these institutions or the creation of new ones sufficient to meet the expected increase of enrollment is out of the question." After this pragmatic view of the situation the HEW brief goes on to say that the aid given to sectarian colleges may not help religion as much as such aid would if given to schools of less than collegiate rank; the "connection between religion and education" the brief asserts, "is less apparent and . . . religious indoctrination is less pervasive in a sectarian college curriculum . . ."

Although there are valid distinctions between aid to colleges and aid to schools of less than collegiate rank one cannot escape the impression that the HEW brief believes implicitly in *encouraging* nonpublic colleges whereas it expresses the utmost reluctance to encourage or even to recognize the public function performed by the nation's nonpublic primary or secondary schools. Such an attitude, of course, reflects the tone and spirit of much of American educational thought.

It may be that Secretary Ribicoff's brief did not adequately assess the strength of the opposition to grants for church-related colleges. During 1962, opposition to direct grants for church-related institutions of higher education was sent to Congress by the following organizations: the National Congress of Parents and Teachers, the National School Boards Association, the American Association of School Administrators, the American Vocational Association and the Council of Chief State School Officers.

The American Council on Education has endorsed unreservedly the Administration's proposals for aid to *all* colleges and universities. The ACE, along with many other organizations working in the field of higher education, would be opposed to the three standards set forth by the American Civil Liberties Union as the prerequisites for a church-related college to obtain Federal funds. The ACLU would require a college to comply with the following three provisions before it could be eligible for aid:

1. Admit all students without respect to religion,

2. Require no course in theology nor attendance at a religious practice,

3. Place the control of the college in the hands of academic and not ecclesiastical officials.

This extreme position seems hard to reconcile with the ACLU's approach to academic freedom. The three requirements, furthermore, seem to impose a philosophy of education on the authorities of a church-related college with no comparable burden being imposed upon those many colleges which require the equivalent of a course in secular humanism.

It is difficult to discover from a review of Congressional activity in 1962 with regard to aid for higher education, whether the church-related issue played a significant role in the defeat of all proposals for aid to public and private colleges and universities. On September 20, 1962, the House of Representatives recommitted the conference report on H.R. 8900 with instructions to remove all provisions for student assistance. This bill, which provided for grants to both public and private colleges, was not openly rejected because it would aid church-related institutions. This church–state factor, however, apparently entered into the vote of 214 to 186 by which any hope for Federal aid to higher education in 1962 was in effect destroyed.

It is significant, however, that on January 30, 1962, the House of

Representatives passed, by a vote of 319 to 79, a bill authorizing broader aid to *all* colleges and universities than H.R. 8900 but with no student scholarship or loan provisions. It is doubtful, therefore, that the opposition of the National Education Association to the granting of financial aid to *private* colleges was decisive in the vote of September 20, 1962. Furthermore, the NEA's position was not exclusively based on opposition to aid for church-related colleges, but to *all* nonpublic institutions of higher learning.

In 1961, there were 2,040 colleges and universities in the United States of which only 721 were publicly maintained. The NEA's recommendation would be to give grants to the 721 public institutions but only loans to all private colleges and universities.

Such a position has never been adopted by any educational association which represented America's colleges and universities. The American Council on Education whose member organizations represent more than 90 per cent of student enrollment in the United States, has always firmly supported aid for all colleges—private, public or church-related.

After the defeat of Federal aid for colleges in 1962 the American Council on Education reaffirmed its opposition to the exclusion of private colleges from Federal assistance. It is difficult if not impossible to evaluate the strength or the depth of the support which the NEA outlook can muster. The NEA approach clearly does not reflect the views of the vast majority of leaders in higher education. Nor is it consistent with what various states are attempting to do to assist *all* colleges as, for example, in the college-aid plan of New York state.

The future of Federal aid for higher education may depend on some clarification of the church-state issue with regard to religiously oriented colleges, but it seems fair to state that a bill to aid *all* colleges could be enacted. Sound legal precedent to support the constitutionality of such a bill is available.

Only the future can reveal what policy the national government will adopt if or when it decides to give assistance to the four million American youths who are full-time students at institutions of higher education. It seems improbable that such a policy would deny aid to the 41 per cent of America's collegians who attend nonpublic colleges and universities.

THE CATHOLICS' JUSTIFICATION
OF THEIR CLAIM

In the nation-wide controversy over Federal aid in the late 1940's and again in 1961, the Catholics of America were called upon to justify their claim to some type of participation in the program of massive assistance to education which the Federal government might initiate. In the late 1940's the Catholic "case" rested almost entirely on the assertion that *some* part of Federal aid should be allocated to those public welfare benefits in which private school pupils may constitutionally share. This position, relying heavily on the then recently decided *Everson* case, was legally beyond challenge. But it is not certain that even this token noneducational assistance to private schools could have survived all the assaults of the antiprivate school lobby within Congress. In any event, the petition for "fringe benefits" for nonpublic school children did not produce a feasible method by which Federal aid could be enacted in a manner satisfactory to most interested parties.

In 1960 and thereafter, Catholic spokesmen urged consideration of long-term, low-interest loans rather than an allocation for "fringe benefits." The petition for loans, patterned along the lines of the NDEA formula, represented something less than what had been sought by Catholic officials a decade previously. Under bills favored by Catholic authorities in the late forties, 10 per cent of the funds allotted to each state would be earmarked for the furnishing of nonreligious textbooks, bus rides and health aids for *all* children with the proviso that the Federal government could, as in the School Lunch Act, distribute these benefits directly to nonpublic school children in those states where such distribution would be forbidden by law.

Despite the fact, however, the Catholic spokesmen have never requested more than child-welfare benefits and long-term loans under any proposed Federal aid program, Catholics in America have been required to justify their claim as if what they were asking was not a token participation but rather full partnership in the funds available for public schools. Catholics have consequently assembled arguments and constructed a sorites which logically is calculated to justify not merely the token acknowledgment which Catholics seek in the Federal aid program, but rather the total subsidization of Catholic schools. There is, therefore, an unreal quality in the debate about Catholic schools and Federal aid. Catholics advance reasons why they should receive total financing for their schools, while their opponents offer arguments which in effect urge that parochial schools should not be publicly financed and in fact should not be encouraged.

It may be that the broadening of the argument to this extent is inevitable, because the real issue does not center on what the Supreme Court ruled or left open in *Everson*, but on the basic public policy question of whether the Federal government should encourage or discourage nonpublic schools in America. Both sides to the Federal aid debate operate on the assumption that the Federal government cannot possibly begin a program of aid to education without adopting a fundamental policy of encouragement or discouragement of private schools. This issue is the heart of the matter and it seems unlikely that it can be resolved by skirmishes over the exact meaning of the establishment clause, a question which, however one views the situation, does not supply the solution for the overwhelmingly important question of what attitude the national government should adopt towards private and church-related schools.

If the principle involved is important, the factual consequences of the Federal government's decision on the place of private schools will also be most significant. For the sheer size of the Catholic school system suggests that it cannot be ignored without vitiating a significant part of the purpose of Federal aid to education.

The teaching personnel involved in Catholic education in 1961 is indicated below:[12]

	Lay Teachers	Religious or clerical teachers	Total
Elementary Schools	32,723	78,188	110,911
Secondary Schools	12,470	34,153	46,623
Colleges and Universities	17,240	8,293	25,533
	62,433	120,634	183,067

The enrollment in Catholic schools is likewise an indication of the fact that to ignore the private school in any Federal aid bill is to deny the benefits of a long-awaited development in education to every seventh or eighth child in America. The total student population of Catholic schools is as follows:

	No. of Catholic schools 1961–62	Total enrollment 1961–62	Estimated enrollment 1962–63
Elementary	10,631	4,445,288	4,560,000
Secondary	2,376	937,671	1,002,000
Colleges and Universities	238	326,160	355,000
	13,245	5,709,119	5,917,000

The astonishing extent and growth of the Catholic school system may suggest that Federal encouragement or discouragement may not after all be of such momentous consequence. Nor is it all certain that partial government subvention would encourage the Catholic or any other church-related school system. It is significant that in England, after most generous state aid was given to Anglican and other sectarian schools in 1902, the enrollment in Anglican schools declined from 1,750,094 in 1911 to 859,426 in 1958.[13] Put another way, one notes with amazement that the Church of England's schools *without* state aid prior to 1902 educated more than one-half of the nation's pupils whereas in 1958 after more than fifty years of generous state subsidization these same schools educated less than 20 per cent of the school children of England.

Catholics in America have been challenged to show that they are justified in their request for participation in Federal aid. Their arguments and their attempts to refute their opponents are worthy of the most serious reflection. One of the principal difficulties which Catholics have encountered in attempting to communicate the reasons which, in their judgment, justify their claim to some partial aid for their schools arises from the fact that Catholics find it difficult to separate out from their argument on behalf of Federal aid for Catholic schools those elements which are known to them only from specifically Catholic beliefs or from what Catholics regard as the natural moral law. Those non-Catholics who have been sympathetic to the Catholic position on the education issue have remarked that the Catholic "case," arguing from Catholic and natural law presuppositions, is persuasive and almost self-evident. But its self-evident qualities are obscured when viewed in the light of legal, constitutional and educational premises commonly accepted by non-Catholic Americans.

The Catholic case for publicly financed sectarian schools is developed along two lines of reasoning. The first stems from Catholic principles involving parental and ecclesiastical rights coupled with the notion of distributive justice; the second relies on constitutionally guaranteed religious freedom, traditional ideas of unfairness in taxation and the religiously pluralistic nature of American society. Although theoretically one could attempt to separate these two considerations, such a separation is unrealistic. The fact is that partisans on both sides of the controversy have deeply held convictions about the nature and purpose of life and therefore of education.

The case from ecclesiastical and parental rights, coupled with the notion of distributive justice:

If one follows the first line of reasoning the Catholic claim for state aid requires little debate. As Pope Pius XI put it in his 1930 encyclical on education: "Let no one say that in a nation where there are different religious beliefs, it is impossible to provide for public instruction otherwise than by neutral or mixed schools. In such a case it becomes the duty of the State, indeed it is *the easier and more reasonable method of procedure,* to leave free scope to the initiative of the Church and the family, while giving them such assistance as justice demands."[14] [Emphasis supplied.] It is understandable that some Catholics, in arguing on behalf of Federal aid for sectarian schools, assume and assert that the granting of such aid is "the easier and more reasonable method of procedure" and that it is something which "justice demands." It is likewise understandable that many non-Catholics, even if they concede the merits of the Catholic position as Pope Pius XI stated it, feel that it has no applicability to the American scene. One cannot escape the impression that, in the national debate over aid to Catholic schools, the real issue is not the theoretical validity of the Catholic position but rather its relevance to the American scene.

It seems clear, therefore, that Catholics in urging the validity of their case on the basis of parental rights and distributive justice have been to some extent talking to themselves. They use terms that are meaningful to them but which often do not seem to raise even a serious doubt in the minds of those millions of non-Catholics who have simply assumed that all tax support must, as if by the canons of American democracy, be granted only to public schools. Catholics on the other hand, can rightfully insist on this approach since it is grounded in the basic principles of the natural law and of the Catholic faith.

Yet fearful dilemmas and temptations confront Catholics as they attempt, almost for the first time in American history, publicly to discuss why a monopoly on education by the public school is undesirable and unfair. Here are some of the questions they must answer to their own satisfaction as the battle lines over Federal aid and nonpublic schools become more sharply drawn:

How strong and insistent should the Catholic position be on the Federal level when the fact is that, on the state level, no government has ever aided private schools within the last four to six generations? Can a public policy of a century's duration be overcome by one new Federal law?

To what extent should a Catholic citizen permit a candidate's expressed views on aid to parochial schools to influence his judgment in voting for or against the candidate? Is it desirable in any case to allow the question of aid for church-related schools to become a political issue?

If some aid is eventually granted to Catholic schools when, if ever, would the amount of such aid become a purely political question on which church leaders should, as on other political questions, refrain from comment?

One could enumerate other difficult questions which in the near future will confront Catholics. These questions are raised at this point to illustrate the fact that the line of reasoning so often taken by Catholics tends to be oversimplified and sometimes leaps to broad conclusions with profound implications unrealized by their advocates. Let us now review the Catholic case, noting first the line of reasoning which employs concepts derived from Catholic and natural law notions and then constructing a line of argumentation from those legal, constitutional and educational principles accepted generally by most Americans.

Catholics argue on behalf of state aid for nonpublic schools on the principle that parents have a right to that type of education which they desire for their children. This right was vindicated in the *Pierce* decision, but the scope of a parent's rights as conceived in traditional Catholic thinking cannot be said to have legal justification in American decisional law. The legislative and decisional law of the American nation asserts rather that parents have the right to contract out of the public school but that, if they do, the state is no longer required to assist them with the education of their children.

Reasoning from the parental right is deemed by many Catholic spokesmen to be the most cogent argument available to Catholics in the struggle to have their schools receive some state assistance. The contention that parents have a right to control the content and atmosphere of their children's education is undoubtedly persuasive. It appears, however, that the Catholic claim that parents have a right to "permeate" their children's education with religion at state expense is almost instinctively rejected by many non-Catholics on the theory that the state has no duty or right to supply an education so "permeated."

Indeed it is the "permeation" concept which seems more and more to overshadow and cancel out whatever cogency might exist in the arguments which Catholics advance for their claim to public support of their schools. Everyone would agree with the contention that parents have important and even primary rights in connection with the education of their children, but this agreement disappears when the claimed parental right turns out to be a right to receive at state expense an education permeated by religion.

Another argument traditionally employed by Catholics centers on the notion of distributive justice. Once again there is theoretical acceptance of this idea by non-Catholics until it is perceived that its logic leads to the conclusion that Catholics have a right to state aid for a school permeated by religion. The argument from distributive justice asserts that it is unjust to refuse to return to Catholics that share of the taxes which they contributed to the state for the purpose of education, while at the same time requiring them to send their children to fully accredited schools. This argument necessarily presupposes several other principles from the Catholic philosophy of the state. One such principle would be the belief in subsidiarity, or the insistence that voluntary, nongovernmental agencies should perform all possible public service functions, and that the state should assume the management of these functions only when it is clear that private groups are incapable of handling them.

THE CASE FROM AMERICAN LEGAL, CONSTITUTIONAL AND EDUCATIONAL PRINCIPLES

A legal-constitutional-educational line of reasoning calculated to support the Catholic claim to some part of Federal aid to education would follow this series of propositions, which we will first enumerate and then discuss:

1. The public school in America is forbidden by law to fuse the sectarian—and therefore the sacred—with the secular education which it imparts to its students.

2. Catholics consequently find the secular school inconsistent with certain dictates of their conscience and, as a result, the source of a restriction and even a violation of their constitutionally guaranteed religious freedom.

3. Under any theory of jurisprudence accepted by any significant group in America, it is unjust to inflict a financial penalty on citizens because of the exercise of their religion when the state could, with no added expense and no harm to the common good, relieve them of such financial penalty.

4. The granting of tax money to finance a *small* part of the *secular* program of a church-related school could not (a) undermine the public school, (b) weaken national unity or (c) cause a proliferation of sectarian schools.

The Public School Is A Secular School

When American law in the last century decreed that the common school must not teach anything "sectarian" there was no intention of ruling out the teaching of the sacred or the religious. Only those doctrines unique to a particular "sect" were proscribed. Actually the legal ban on "sectarian" teachings probably did not substantially affect the curriculum of the public school until recent years. Within the last generation, however, the term "sectarian" has come to include all that is sacred and religious. The public school today, therefore, is restricted to a curriculum that is essentially and almost exclusively secular.

There is to be found everywhere, even among many Catholics, the greatest reluctance to accept the idea that the public school is the "secular" school. Most Protestants and even secularists will argue that the public school can and must communicate moral and spiritual values which transcend the secular. But even the most ardent defenders of the public school as something more than a "secular" institution are not certain that it has the right to transmit theistic values.

It is difficult to escape the conclusion that the United States Supreme Court itself, even in its irenic *Zorach* decision, ruled that the public school must be secular. Justice Douglas wrote in that opinion that "government may not . . . *blend secular* and *sectarian* education."[15] Justice Rutledge, dissenting in the *Everson* case, stated that "children are not sent to public schools under the Pierce doctrine . . . for the reason that their atmosphere is *wholly* secular."[16] [Emphasis supplied.]

It is impossible to suggest any legal or constitutional theory by which a public school teacher could transmit other than a secular education. While a teacher may inspire by personal example and by inculcating respect for sacred truths, even the collective conduct of several such teachers cannot remove from a public school the label of "secular."

Catholic reluctance to push the concept of the "secular" school to the limit of its logic derives from the fact that more than one half of all Catholic children attend the public schools of our nation. Quite understandably Catholics do not wish to add to the conceded secularization of these schools by placing new inhibitions upon their administrators and teachers concerning the teaching of theistic or sacred truths and values. But can Catholics have it both ways—urging the secularization of the public schools when arguing for tax support for parochial schools and encouraging the communication of religious and theistic values when dealing with the mission of the public school?

If the public school is by law and in fact a secular school does it follow that secularism is "established" in the nation's schools? Catholics once again have been hesitant in pressing this accusation. But if Catholics are to obtain financial support for their own religiously oriented schools they must first persuade the American people that for Catholic children the public school is a clear and present danger because it is so secular as to be, in effect, anti-religious.

If this standard of opposition to the public school is thought to be too rigorous, then how opposed must Catholics be to the secular public school before they can claim that their conscience refuses to allow them to permit their children to participate in the school offered by the state? This question leads us to the second point in our line of reasoning: the rights of conscience and religious liberty in confrontation with the school which, to repeat Justice Rutledge's phrase, is "wholly secular."

Conscience, Religious Freedom and the Secular School

CONSCIENCE AND OBEDIENCE TO LAW. It is uncertain what American law would hold if tomorrow the nation's Catholics came to the conclusion that they could no longer in good conscience allow their children to attend any public school. There exists practically no American legal precedent on this subject. The Amish and a few comparable sects have resisted attendance in ultramodern school buildings, but otherwise there has been no instance of any group which asserts that the tax-supported state school violates their conscience because it divorces the sacred and the secular and teaches only the latter.

Thus when Catholics state that they cannot "in conscience" send their children to non-Catholic or public schools they are not necessarily speaking in a way which would bring them within the legal category of conscientious objectors to a particular state-sponsored compulsory program. How much objection in conscience would Catholics have to possess before the state would be required under the Constitution to excuse them from public school attendance and yet not to penalize them financially because of their religious scruples?

Obeying one's conscience does not, of course, automatically grant immunity from the law—even if by obedience one's conscience is violated. The Mormons felt required, under pain of everlasting damnation, to enter into plural marriages, but the Supreme Court of the United States held firmly that unity is one of the essential qualities of the marriage contract and that even the voice of conscience could not justify bigamy.[17]

Similarly the Supreme Court in 1961 ruled that those who, for reasons of conscience, observe a day of worship and total rest on Saturday may not transact business on Sunday. A law is not unjust or coercive of conscience, Chief Justice Warren wrote, if it does not compel an act forbidden by conscience but only renders "the practice of . . . religious beliefs more expensive."[18]

The flag salute cases, however, lend some support to the Catholic parent's assertion that state-created pressure to send his children to the secular school, because of an economic boycott on the church-related school, violates his conscience. As is well known, the U. S. Supreme Court reversed itself with respect to laws requiring children, who were Jehovah's Witnesses, to salute the flag; in 1943, the Supreme Court, vacating previous rulings to the contrary, held that it is unconstitutional to require a pupil to salute the flag when he has conscientious objections to such a practice.[19]

If children with religious scruples over the performance of certain *secular* practices within the public school have a constitutional right to be excused from such activities does it follow that the Catholic, opposed in conscience to the secular approach to life and learning dominant in the public school, can also be said to have a constitutional right not to be coerced into participating, contrary to this conscience, in such a program?

An affirmative answer to that question could not at present be inferred, but the reflections of Justice Frankfurter, dissenting against the majority opinion which granted an exemption from the flag salute to children conscientiously opposed to the practice, is significant. Justice Frankfurter sees the consequence of the Court's bowing to the religious scruples of a minority and raises this question: "Parents who are dissatisfied with the public schools . . . carry a double educational burden. Children who go to public school enjoy in many states derivative advantages . . . What of the claims of equality of treatment of those parents who, because of *religious scruples, cannot* send their children to public schools? What of the claim that if the right to send children to privately maintained schools is partly *an exercise of religious conviction*, to render effective this right it should be accompanied by equality of treatment by the state. . . ." [Emphasis supplied.][20]

If the Catholic claim to partial tax support for their schools is to be grounded on the argument from conscience it would appear that at least the following must be shown to be facts: (1) The public school is so secular that, in Justice Frankfurter's words, Catholic parents "cannot . . . because of religious scruples" allow their children to attend. (2) The secular school demands an expression of beliefs or state of mind which is inconsistent with the fundamental attitudes and beliefs of a person committed to a supernatural view of life. (3) Irreparable harm will most probably be done to a Catholic child attending a secular public school because he will learn nonsacred truths in such a manner that his faith will be impaired.

If one hesitates to agree that these three assertions can be verified, as understandably one might, then the validity of the argument from conscience should be reconsidered.

It seems clear, therefore, that the Catholic case for some share of Federal aid cannot rely on a clear-cut legal case of the Catholic conscience being violated by enforced attendance at a secular public school. Catholics cannot, moreover, identify their case with that of the person who, conscientiously opposed to war refrains from any direct preparation for war. The Catholic, in other words, has not said and perhaps cannot say that he is a "conscientious objector" to the secular school. If the Catholic did or could his case might be radically different.

RELIGIOUS FREEDOM AND THE SECULAR SCHOOL. Although Catholics cannot claim in the strict sense that participation in the secular school violates their conscience, they do claim that the denial of state funds which leads to the enforced attendance of their children at secular schools infringes, impairs or restricts their religious freedom. Here again, however, it appears that Catholics have not drawn up a careful bill of particulars concerning their feeling that their religious liberty is, under present conditions, being curtailed.

Jehovah's Witnesses have contributed new horizons to religious freedom in the score of cases which they have carried to the United States Supreme Court within the last generation. In briefest summary, the rights extended to the Witnesses guaranteed their immunity from arrest while preaching in public streets or parks. The language of the Supreme Court, however, in broadening the right to make the public park a pulpit is often so sweeping that one can conclude that *any* restriction on religious preaching or practice must have a justification of a most substantial nature.

Catholics in this matter face a serious dilemma. If they assert that maintaining their children in a Catholic schools is an exercise of their religious freedom, then their request for tax support for such activity runs squarely into the prohibitions of the establishment clause. If, on the other hand, Catholics ground their claim to public support of their schools strictly on the *secular* contribution which these schools make to the state by educating its future

citizens, then they may not logically urge that their religious freedom is restricted if the state, for reasons of expediency or economy,
decides to finance only the public school.

The argument from religious freedom cuts both ways because it
is not certain what relation the second part of the First Amendment—the free exercise clause—has or should have to the first
part, the establishment clause. Many noted scholars have argued
that the extension of religious freedom is the *main* purpose of the
First Amendment, and that therefore the establishment clause is
merely instrumental to the broadening of the horizons of religious
liberty. The Supreme Court, however, has not adopted this theory
and, in fact, in several instances (including the prayer decision in
June 1962) has reaffirmed its conviction that the establishment
clause stands independently of the free exercise clause and by itself
creates rights which can be infringed even in the absence of an
infringement of the free exercise clause.

Under this construction of the First Amendment it is difficult
to see how the Catholic can claim that the denial of state support
for church-related schools is a violation of his free exercise of
religion. At least, if it *is* a violation then the financing of these
schools would also violate a right in the non-Catholic to have the
establishment or no-aid-to-religion clause observed. If the no-aid-
to-religion doctrine is an absolute, then it is not possible to have
state money finance, even in part, the exercise of anyone's religion.

But can the Catholic utilize the new interpretation of the establishment clause and assert that his right to be free of the establishment of *any* religion—including that of secularism—is being infringed by a dominance of secular values and ideals in the public
school which amounts to an establishment of religion in the strict,
constitutional sense? It might be difficult to gain acceptance of this
idea but certainly its potentialities, under present law which views
the establishment clause as conferring rights independently of an
infringement of religious freedom, seem to be very great.

If then it is not possible, in the present state of the law, to prove
that the Catholic whose child, because of economic coercion,
attends the secular school or that the Catholic who pays "double
taxation" for his child's education in a Catholic school are the
victims of an infringement of their religious freedom, is it nonetheless arguable that *some* specific constitutional rights of these

Catholic parents are being infringed? This, of course, is the crucial question—and the answer, as of now, appears to be "No."

There may be involved, however, a denial of equal protection for the parent whose children in the parochial schools are denied, because of their faith, the "benefits of public welfare legislation," as the *Everson* decision put it. One may claim also that such a denial would offend the "free exercise" clause, but neither the *Everson* opinion itself nor the state decisions which followed it are very clear as to the extent of the coverage of "public welfare benefits."

One cannot help but feel, nonetheless, that there is a breadth and scope in the "free exercise" clause which is capable of expanding to include that religious motivation which causes a Catholic parent to send his child to a church-related school. But such expansion is the work of the future. It is clear that contemporary collective Catholic thought and conscience feel that the parochial school is an inherent part of the exercise of their religion. What is needed is to translate this conviction into juridical language and constitutional law. Such a task may not be achieved in one generation, because of the school problem, which took at least four generations to become a national dilemma, may require that same amount of time to unravel itself into an equitable solution for a pluralistic society.

If arguments from the imperatives of conscience, the desirability of having an unfettered religious freedom and the right to be free from the establishment of secularism are potential rather than actual legal and constitutional doctrine at this time, the claims of conscience and religious liberty are nonetheless the very essence of the Catholic complaint and petition. If, however, it is not now possible to bring these arguments to full flower, it is feasible to develop and expand a corollary of these arguments: the idea that the state cannot penalize citizens for exercising their religion in an area in which the state imposes a compulsory law as it does in education. This leads to our third point in the legal-constitutional-education "case" for the Catholic position.

Financial Penalty for Religious Practice

Under any theory of American Jurisprudence it is unjust to inflict a financial penalty on citizens because of the exercise of their

*religion when the state, could, with no added expense and no harm
to the common good, relieve them of such financial penalty.*

Both sides to the debate over Federal aid for Catholic schools
invoke the fact of compulsory education laws. Catholics urge that
it is unfair to compel them by law to educate their children and
yet to deny financial assistance to the only type of school suitable
to their conscience. Opponents of aid for sectarian schools insist
that, since the children who attend parochial schools are legally
required to do so, the state, in the granting of a subvention to this
required attendance, would be aiding a religion.

But is the fact of compulsory attendance laws really relevant to
the debate? If tomorrow it were deemed unnecessary to have such
laws, as well it might be, attendance at public and parochial schools
would probably not be affected. And would the repeal of laws requiring attendance at school change the nature of the debate over
the advisability of Federal aid going to Catholic schools?

As a concrete example let us assume that a particular state made
a rule that no one need attend school after the ninth grade. Youths
in the three remaining years of high school in this state would attend school voluntarily and not because it is their legal duty. The
state would encourage such attendance by making good educational
facilities available. Would the absence of legal compulsion permit
the state to extend the G.I. tuition-scholarship plan down to the
secondary school?

Actually many seniors in high school today, being over sixteen
years of age, are no longer required to attend school. Could a bill
be enacted to provide some type of special secular training for *all*
high school seniors who attend *any* high school but who are no
longer legally required to do so?

It seems clear that little thought has been given to these questions because both parties to the Federal aid debate have been
anxious to exploit whatever relevance there is for their side of the
struggle from the existence of laws requiring school attendance.

When education became compulsory about a century ago, the
foreseeable inconvenience to some was mitigated by a great emphasis on the idea that the required education would be free. The free
public school and the free public library emerged together in
American life as symbols of democracy. No one seems to have
raised the point that the ideal of a "free" education was basically
compromised by providing only one type of school and that con-

cededly contrary to the conscience and religious faith of a substantial minority.

Today, however, the twin concepts of a compulsory but free education, revolutionary ideas a century ago, have long since been accepted as beyond dispute. But can the American state retreat from its historic commitment of giving a "free" education to the children of *every* citizen when some citizens insist that the free state school violates their deepest beliefs and those of their children?

As we have seen, the arguments from conscience and religious freedom have not yet reached the clarity and status of an undeniable constitutional right, but by what theory of law or of society can a state refuse the right to a "free" education to those for whom the one secular type of schooling is not acceptable for reasons of conscience?

The state is not being asked by those who seek aid for nonpublic schools to spend any money which it has not already committed itself to spend.

If the state were scrupulously devoted to its pledge of giving to *all* children required to attend school a free education it could, with no violation of the separation of church and state, set aside for each child who, for reasons of conscience withdraws from the public school, a sum of money equal to the sum expended on every child who attends the free schools. Is it not just to place in a trust fund, so to speak, the cost of a free education which is each child's right as a future American citizen? If that child, acting through its parents, decides that he will follow the state-prescribed curriculum of secular learning in the atmosphere of a sectarian school it seems to be totally arbitrary and unjustifiable to cut off the child's right to a free education because he and his guardians hold, as part of their religious faith, that the secular and the sacred are inextricably intermingled.

None of the philosophies of law which are current in America can justify the exclusion of an ever growing body of children from the financial benefits to which they are entitled and to the expenditure of which the state has committed itself. Such a financial penalty on parents and children because they have by their conscience a different philosophy of education from the majority seems to be such an inherent injustice that law and society would desire to remedy it within the foreseeable future. The least that the state should be doing is seeking ways by which it can carry out its pledge to every child that it will have a free education.

One reason which could justify the boycott of nonsecular schools would be a finding that such schools do harm to the common good. Some few commentators on the matter imply darkly that such is the fact though they, somewhat illogically, do not feel that any further discouragement of nonsecular schools is necessary. The issue of private schools and the common good leads to our fourth point in a case for aid to Catholic schools built on a legal–constitutional–educational foundation.

Tax Money and Secular-Program Support

The granting of tax money to finance a small part of the secular program of church-related schools could not undermine the public school, weaken national unity or cause a proliferation of sectarian schools.

It should be noted that here, once again, emphasis is placed on the fact that the only real issue presently in controversy in America is a *small* subvention for the *secular* aspects of church-related schools. It would appear that those who hold, with Justice Frankfurter, that the public school developed "as a symbol of our secular unity" and that it is now the principal promoter of unity in the nation look on any development which might possibly be adverse to the public school as a serious threat.

COULD PRIVATE SCHOOLS UNDERMINE PUBLIC EDUCATION? An example of the almost mystical qualities attributed to the public school can be seen in the testimony given to Congress in March, 1961, by Methodist Bishop John Wesley Lord on behalf of Federal aid to public schools as noted above (p. 181). No line of reasoning, however logical, can be expected to effect any rapid change in the attitudes revealed by Bishop Lord, whose views reflect an outlook on the public school not at all uncommon in America.

The most intractable subject in the entire discussion of Federal aid for Catholic schools centers on the implied criticism of public education which the very existence of Catholic schools signifies. As a result of this implied criticism, the request of these schools for some financial assistance is not judged on its merits, but rather on what effect the granting of such a request would have on the prestige of the public school. As Reinhold Niebuhr put it: "Protestants are inclined to be unyielding on problems of the public school because they suspect the hierarchy, at least, of being inimical to the whole idea of the public school system, which Protestants, as well as our secular democrats, regard as one of the foundation stones of our democracy."[21]

It is frequently asserted by opponents of Federal aid for Catholic schools that an allotment of funds to private schools will mean that less money will be available to the already under-financed public school. Aside from the fact that this objection does not confront the hard question of the validity of the claim of the nonpublic school for state aid, the objection carries with it the assumption that encouraging private education will inevitably diminish the position of esteem now held by public education.

Could not this objection to aid for private schools be met by the adoption of a provision in the enabling legislation that public schools will receive a fixed sum graduated upward each year by means of an appropriate formula? If a guarantee of such increment for the public schools for a ten-year period were agreed upon, it is difficult to see how the granting of some assistance to private schools would cause the budget of the public schools to be lessened.

The public school was "undermined" in a certain sense when the Supreme Court in its 1925 *Pierce* decision ruled that no state had "any general power to standardize its children by forcing them to accept instruction from public teachers only."[22] Virtually no opponent of Federal aid to private schools has asserted that these schools, whose number and student population have about doubled in the period from World War II to 1963, constitute a threat to the public school. Is it not a fair question to ask, however, whether at some point privately financed schools will be so numerous as to represent an undesirable challenge to the prestige, function and mission of the public school? This question leads us to the second anxiety which troubles opponents of state aid for private schools: would such aid weaken national unity?

PRIVATE SCHOOLS AND NATIONAL UNITY. The theory that public schools have as a part of their mission the unifying of their students never makes it clear whether the pupils become unified by merely mingling together or whether the mystique or the instruction of the public school produces the unifying effect—an effect which somehow is different from the universally deprecated "conformity" which is said to afflict American youth.

Assuming that the public school is so indispensable to the moral unity and cultural future of America, then *every* precaution should be taken to prevent a decline in its student population or public prestige. The assertion that the public school is the vehicle by which the ideals of democratic living and the traditions of America are communicated proves too much; it proves in fact that the Oregon school case was wrongly decided. Or, at least, it proves that some appropriate and effective measures should be taken so that, notwithstanding a continued denial of tax support to private schools, the number of these schools and their student population not increase substantially beyond their present proportion vis-à-vis the total public school enrollment.

If, furthermore, the opponents of public aid for Catholic schools base their opposition on the presumed need which the nation has of the public schools for the purposes of creating national unity, is it not logical to ask when or whether national unity will have become so secure that more young Americans can attend nonpublic schools with no resulting serious threat to the maintenance of national unity? Will America be ready in another generation or in two generations to absorb the existence of more private schools? Or will national unity always have as its indispensable partner the public school?

Confronted with this type of formless and therefore formidable objection to the petition for some public support for the Catholic school, the advocate of such support can only ask some fundamental questions: Is there any evidence beyond mere conjecture that the public school promotes national unity more than the nonpublic school? How is it assumed that the church-related school, which can teach more freely about the religious foundations of American democracy than the public school can, is thought to be less capable of promoting national unity than the public secular school? How can the promotion of national unity be a part of the task of the public high school teacher when the imposition of such a task on a public university professor would be deemed an intolerable infringement on academic freedom?

If the allegation that the preservation of national unity depends on the preservation of the public school seems to wither away upon analysis, the often expressed fear that aid for private education would cause a proliferation of sectarian schools is even more evanescent.

PUBLIC AID AND A PROLIFERATION OF SECTARIAN SCHOOLS. Dean John C. Bennett, one of the most balanced of all Protestant students of church-state matters, expresses his fear of the consequences of granting public aid to church-related schools in these words:

I believe that even more important is the consideration that decisive encouragement of parochial schools through public financial aid would have a destructive effect on the public school and on education generally . . . I am told by those who have studied the matter most closely that we could not expect to have fewer than five or six systems of parochial schools competing for the resources of the community in the large or middle sized cities. This would be divisive; it would be expensive and it would also mean that every system would be educationally weak. . . . Such a development would drain off from the public school the teachers of strongest religious commitment and so public education would be more secularized than it is now.[23]

The assumptions and conclusions contained in this series of predictions are significant. Is there not contained in this prophecy the assumption that many Protestants are experiencing a profound dissatisfaction with the public school—and that even the small amount of aid which the state might offer to private schools would be sufficient to induce these Protestants to create their own schools? There is also the supposition here that competition among school systems would not improve the quality of these schools. Such an assumption is not verifiable on the college level, where a healthy rivalry has brought diversity and added distinction to American higher education.

Only some eight religious sects have ever operated church-related schools in America within the last century. If there is reason to believe that a partial subsidy from the government would elicit enough enthusiasm from many religious groups so as to cause a "proliferation" of sectarian schools, as is so often alleged, then the parents, who presumably need only a little financial encouragement to embark on the burdensome task of opening and maintaining their own schools, must feel deeply that, under present conditions, their ideas and hopes about education are being drastically repudiated by public educational officials.

Such, in briefest review, are some of the major points which must be included and expanded upon in the great "Brandeis brief" which needs to be written to support the case of the Catholic claim to a share of the public school fund. The original "Brandeis brief" hardly touched upon the legalistic aspects of the challenged Oregon law regulating the conditions under which women could be gainfully employed in that state. Brandeis elaborated upon the economic, medical and sociological reasons for the Oregon statute designed to protect the health of women employees against the danger of excessively harsh working conditions. Brandeis won the case; the law was sustained because circumstances had changed.

The school question will be solved in a similar manner. The solution will accommodate the facts, circumstances and needs of the nation's school children with the requirements of a Constitution which was designed both to prevent the establishment of any church and to guarantee the free exercise of religion.

CHAPTER SEVEN

Sunday Laws, Sabbatarians and the Constitution

Every fair-minded American is distressed when a claim based on religious freedom made by one's fellow citizens is not granted by the state. Religionists and agnostics are disturbed that the desires of conscientious parents to have religious symbols and even religious instruction in the public schools cannot apparently be satisfied. Non-Catholics are troubled that Catholic parents must finance their own schools. Even if one is persuaded that the separation of church and state forbids any change in these two situations, there is nonetheless a regret that complete religious freedom, as various groups understand that concept, cannot be granted to everyone. Similarly, there is concern over the fact that Sabbatarians are not permitted to work on Sunday in order to make up for the financial detriment they incur because they refrain from labor in order to worship on Saturday.

It seems harsh indeed that the claims of Protestants for religion in public education, the requests of Catholics for assistance for parochial schools and the petitions of the Jewish community for an easing of the Sunday laws have all been rejected, in whole or in part, by a Supreme Court interpreting a Constitution which forbids any law prohibiting the "free exercise" of religion. One can hope that the Supreme Court, a "novice" in working with the establishment clause, may in the near future work out a harmonization of the imperatives of that provision of the First Amendment with the letter and spirit of the free exercise guarantee of the same Amendment. Until that time, however, pluralism in religion in America is a sociological but not a legal reality.

The emergence of the predicament of the nation's non-Sunday observing religionists during the late 1950's came as a surprise to almost all observers of the religious scene in America. Although it was commonly known that Orthodox Jews and Seventh-Day Adventists observed Saturday as their day of rest and worship there was no widespread understanding that these two groups felt that they were constitutionally entitled to be exempt from Sunday laws which would prevent their laboring on Sunday. Indeed, it does not appear to be certain just when the Jewish community in America came to the decision that they should be immune and hence should litigate to obtain a vindication of this asserted right.

It is, however, most unfortunate that the first request ever brought in American history by the Jewish community to the United States Supreme Court was refused. In May, 1961, in four cases dealing with Sunday laws from three states, the nation's highest tribunal ruled that laws prohibiting labor on Sunday violate neither the establishment nor the free exercise clauses of the First Amendment. Before we come to an analysis of those opinions, however, some observations on the background of the Sunday law question seem appropriate.

BACKGROUND OF SUNDAY LAWS

The existence of Sunday as a day of rest is perhaps more universally accepted in many nations than any other custom derived from Christianity. In all the nations colonized by the European powers the Western concept of Sunday took root to such an extent that it has been estimated that possibly half the human race now observes Sunday as a day of rest.

In Western Europe, the custom of Sunday as a holiday is so deeply imbedded that any substantial modification of the practice seems unthinkable. American law reflects the Puritan, Old Testament attitude towards the one day in seven on which man should worship and rest. It is doubtful if the laws of any other nation are as restrictive of Sunday activities as those of the eastern and central states of America. It is not entirely clear why Protestant or Puritan theology resulted in such Draconian jurisprudence, but Sunday legislation still reflects, more perhaps than any other part of America's civil law, the religious and ecclesiastical compulsions of a rigorously Protestant society. It is curious to observe that in many European nations with minimal legislation regulating conduct on Sunday there seems to be far less commercial and retail activity than in the most strictly regulated American states.

It is easy to see therefore that the Jewish community and those Christian sects which observe Saturday as the Sabbath confront the prestige of an almost world-wide, centuries-old, tradition-laden institution when they claim an exemption from Sunday laws. The small number of those asserting the claim adds to the difficulty of communicating the theological premises of the Jewish and Seventh-Day Adventist position. Of the world's 12,500,000 Jews 5,510,000 are in the United States, of whom 42 per cent or 2,339,000 reside in New York State.[1] Seventh-Day Adventists numbered in 1960 330,000 adult members, while 12,265 persons of three other sects also identified themselves as Sabbatarians.[2]

One of the basic difficulties in the controversy over the exemptions sought by the Sabbatarians centers on the very definition of the term "Sabbatarian." If by this name we designate a person who for religious reasons may not work on Saturday without a violation of his conscience then clearly the state should not compel him to work on that day—short of an unavoidable emergency in which the absence of his contribution would cause great harm to the public good.

If the term Sabbatarian means only a person who is required to worship for a period on Saturday but may then work at his usual occupation, we have a situation similar to that which the Catholic faces on a holy day such as Ascension Thursday when attendance at Mass is required by Church law but servile work is permitted if it is not reasonably possible to be excused from it. If, on the other hand, a person is required to refrain from labor on Saturday and *by this means* to worship God, a new dimension is added to the concept of Sabbatarian.

The civil law of America, since it knows no heresy, is not required to judge whether the conscience of any citizen is in conformity with the beliefs he professes. But if the beliefs he claims as his own clash with the dictates of the law, then the civil power should seek in every way possible to provide relief. Actually, however, the Sabbatarian cannot claim any such head-on collision. Civil law in America never compels anyone to work on Saturday—except possibly in the armed forces. The Sabbatarians of America now claim, however, that any *one* fixed day of rest for *all* citizens penalizes them in an economic way—unless, of course, the day chosen were Saturday. But if Wednesday or Sunday is chosen to provide a common day of leisure for *all* citizens, then the Sabbatarian claims that he is being treated unfairly because he, in addition to the common day of rest, must also refrain from labor on Saturday. The United States Supreme Court, as we shall see, unanimously rejected this cornerstone premise of the Sabbatarian case since, as even dissenting Justice Douglas said, the "state can, of course, require one day of rest a week: one day when every shop or factory is closed."[3]

The Sabbatarian claim has been totally or partially recognized in the laws of at least twenty-one states, wherein permission is granted for work on Sunday for those whose religion compels them to refrain from work on Saturday. Most of these laws, however, qualify the privilege of working on Sunday by insisting that the public peace may not thereby be disturbed, and in many states the exemption from Sunday laws does *not* extend to retail merchants. It is from the complaints of this latter group that all the recent legislative and judicial controversies have resulted.

No state court in American history has ever held that Sabbatarian merchants have a constitutional right to do business as usual on Sunday if they refrain from business on Saturday. While some state legislatures have been generous in concession to self-employed Sabbatarian merchants, the states with a significant number of such persons in their population—such as New York, Massachusetts, New Jersey and Pennsylvania—have not granted the relief sought by the Sabbatarians in those states. The New York experience is especially noteworthy.

In 1950, the highest court in New York upheld the conviction of two Orthodox Jewish retailers for selling uncooked meat on Sunday in violation of law. The United States Supreme Court refused to review the decision of New York's Court of Appeals, giving as its reason the "want of a substantial federal question."[4]

Following the directive of New York's highest court the convicted Sabbatarians and their coreligionists went to the legislature for the relief requested. On March 30, 1958, by a vote of 85 to 61, the New York state legislature refused to enact the Asch-Rosenblatt bill which would have allowed merchants in New York City to conduct business as usual on Sunday if, because of religious reasons, they refrained from work on Saturday. *America*, the national Catholic weekly, editorialized just prior to the defeat of this bill, in this manner: "Perhaps New York City might try a one-year experiment with Sunday openings in a limited section where there is a heavy concentration of Jewish merchants and a predominantly Jewish population. If during this period it is established that Jewish shops are actually closed on Saturdays, a relaxation of the Sunday-closing law would seem to be in order in their cases. If, on the other hand, it is discovered that Jewish shops still remain open on Saturdays, there would be solid reasons why no exceptions to the Sunday-closing ordinance should be tolerated. Why should one group of merchants have the competitive advantage of doing business on Sundays as well as Saturdays?"[5]

This editorial raises two of the concrete problems involved in granting Sunday opening privileges to self-employed Sabbatarians: (1) How is the law expected to enforce Saturday closing by those who open on Sunday? (2) Would concessions to the self-employed retailer give him an unfair competitive advantage over his fellow Sabbatarian who is also a retailer but who, because he necessarily employs non-Sabbatarians, cannot operate on Sundays?

It was apparently after their defeat in the legislature of New York that the Sabbatarians decided to take their case to the courts. The decisions which resulted and the 220 pages of opinions from the Supreme Court of the United States that were issued on May 29, 1961, demonstrate in detail that the Sabbatarian claim is now one of America's most complex church–state problems.[6]

The Massachusetts case involved in this litigation illustrates the predicament of the Sabbatarian, and hence a review of that case is relevant. In 1953, ten members of the Orthodox Jewish faith opened the Crown Kosher Super Market in Springfield, Massachusetts. In admitted violation of state law the proprietors of the Crown Market remained open every Sunday from 8:00 A.M. to 6:00 P.M. This grocery store was the only retail outlet within a radius of some twenty miles to offer a complete line of all kosher foods. Its sales on Sunday, however, were not limited to persons desiring to buy kosher foods. Every customer was served with the result that, although the market was open 56 hours on days other than Saturday (when it was closed all day) and Sunday, substantially more than one-third of its weekly gross of $15,000 was obtained from purchasers on Sunday.

A conviction of the officials of the Crown Market for violations of Sunday laws was affirmed by the Supreme Judicial Court of Massachusetts in November, 1957,[7] on the basis of settled precedents of that tribunal and of decisions in 1896 and 1900 of the United States Supreme Court upholding the constitutionality of Sunday laws.[8] After the Massachusetts decision in 1957, the convicted defendants requested that a three-man Federal court be appointed pursuant to a provision in the U. S. Code authorizing such a suit to test the constitutionality of a state statute.

The parties informally agreed to postpone prosecution until after decision from the Federal court. The Crown Market was joined in its brief by the President of the Massachusetts Council of Rabbis, suing on behalf of himself and other rabbis similarly situated, by the International Religious Liberty Association and the Southern New England Conference of Seventh-Day Adventists. The Crown Market's brief was opposed by the Attorney General of Massachusetts, by the Lord's Day League of New England and by the Boston Archdiocesan Council of Catholic Men.

In May, 1959, in a 2 to 1 split, the Federal court declared the relevant Sunday law of Massachusetts to be contrary to the First Amendment of the Federal Constitution. In an unprecedented ruling this tribunal entered a judgment which, it seems fair to say, elicited a good deal of adverse criticism in legal and professional journals.[9] Many jurists questioned the validity and the advisability of a lower Federal court setting aside a state statute, more than once sustained by the state's highest court, and in the face of a 1951 declaration by the United States Supreme Court that in the matter of New York's Sunday law "no substantial Federal question" was involved.

Judge Calvert Magruder, author of the majority opinion, after relating evidence that the Massachusetts Sunday law was, at least originally, a means to sanctify the Lord's Day, stated in sweeping terms: "What Massachusetts had done in this statute is to furnish special protection to the dominant Christian sects which celebrate Sunday as the Lord's Day, without furnishing such protection, in their religious observances, to those Christian sects and to Orthodox and Conservative Jews who observe Saturday as the Sabbath, and to the prejudice of the latter group."[10]

The decision concludes from this assumed wrong that the Massa-

chusetts statute (1) unconstitutionally restricts religious liberty,
(2) deprives the store owner of liberty and property without due
process of law and (3) constitutes "a denial of the equal protection
of the laws forbidden by the Fourteenth Amendment."

Although these unprecedented findings are of such a novel nature
that one would expect a rather lengthy explanation of their justification one finds only some seven paragraphs about the three
revolutionary principles. Sunday laws, we are told, are proscribed
by the "classic statement" from the *Everson* decision of the Supreme Court that "state power is no more to be used so as to
handicap religions than it is to favor them." No reference is made
to the 1952 *Zorach* decision of the same court wherein the tone and
content of *Everson* are substantially modified.

The Sunday law, it is said, violates the religious liberty of the
store owners, the Orthodox customers of the store and the rabbi-
plaintiffs who "would be hindered in their function of supervising
the food to be eaten by their congregations and . . . would also
suffer great detriment in their efforts to preserve in these circumstances, due observance of the Jewish Sabbath and of the dietary
laws of the people of their congregations."[11] Massachusetts, the
decision states, has "no legitimate interest" to safeguard by its Sunday law and as a result the statute "arbitrarily" restricts the liberty
of those affected by it.

Although the majority opinion in the Crown Market case seems
to accept the theory that the state must isolate and insulate itself
from religion, yet the majority view does place its accent on the
greatest religious liberty for every individual. The difficulty with
unqualified support for this principle, however, is that granting
unrestricted religious liberty to everyone has two effects: it costs
the state more, and it leads to violations of the religious liberty of
other groups. In connection with the modification of Sunday laws,
for example, the state must supply additional police and fire protection for those who carry on business on Sunday as usual. Added
expense will be involved in ferreting out the inevitable racketeer
who will exploit unabashed commercialism on Sunday. Secondly,
if Sabbatarians expect to recoup the losses of Saturday by business
on Sunday many non-Sabbatarians will inevitably have their day
of worship infringed upon.

Judge Magruder's opinion is the only decision in American jurisprudence which acknowledges the validity of the constitutional

argument of the Sabbatarians. Six months after Judge Magruder's decision another three-judge Federal court in Philadelphia affirmed the constitutionality of Pennsylvania's Sunday laws, as strengthened by rigorous enforcement penalties enacted by the legislature in 1959.

This December, 1959, Pennsylvania opinion involved a large department store in a suburban area employing some 300 persons and remaining open seven days a week.[12] About one-third of its business was done on Sunday. This corporation sought an injunction from a Federal court against the enforcement of a law enacted on August 10, 1959, which clarified and strengthened Pennsylvania's prohibition of work on Sundays. The 1959 Act was admittedly lobbied through by merchants in an attempt to regulate business competition by halting the vast commercial Sunday sales of the suburban giants.

Judge William Hastie of the Federal Circuit Court of Appeals ruled that the 1959 legislation was constitutional—although concerning some points of interpretation, the case was remitted to the state courts of Pennsylvania. Judge Hastie ruled that the Pennsylvania law could not be held invalid as a violation of religious freedom in view of the fact that the United States Supreme Court, in refusing to review a similar New York law in 1951, stated that it dismissed the New York appeal "for want of a substantial Federal question." Furthermore, Judge Hastie noted, the same court had thrice refused to review state Sunday closing laws even when there were involved "even near whimsical classifications." Judge Hastie in effect decided that no court less than the United States Supreme Court could rule that there is a First Amendment problem in Sunday legislation.

Judge Hastie made no attempt to explain how Federal Judge Magruder reached a different result and found the Massachusetts Sunday law unconstitutional except to say bluntly that Judge Magruder's "opinion disposes of this problem of controlling authority in a brief footnote which is not elaborate enough to make the court's reasoning clear to us."[13]

Federal District Judge George A. Welsh, agreeing that the 1959 Pennsylvania Sunday law does not violate religious liberty, dissented from the view of Judge Hastie and District Judge John W. Lord, Jr. but only because he felt that the Pennsylvania legislature could not enact such a law without a popular referendum.

Such was the state of the law when the United States Supreme

Court agreed to pass on the constitutionality of Sunday laws. The claims of Sabbatarians, however, were not the only issue in dispute in the several states when the enforcement of Sunday laws had become a problem. Equally complex was the challenge to Sunday legislation by suburban discount houses whose very survival depends on high volume and massive week-end sales. It is unfortunate that the strictly economic issue raised by suburban retail giants became intermingled with cases involving the right to religious freedom of Sabbatarians. It is likewise regrettable that, because of this intermingling, many people now identify the petition for a modification of Sunday law legislation with commercial interests whose basic purpose is financial gain and not the extension of religious freedom.

The intertwining of the demands of the proprietors of highway discount stores for the right to operate seven days a week with the request of sincere Sabbatarians to conduct their business on Sunday rather than on Saturday may well have been instrumental in producing a Supreme Court decision adverse to both petitions. It seems improbable that, without the aspect of commercialism present in some phases of the four Sunday law cases litigated in 1961, the Supreme Court could deny that Sunday laws impose an indefensible restraint on the religious freedom of those persons whose day of worship is Saturday. With this affirmed let us examine the precise holdings in the May 1961 rulings of the Supreme Court on Sunday laws.

THE SUPREME COURT'S DECISIONS

The basic contention of the Sabbatarians in the four Sunday law cases was that any law which makes the cessation of labor on Sunday a requirement under penalty of punishment aids the Christian religion and therefore is unconstitutional. Chief Justice Warren ruled firmly that Sunday closing laws do not discriminate against Orthodox Jews but only make "the practice of their religious beliefs more expensive." In a nation, the Chief Justice continued, "made up of almost every conceivable religious preference it cannot be expected, much less required, that legislators enact no law . . . that may in some way result in an economic disadvantage to some religious sects. . . ."[14] The states, the court held, are not forbidden to have laws which assist religion so long as these laws have an adequate secular purpose and this purpose cannot be carried out by any other reasonable means.

Two of the cases involving Sunday laws concerned owners of highway discount stores who were open for business seven days a week. These two cases were decided by a vote of 8 to 1, with only Justice Douglas voting to declare the statutes unconstitutional. The other two cases involved Orthodox Jewish owners of a kosher supermarket in Massachusetts and of small retail stores in Philadelphia. In these two cases Justices Brennan and Stewart joined dissenting Justice Douglas and voted to declare these laws unconstitutional as against the Sabbath observers.

The Sabbatarian arguments focused on three issues: (1) the establishment of religion, (2) the free exercise clause, and (3) equal protection. The Supreme Court rejected all three arguments, with Chief Justice Warren writing the prevailing opinion in all four cases.

1. On the establishment argument the Court conceded that the Sunday laws in question had a religious origin but stated: "The present purpose and effect of most of (these laws) is to provide a uniform day of rest for all citizens; the fact that this day is Sunday, a day of particular significance for the dominant Christian sects, does not bar the state from achieving its secular goals. To say that the states cannot prescribe Sunday as a day of rest for these purposes solely because centuries ago such laws had their genesis in religion would give a constitutional interpretation of hostility to the public welfare rather than one of mere separation of church and state."[15] The Court ruled therefore that the state, in an effort to promote laudable secular aims within its competence, is not barred from achieving these objectives in ways which may incidentally benefit religion. As Justice Frankfurter put it in his concurring opinion: ". . . not every regulation, some of whose practical effects may facilitate the observance of a religion by its adherents, affronts the requirement of Church–State separation."[16]

Only Justice Douglas was persuaded by the contention that Sunday closing laws violated the establishment clause. It is significant to note that Justice Black, who wrote the stringently separationist language in *Everson* and *McCollum*, sees no problem of establishment or of free exercise of religion in Sunday laws which clearly aid the Christian religion by fixing Sunday as a day of universal rest.

2. The Court, through Chief Justice Warren, similarly rejects

the allegation that Sunday laws unconstitutionally infringe on the religious freedom of those who worship on Saturday but who are prohibited from work on Sunday. The argument of the Sabbatarian in this connection centers on the undeniable fact that grocers and retail merchants are clearly at an economic disadvantage if they must suspend business on Saturday because of their faith and on Sunday because of the law. The point overlooked in this contention, however, the Court points out, is that Sunday laws do not render illegal the actual practice of the Sabbatarian's religion; the only restriction placed on religion by these laws is that imposed on the self-employed merchant, who, if he is a Sabbatarian, may not operate on Sunday to recoup the losses he may have incurred by closing on Saturday.

The Chief Justice, however, did assert that a state should seek to avoid even indirect burdens on religion. His language on this point is most important since it may well form the basis of a subsequent suit by Sabbatarians: "If the state regulates conduct by enacting a general law within its power, the purpose and effect of which is to advance the state's secular goals, the statute is valid despite its indirect burden on religious observance *unless a state may accomplish its purpose by means which do not impose such a burden.*"[17] [Emphasis supplied.] It would appear from this qualification on the police power of the state that, if Sabbatarians can show that the general purposes of Sunday closing laws can be achieved "by means which do not impose . . . an indirect burden on religious observance" then the state will be constitutionally required to adopt a law which accomplishes the ends of Sunday legislation while imposing no disadvantages on Sabbatarians. The principle enunciated by Chief Justice Warren is, of course, also applicable to the issue of tax support for secular educational purposes in nonpublic schools.

Sabbatarians anxious to take advantage of the qualification noted by Chief Justice Warren must also, however, confront another principle set forth by the same judge: ". . . . reason and experience teach that to permit the exemption (from Sunday laws) might well undermine the state's goal of providing a day that, as best possible, eliminates the atmosphere of commercial noise and activity."[18]

Justices Douglas, Brennan and Stewart were persuaded that the Sabbatarian claim of an infringement of religious freedom was valid. Justice Douglas felt that the "dominant religious group" has been allowed "to bring the minority to heel because the minority

. . . does not defer to the majority's religious beliefs."[19] Justice Brennan protests that Sunday laws mean in effect that "no one may at one and the same time be an Orthodox Jew and compete effectively with his Sunday-observing fellow tradesmen." The law, Justice Brennan feels, thus makes "one religion economically disadvantageous."[20] Justice Stewart joins these two justices in dissent, asserting in a one-paragraph opinion that "no state can constitutionally demand . . . an Orthodox Jew to choose between his religious faith and his economical survival."[21]

3. Eight justices considered and repudiated the charge that the Sunday laws in issue, being arbitrary and unreasonable in the subject matter of their inclusions and exclusions, violated the equal protection of the laws. Justice Douglas did not consider this point, having concluded that the statutes in question violated both the establishment and free exercise clauses of the First Amendment. It is not surprising that the Supreme Court did not concede the alleged unreasonableness of the Sunday-closing laws; similar contentions about other laws have been almost universally rejected by the court for at least a generation.

Related to this aspect of the Sunday law cases is the important fact that Sabbatarians in the nature of things seek an economic advantage over their competitors. This element of the Sunday law cases was never fully clarified in the 2,000 pages of briefs or the 220 pages of opinions. If exemptions to Sunday laws were granted to Sabbatarian merchants they would receive not an equalization of their economic position in relation to the non-Sabbatarian but rather a distinct economic advantage. As Justice Frankfurter put it in his 93-page concurring opinion: "If it is assumed that the retail demand for consumer items is approximately equivalent on Saturday and on Sunday, the Sabbatarian, in proportion as he is less numerous, and hence the competition less severe, might incur through the exception a competitive advantage over the non-Sabbatarian, who would then be in a position, presumably, to complain of discrimination against *his* religion."[22] It should be noted that the Sabbatarian would still enjoy this economic advantage even if the law accepted completely his logic and chose Wednesday, for example, as the common day of rest instead of Sunday. In such event the Sabbatarian would still claim the right to open on Wednesday and close on Saturday.

In view of the inevitable financial advantages of being a self-employed Sabbatarian merchant in a society which recognized the claim of this group to conduct business on the common day of rest, the state would have the difficult task of determining who is "conscientious" and who is "commercial". The laws of the states which currently exempt from Sunday laws persons claiming another day as their Sabbath require the claimant to "conscientiously" observe another day. Administrative difficulties have appeared in the enforcement of this requirement as is evidenced in a 1956 decision of the Michigan Supreme Court denying the good faith of an allegedly Sabbatarian owner of three stores who reaped the benefits of Sunday sales in one store operated by himself, closing on Saturday and opening on Sunday, and the benefits of Saturday sales in the other two stores operated by agents, opening Saturdays and closing on Sundays.[23]

Several observations and conclusions on the Sunday law cases seem appropriate:

1. The four decisions make it clear that the state need not remove every direct or indirect benefit to religion when it legislates for a legitimate secular purpose.

2. Although Sunday laws were categorized by the Court as civil regulations designed to provide a common day of rest the Court also made it clear that a *partially* religious Sunday law—one for example intended to facilitate participation in religious services —would not for that reason be struck down if it had a simultaneously valid civil purpose. As the Chief Justice put it: "Because the state wishes to protect those who do worship on Sunday does not mean that the state means to impose religious worship on all."[24]

3. The Court did not rule out the possibility of a violation of the First Amendment by a particular Sunday law if it can be demonstrated that the purpose of the law as "evidenced either on the face of the legislation, in conjunction with its legislative history, or in its operative effect, is to use the state's power to aid religion."[25]

4. While the "no-aid-to-religion" thesis of the *Everson* and *McCollum* decisions was not explicitly qualified in the Sunday law decisions it is interesting to note that, of the two justices still on the Court who participated in those decisions, one (Justice Black) sees no church–state problem in Sunday laws whereas Justice Douglas, despite his authorship on the accommodation theory of church–state relations in the *Zorach* opinon, rejects Sunday laws as violative of both of the religious guarantees of the First Amendment.

5. The 8-to-1 and 6-to-3 majority opinions constitute a clear repudiation of the doctrinaire interpretation of the First Amendment advanced by the American Jewish Congress and the American Civil Liberties Union. The Supreme Court has refused to accept the implications which these two organizations have sought to read into the famous words of *Everson*: "The 'establishment of religion' clause of the First Amendment means at least this: Neither a state nor the Federal Government . . . can pass laws which aid one religion, aid all religions, or prefer one religion over another." The Sunday law decisions have made it clear that, despite the cited generalizations from *Everson*, the state may provide for the common good in a manner which may indirectly aid a religion or even prefer one religion over another.

6. One cannot but regret that the claim of the Sabbatarian for freedom from an economic penalty because of the exercise of his religion was rejected by the nation's highest tribunal. Justice Brennan has a valid point when, in his dissent, he asserts that a majority of the court has "exalted administrative convenience" and that it "conjures up several difficulties with such a system (granting Sunday-law exemptions to Sabbatarians) which seem to me more fanciful than real."[26]

SUNDAY LAWS AND THE STATE LEGISLATURES

The Supreme Court opinions made it clear that the states could grant liberal exemptions from Sunday laws to those who observe another day of worship. In fact, Chief Justice Warren asserts that this course of action "may well be the wiser solution to the problem."[27] Although about one-third of the states have some type of exemptions for Sabbatarians, many legislatures, after the Sunday law cases were decided, were in doubt about what "solution" to adopt or even about the extent and nature of the "problem."

Prior to the 1961 decisions, the law of twelve states had exemptions from Sunday-closing statutes which were apparently satisfactory to all Sabbatarians; these states were Connecticut, Illinois, Indiana, Iowa, Kentucky, Maine, Michigan, Ohio, Oklahoma, Virginia, West Virginia and Wisconsin. Typical of these laws is the following exemption clause from Ohio's Sunday legislation: "This section (prohibiting work on Sundays) does not apply to work of necessity or charity, and does not extend to persons who conscientiously observe the seventh day of the week as the Sabbath, and abstain thereon from doing things prohibited on Sundays."[28]

One never hears of problems in the twelve states which allow Sabbatarians, including self-employed retailers, to conduct business on Sunday. In these states, groups of merchants presumably self-regulate their activities so that no substantial problem arises in the apparently rare case where a Sabbatarian desires to conduct his business on Sunday.

In other states, however, and particularly in New York, Pennsylvania, New Jersey and Massachusetts, no happy entente between legislators and Sabbatarians has been reached since the May, 1961, Supreme Court decisions. The controversy in all these states over the unhappily named "Blue Laws" has been complicated by such collateral issues as the desirability of local county option, the effectiveness of various, special-interest lobbies and the basic fact that no one can pretend to be able to predict with any accuracy what effect, if any, a "liberalization" of Sunday laws in favor of Sabbatarians might produce. Hence state legislatures continue to grope for "compromise" solutions while Jewish groups persevere in their search for exemption statutes, Protestant bodies divide over the basic issues and Catholic spokesmen express misgivings over the threat of added commercialism on Sunday.

It seems clear that the struggle to obtain a "fair Sabbath" law from the legislatures in eastern states has become symbolically and psychologically important to the Jewish community. The failure to secure such legislation in New York state is, quite understandably, a source of discomfort to those who annually petition for exemptions for Sabbatarians. Events in the Massachusetts legislature in 1962 prompted this comment by David Danzig, program director of the American Jewish Committee, writing in the September 28, 1962, issue of *Commonweal* in a symposium on "The Jew in American Society": "After the recent incident in Massachusetts it will be all the more difficult to convince Jews of the moral superiority of recourse to the legislature. Jews were able, briefly, to obtain from the Massachusetts legislature an exemption from the Sunday-closing laws for observers of the Saturday Sabbath. Then the Catholics spoke up, and the legislature hastily reversed itself."

Although very few Catholic writers have made statements on Sunday-closing legislation, some writers from the Jewish community feel that the Catholic attitude is the sole cause for the failure of some states to enact exemptions for Sabbatarians from Sunday laws.[29] While the effect of Catholic activity in this area is debatable it is true that the Catholic community in general seems to feel that the pressure to modify Sunday legislation is another application of the secularistic concept that the government may not encourage religion or promote morality. There is, moreover, the fear among Catholics—and many others—that concessions to sincere Sabbatarians may lead to ruthlessly competitive practices and Sunday "bargain days" which will inevitably force more and more Sunday observers to work full-time on their day of worship.

Even, however, if all religious groups were persuaded and enthusiastic about the implementation of the rights asserted by Sabbatarians to conduct business on Sunday, the claims of these religionists must still win the approval of unionist and mercantile groups who quite properly want specific information on how Sabbatarians' business on Sunday is likely to affect their own interests.

The problem should be confronted with the confident expectation that America, like England and other nations,[30] can work out an accommodation and harmonization of interests so that those conscientiously opposed to labor on Saturday may not be unreasonably penalized or benefited for following the dictates of their conscience.

More important, however, than the co-operation which all should give to sincere Sabbatarians so that they will not be economically disadvantaged by their faith is the understanding which all believers and nonbelievers should seek to extend to the people of the Jewish community for whom the very existence and legal force of Sunday as a holiday is a reminder of the Christian civilization in which they live.

It may well be that the customs and laws surrounding Sunday in Western culture are so interwoven with the life and history of European and American nations that no court decree or statutory rule can effect any substantial change in the attitude of the citizenry towards Sunday. But at least the claim of the Sabbatarian, unfortunately not completely clarified and not granted legal recognition in the 1961 Sunday law cases, should act as a constant reminder that all should be sensitive and sympathetic to the differences which those who follow Judaism have with an American society, once predominantly Protestant and now religiously pluralistic.

CHAPTER EIGHT

Conclusions and Recommendations

CONCLUSIONS

Even the most summary review of church–state relations in America will reveal overwhelming evidence that there are vast, noncontroversial areas where an almost universally accepted understanding on church–state matters exists in the American mind. The remarkable consensus on moral and religious ideas which underlies this understanding on many church–state issues has, until recently, been almost unchallenged and in fact virtually unexplored.

Whenever conflicts arise out of hitherto settled legal–moral or church–state issues the contemporary tendency is to attempt to resolve all these problems by immediate reference to the First Amendment and to the United States Supreme Court. The wisdom of employing the establishment and free exercise clauses of the First Amendment for such purposes is open to question. In a relationship as profound and complex as that between church and state it should not be expected that one set of legal–moral or constitutional principles will render self-evident the rights of all interested parties.

In relationships less complex, such as marriage or even in a legally certified labor–management contract, no body of principles can be devised by which all the rights of the parties involved can be legally determined. Some rights in every such relationship must in the nature of things remain as moral or social rights rather than judicially enforcible or even legally identifiable claims.

The central question is every relationship involving two persons or two groups centers on the expectations of the persons involved. In church–state relations in America the source of tensions resides in the fact that neither the churches nor the American state have a sufficiently clear concept of what they should or do expect from each other. The churches have as their primary expectation from the state a freedom to practice and propagate their faith. The state on the other hand has as its primary expectation the formulation by the churches of virtuous and patriotic citizens. But beyond these oversimplified generalizations it is difficult to say much more about what the churches and the state in America should seek or expect from each other.

In a sense the churches expect neither to receive from nor to give anything to the state. The mission of a divinely established religion is not to form virtuous citizens but to bring salvation and redemption to the children of God. On the other hand the state, as the guardian of the temporal order, is autonomous in its own sphere and as such need have no expectations of the churches. Once again, however, these broad generalities are of little use when one contemplates the question of what values the state should maintain and support in building among its citizens that moral consensus upon which the legal bases of society must rest.

Every state that is not totalitarian confronts the fact that no just government can devise and impose on its people those moral standards which appear wise to the legally constituted officials. Nor may such officials accept the majority view, in the manner of a Gallup poll, as the wisest moral view to follow. Public authorities in any just government must look to the moral standards inherited and believed in by the people who make up the governed. In so doing the government seeks to preserve the inner sources of its unity while at the same time benevolently facilitating the continuation and even the deepening of the religious and moral values of its people.

In a modern pluralistic democracy the state is faced with a situation which is new in human history. Seldom if ever before, have there been nations without the existence of deep social and even legal barriers between the members of different religious faiths. Contemporary democracies—and especially the American state —have not really thought through the expectations which they

could or should have of the religious bodies in their midst. It is an
easy answer to say that America's unity is of a secular nature and
that consequently the American state need have no expectations
of the churches. But such a conclusion does not really wrestle with
the profound, complex and undeniable fact that America's unity,
even if it can be called secular, derives from ideals whose presence
in Western culture is attributable ultimately to the Jewish and
Christian religions. A central question therefore in church–state
relations is the extent to which the American state has relied and
should continue to rely on the invisible but real moral influence
of the churches and synagogues of America.

Can any guidelines then be given by which the state can be just
to the churches and, without abrogating any rights of nonbelievers,
encourage those religious values on which the moral standards of
the citizenry are based?

Four intertwined theories on the legal aspects of church–state
relations are distinguishable in the ever more abundant literature
about the place of religion in relation to government in America.
We will first identify them and then try to assess their content and
value. These theories propose: (1) the *absolute* separation of
church and state; (2) a state that is neutral as between religion
and irreligion; (3) cooperation between church and state; (4) a
state that refuses to employ religion or irreligion as the basis for
any classification.

The Absolute Separation of Church and State

Like all theories advancing absolutes the contention that the
First Amendment means an *absolute* wall of separation between
church and state is attractive by reason of its simplicity. But like
some other absolutes urged by American jurists it cannot resolve
all the conflicting claims in church–state relations. The advantages
of such a thesis include the following:

1. The state assumes an absolutely impartial attitude between
religion and irreligion and thus, theoretically at least, allows all
creeds to compete in the marketplace of ideas.

2. In a newly pluralistic society the application of the doctrine
of *absolute* separation precludes the use of state power and governmental machinery to advance the religious beliefs of those believers
or nonbelievers who, by reason of their persuasiveness or their

numbers, would be able to engage the state's energies for their own purposes.

The disadvantages of the theory of *absolute* separation include the following:

1. Such an interpretation of the establishment clause tends to narrow the expansion of the "free exercise" of religion clause and may, as a result, actually place the enormous power and prestige of the state against what otherwise would be a spontaneous collective manifestation of faith or disbelief.

2. A logical application of the absolute separation thesis would necessitate the abolition of innumerable benefits to religion, the granting of which cannot be explained or rationalized on any other basis than by a desire on the part of the state to favor the implementation of religious freedom.

State Neutrality to Religion

The most articulate and balanced advocate of the theory of state neutrality towards religion has been Professor Wilber G. Katz of the University of Wisconsin Law School and former dean of the University of Chicago Law School. Professor Katz writes: "The basic American principle of church–state relations is neither separation of church and state nor impartial benevolence towards religion; it is the principle of religious liberty, which requires strict government neutrality with respect to religion."[1] Government neutrality, in Professor Katz's reasoning, would permit the freedom to worship in public schools and the right to have state subsidies for church-related schools.

This thesis has been criticized as an attempt by its advocate to pummel "a dead horse of absolutism with an absolutism of his own."[2] This theory of neutrality has also been deemed inadequate because it does not seem to come to grips with the contention that the financing of a sectarian school by the state is deemed by some to be an injustice to the believer and to the nonbeliever whose tax money is spent to advance sectarian doctrines which he believes to be erroneous.

The neutrality thesis, however, can at least be viewed as an interpretation of the First Amendment which resolves some but not all of the dilemmas that arise from the twin guarantees of freedom *from* religion and freedom *of* religion.

Cooperative Separationism

This view of the First Amendment is open to the obvious criticism that the whole thrust and purpose of the separation idea is weakened and in fact eroded by the fluidity and amorphous nature of the concept of "cooperation" between church and state. To urge "cooperation," furthermore, seems to imply or assume the desirability of that very interdependence between church and state which the concept of separation is designed to interdict.

As an expression, however, of the traditional role of church and state in American history the term "cooperation" is not an inaccurate or an inappropriate word to describe this relationship. Aside from some Catholic and other advocates of state aid for sectarian schools who have endorsed "cooperation" between church and state Professor Paul G. Kauper has written cogently about the usefulness of "cooperative separation."[3] "Cooperation," however, like "neutrality," has no juridically established definition and is consequently only a theory by which an attempt is made to explain the inner meaning of the First Amendment. But clearly all plausible theories and theses on which to base a church-state jurisprudence for a pluralistic America are valuable.

Religion as No Basis for Classification

At the height of the Federal aid controversy in 1961 Professor Philip Kurland wrote an article on church and state in the *University of Chicago Law Review* which was later issued as a book entitled *Religion and the Law.*[4] The argument on church–state relations advanced by Professor Kurland—a doctrine admittedly in search of authorities—urged that the First Amendment was intended to prevent the state from making religion or irreligion the basis of any state action or nonaction. In a detailed study of all Supreme Court decisions on church–state matters, Professor Kurland found a good deal to justify his thesis but also many areas where it was not certain that his thesis was accepted or would be accepted by the Supreme Court.

The doctrine that religion should not be basis for any classification by the state means apparently that the state may subsidize the secular education of a nonpublic school even though it is permeated with sectarian teaching. But the same doctrine apparently would not permit the state to grant the Sabbatarian an exemption from a mandatory day of rest statute even though the denial of the exemption would result in a financial penalty to the Sabbatarian.

Such in brief are four of the concededly tenuous and not mutually exclusive theories that look towards a deeper understanding of the place of the First Amendment in a pluralistic society. If one feels that the meaning of these theories leaves something to be desired, he is but reflecting what every observer of church–state jurisprudence has concluded. As F. Ernest Johnson put it: "In a fairly long professional life devoted largely to studies and activities in controversial fields I have found no problem so confused, so lacking a 'universe of discourse'—even with respect to agreement of the meaning of the terms used in the argument—as the problem of church–state relations in the United States.

"It seems to me that our most urgent needs are a great measure of agreement as to the true nature of the issues and a much clearer understanding by the contending parties of *what their opponents are trying to say.*"[5] [Emphasis supplied.]

All too frequently the "contending parties" in America's church–state controversies do not really understand "what their opponents are trying to say." For this reason some groups are seeking more and more to have the courts supply a formula for the harmonization of the competing rights of believers and nonbelievers. American courts must ultimately base their conclusions on a public policy which is not spelled out in the First Amendment. And in so doing the courts and particularly the United States Supreme Court are required to issue statements whose impact is incalculable. It is not the legal ruling on some relatively restricted religious practice which enters into public opinion, but rather the tone and atmosphere of the opinions which accompany the actual ruling of the court.

The spirit and wording of the *Zorach* opinion is an example of the enormous influence which a Supreme Court opinion can exert. In an excellent study entitled *Zorach v. Clauson: The Impact of a Supreme Court Decision,* Professor Frank J. Sorauf writes: "This impact of *Zorach* beyond the bounds of the facts it decided and the rules it enunciated illustrates how Supreme Court precedents, as soon as they leave judicial hands, enter into another realm of policy-making and become symbols in political debate and deliberation."[6] Professor Arthur E. Sutherland, Jr., in an article on the School Prayer case in the November, 1962, issue of the *Harvard*

Law Review, comments in the same vein when he notes: "Some of the more startling connotations of the *School Prayer* opinions may come to be explained as springing from *obiter dicta,* unnecessary to the actual decision. But church–state cases have seemed to attribute unusual authority to dicta; even by-the-way judicial remarks about religion in schools are not readily brushed off. . . ."[7]

The fact that incidental observations of the Supreme Court in church–state decisions are seized upon for polemical purposes by partisans in church–state controversies is but another indication that there is no "universe of discourse" in this area. Are there then any principles for a dialogue between believers and nonbelievers, the use of which would make lawsuits less necessary or more meaningful in their results? Following are some suggestions and recommendations for all groups which, if followed, may diminish the abrasive nature of controversies in the church–state area.

RECOMMENDATIONS

For All Citizens

Anyone seeking to understand the relation of government and religion in America must recognize the uniqueness of the role of religion in the United States. As Peter F. Drucker has perceptively noted: "Organized religion plays a part in our society which is altogether unknown elsewhere. . . . This dual relationship: strictest separation between church and state and closest interpenetration of religion and society, has been characteristic of this country from the start to its independence. . . . It is basic to the American creed that a society can only be religious if religion and the state are radically separated, and that the state can only be free if society is basically a religious society. . . ."[8] Mr. Drucker concludes that "the basic relationship between religious life and political power cannot . . . be founded on a purely negative policy of nonencouragement. It requires a positive policy of impartial encouragement of all religions and of all truly religious life and activity in American society."[9]

A policy of "nonencouragement" of religion is today advocated by many strict church–state separationists, but Mr. Drucker, an astute critic of Americans, feels that "impartial encouragement of all religions" is necessary to preserve a free society.

Although one could disagree with some of these conclusions there are present here clearly important implications for the state because, as Mr. Drucker puts it, the "United States is . . . the only country of the West in which society is conceived as basically a religious society."[10] If one agrees with this interpretation of the religious character of American society, it would seem to be difficult to deny its corollary that—within the framework of strict separation—the state should "always sponsor, protect and favor religious life in general."[11] If one rejects the conclusion that American society cannot be free without religion, then he must sustain the burden of showing that purely secular values are sufficient to carry forward the ideals and purposes of American society.

The attempt to identify and analyze all the paradoxes and inconsistencies that characterize the basic relationship of American society to religion reveals once again that the unexplored areas are vast. It would appear that the only responsible and just attitude for all citizens to assume is one of respectful if critical evaluation of the conflicting theories on the difficult question of the relationship of religion to the needs of American society. Is it not reasonable to suggest that all citizens in their thinking about church–state matters seek to promote a relationship between government and religion which is certain to guarantee the preservation of a free society? Is it certain that such a society can be maintained if a policy of "nonencouragement" to religion is pursued?

The basic problems therefore confronting every person who desires to take a position on church–state relations are far deeper than the legal issues and court decisions in which too many persons and partisans seek to take a refuge. The fundamental issues center on the nature of American society and the needs which it has if it is to remain free.

For Protestants

The foregoing suggestions for all Americans have more application to Protestants than to the members of other faiths in America. For it has been Protestants who have formed and fashioned the unique American state, a religious society one of whose basic tenets is paradoxically a wall of separation between church and state. As the consensus which made America a "religious" society continues to fragment, American Protestants are being forced to make some hard decisions as to how impenetrable the wall of separation can be without at the same time allowing an erosion of the religious nature of the unity and basic ethos of America.

The Protestant community in America has not had the need nor the occasion to think out a consistent church–state policy. It has been generally assumed by Protestants that the American state, being traditionally benevolent to religion, would be a partner and a friend to the Protestant religion. The abolition of Protestant-inspired religious exercises such as Bible-reading in the public schools seems to shatter the preconception of some Protestants that American democracy and Protestant Christianity are inseparable and mutually dependent. If there is any other phenomenon which disturbs Protestants it is the sight of undeniably strong non-Protestant power and prestige. Quite understandably the appearance of a non-Protestant challenge to the marriage or merger of Protestant Christianity and American democracy is bewildering and upsetting to the convinced Protestant. Some few Protestants have sought the aid of the law to prevent non-Protestant and particularly Roman Catholic groups from securing benefits or status, the granting of which could arguably be a violation of the wall of separation between church and state.

But the Protestant argument that the Roman Catholic citizen is not entitled to aid for parochial schools means logically that the public school may not promote even the most innocuous nonsectarian religious exercise. Hence the Protestant confronts the question of whether or not his resistance to the rise of non-Protestant forces will be so strong that it will bring about the secularization of public education and eventually the destruction of the religious nature of American society.

Nothing in Protestant theology or in Protestant history makes it easy or perhaps even possible for the Protestant community to accept the notion of a state whose attitude towards religion is so noncommittal as to be in effect almost hostile. Yet such an eventuality could result, if the wall of separation theory becomes the absolutely controlling principle in church–state relations.

Secularism or, as Protestants (at least unconsciously) view it, the de-Protestantization of America has been and is a fear of no small moment to American Protestants today. It may be that in the near future, they will have to choose and accept true religious pluralism or see the "deconsecration" of the nation.

Protestants more than any other religious or nonreligious group in America will be called upon to change their attitudes and yield on certain church–state arrangements and traditions. It will be quite understandable if some of them feel that yielding on certain issues would involve a compromise of principle. Those who so feel have the burden of persuading their fellow citizens of the validity of the principles which are assertedly compromised. If confusion and disagreement about the basic principles involved continue among religious groups, it seems possible that serious harm to the public peace and to interreligious harmony will eventuate.

For Catholics

If Protestants in America are sometimes bewildered by the abruptness of the transition of America from a pan-Protestant nation to a pluralistic society, Catholics are often no less bewildered by the sudden emergence of an era in which Catholics are expected to assert their views and claims in church–state matters. Catholics have, as a result of their bewilderment, not infrequently declared their support and even their attachment to the unofficial "establishment of all religions" which has characterized America until the very recent past.

Catholics, even more than Protestants, fear the disestablishment of religion and the canonization of secularism as the nation's official church–state philosophy. If many Protestants have assumed and asserted the indispensability of religion for the American way, Catholics have an even deeper feeling on the inseparability of religion and American morality. It may be that Catholics, a minority whose patriotism has sometimes been challenged, have embraced to a greater degree than non-Catholics the notion of the indivisibility of religion, patriotism and public morality. Some Catholics consequently express deep anger when the Supreme Court or another government agency issues decisions disestablishing religion; such decisions shatter the neat thesis subscribed to by so many Catholics that the progress of religion and the progress of America are inseparably joined.

Catholics in America have in many ways a more difficult adjustment to make in their church–state thinking than other groups of believers or nonbelievers. As a result, widespread misunderstanding and indignation on their part can be anticipated as the Supreme Court and other government agencies continue to carry out their assigned task of trying to reconcile conflicting claims in the church–

state area with the demands of the Constitution. The following suggestions therefore seem appropriate for Catholics:

1. Because of the complexity and uniqueness of the church–state dilemmas which confront America today, Catholics should avoid the omnipresent temptation to oversimplify the issues. Even more importantly Catholics should resist the temptation to act on the principle that what is good for the Catholic Church is good for America. If there is some truth in the assertion that many Protestant groups in American history have tended to identify the advancement of the nation with the advancement of pan-Protestantism, it is equally true that Catholics must avoid a comparable identification.

2. Catholics must be careful not to be—or to convey the impression that they are—preoccupied with their own interests (such as Federal aid for Catholic schools) to such an extent that these interests tend to dominate their whole approach to virtually all issues. An obsession by any group about its own rights is likely to impair the good citizenship and, indeed, the civility of such a group.

3. In view of the complexity of church–state issues and the current searching for appropriate Catholic attitudes, it is proper for Catholics to remain calm and, without a trace of hysteria, to prepare themselves for a long series of church–state decisions. As legislative and judicial opinions continue to be issued on all manner of church–state problems, Catholics will encounter serious temptations to speak or act in an un-Christian and even uncivil way about the magistrates who will interpret church–state law as it appears to them. Because of the richness and depth of the metaphysical and theological traditions which Catholics have inherited, they will be instinctively inclined to judge harshly of some jurist who will decide profound church–state problems by the use of a few simple principles. Catholics will be tempted, as they have been in the past, to call these solutions "absurd," "asinine," "un-American," and even "anti-Christian." Increasing the temptations of Catholics to be harshly critical of decisions which may in part derive from secularistic premises is the deeply rooted fear of secularism and the knowledge that, as Reinhold Niebuhr put it, "our Protestant heritage disintegrates into secularism much more easily than Catholicism does."[12]

4. Catholics, more than the protagonists of differing church–

state viewpoints, are inclined to assert the Catholic claim as an absolute and dismiss the objections to it as the products of secularistic or bigoted minds. One of the principal examples of a cavalier attitude by Catholics with regard to an honestly debatable point is the Catholic emotionalism centering on the "permeation" issue. The central contention of those who object to public financing for Catholic schools is the undeniable fact that secular instruction in a Catholic school is "permeated" by a Catholic atmosphere and Catholic attitudes. No Catholic would want to deny the fact of permeation and, indeed, would be disturbed if a Catholic school did not seek to interfuse and permeate Catholic values with secular instruction.

But the argument centering on permeation deserves a reasoned answer and not an emotional "brush-off." It is true that some non-Catholic writers have sought to ridicule certain examples in Catholic textbooks where sectarian teaching is clumsily injected into the instructional material employed in a purely secular subject. This tendency to cite the more obtrusive examples of "permeation" may be present in the study by George R. La Noue entitled "Religious Schools and 'Secular' Subjects" published in the *Harvard Education Review* (Summer, 1962). But the basic contention of Mr. La Noue and those who are troubled about the permeation issue deserves more careful analysis than it has received from some Catholic writers. Certain Catholic polemicists seem uncertain whether it is better to confess the permeation and claim that the banning of permeation would violate the religious freedom of Catholics, or to deny the permeation and claim that secular subjects are taught in Catholic schools in a manner identical with their treatment in publicly financed schools. Regardless of which choice is made, there are implications which not all Catholics have as yet fully appreciated.

5. If there is any single suggestion or warning that is appropriate for Catholics, it is the counsel not to contemplate the use of the power of population or politics to secure the ends which they may seek. This suggestion, however, must be pondered against the background of the startling generalization made by the very perceptive editor of the London *Tablet*, Mr. Douglas Woodruff. Writing about church–state problems on the continent of Europe Mr. Woodruff concludes: "The vindication by the church of the right to maintain schools is the basic reason for the existence of

Catholic political parties. They are not needed except where there is a danger of anti-Christian parties turning the machinery of the state against religion by claiming a state monopoly for education."[13]

In every nation of the West with a religiously pluralistic population the problem of religion in education has become a part of, and been resolved by, the political process. Can Americans avoid such an eventuality? Catholics more than any other group hold the answer to that question. The basic attitudes of Americans seem to be against the very idea that church–state issues should become political issues. If Catholics, consciously or otherwise, turn their church–state grievances into political issues, they must accept the long-range consequences of offending the fundamental sensibilities of their neighbors and fellow citizens.

For Jews

What would have been the attitude of the Jewish community in America on church–state matters if the tides of immigration and several other forces had brought to the United States only Orthodox Jews, the vast majority of whom had remained committed to that faith? In such a situation would the position favoring Federal aid for private schools, which is today supported by some Orthodox rabbis, be the typical view of American Jews? In other words, is the strict separationist view subscribed to by virtually all non-Orthodox Jewish spokesmen today the derivative of non-Orthodox theology? Or is it the end product of a process of reasoning entered into in order to discover and adopt a church–state viewpoint that would appear to be the most advantageous to the Jewish community?

It is difficult to understand why certain rigid church–state separationist views have been embraced so universally by American Jews. There are, to be sure, respectable constitutional arguments to support this position, but the ambiguity in the constitutional authorities does not justify the vehemence with which rigorous church–state separation is endorsed by Jewish spokesmen.

But whatever the ultimate justification might be for the Jewish position, other particans of church–state positions should expect and should encourage members of the Jewish faith to advocate and abide by their position to the full limit of their convictions and resources. Jewish leaders have presumably concluded that the positions they advance are in the best interests of the Jewish community and of the nation. It is consequently their duty to present their views and to work for their adoption.

At the same time, however, Jewish spokesmen have an obligation to address themselves to the contention that public morality and the moral health of the nation may be endangered by that divorce of religion from society which may result from the continuous application of the doctrine of absolute separation of church and state. It is not an adequate answer to state that the home and the church are the natural seedbeds of the moral and religious life of the nation. Americans by tradition and instinct feel the need of a public philosophy publicly endorsed. Those who seek to render this public philosophy non-theistic should bear the burden of demonstrating their conviction that American society will not thereby by harmed. Interreligious harmony will suffer unless there is some easing of the profound anxieties of sincere persons who view judicial and legislative disestablishment of religion as an undermining of the nation's basic morality and unity.

One church–state theory sometimes advanced by Jewish writers is the contention that the nation's Founding Fathers deliberately and consciously set out on a great experiment—the creation of the first truly secular state in Western civilization. Although there is evidence to support this position, there is abundant contrary evidence suggesting that the deism and the rationalism of the Founding Fathers produced a state of which it is true to say, as Justice Douglas wrote in his 1952 *Zorach* opinion, "we are a religious people whose institutions presuppose a Supreme Being."

For Nonbelievers

However truculent the members of any religious body may sometimes become, it seems true to say that all believers in America desire to be fair to the millions of their fellow citizens who are agnostics, atheists or nonbelievers. Justice would seem to suggest that the nonbeliever and even the person with no church affiliation should not be required to support the works of organized religion. If, however, this principle were an absolute, the complaints of the nonbeliever would be substantial indeed. The fact that religionists can give lip service to the principle of total justice for nonbelievers and yet continue to promote and accept government aid for religion is one of the greatest of the paradoxes in church–state thinking in America.

The rights of nonbelievers in America, seemingly conceded in principle by most believers, have attained very little actual recognition in American law. The profound conviction, held by many believers and nonbelievers alike, that the nation's morality and even its unity are grounded in the truths of religion may make religionists reluctant to concede and nonreligionists hesitant to press the otherwise logical proposition that nonbelieving citizens should not be expected to bear their proportionate share of whatever the state expends to advance the cause of religious groups.

The fact that the rights of nonbelievers have attained little legal recognition in America supplies no reason for believers to deny the validity of the claim of the agnostic or nonbelieving citizen. Religionists may argue that the extension of complete legal equality to nonbelievers is a dangerous public policy. But such a thesis, to be just, must be supported by an over-all thesis of church–state relations which could justify a preferred position for religionists over irreligionists. Such a preferred position cannot be unambiguously demonstrated to be the law of America today.

A most appropriate statement with which to conclude a discussion such as this is one made by Reinhold Niebuhr: "Every society needs working principles of justice, as criteria for its positive law and system of restraints. The profoundest of these actually transcend reason and lie rooted in religious conceptions of the meaning of existence."[14] In every church–state controversy, it is well that all parties realize that in our society the "working principles of justice . . . transcend reason and lie rooted in the religious conceptions of the meaning of existence."

Notes

CHAPTER ONE. *Areas of Church–State Cooperation*

1. Kauper, Paul G., "Church and State: Cooperative Separatism," Vol. 60, *Michigan Law Review*, 1961, pp. 1–40, at p. 4.
2. Littell, Franklin Hamlin, *From State Church to Pluralism: A Protestant Interpretation of Religion in American History*, Doubleday & Co., New York, 1962, at p. 99.
3. Stokes, III, p. 454.
4. Quoted in Commager, Henry Steele, *Living Ideas in America*, Harper & Row, New York, 1951, p. 493.
5. Zorach v. Clauson, 343 U.S. 306 at p. 313 (1952).
6. Church of the Holy Trinity v. United States, 143 U.S. 457, 470-471 (1892) and United States v. Macintosh, 283 U.S. 605, 625 (1931).
7. Sperry, Willard L., *Religion in America*, Cambridge (Eng.) Univ. Press 1946, p. 60.
8. General Finance Corp. v. August Archetto, 176 A2 73 (1961); Cert. Denied; 369 U.S. 423 (1962).
9. Everson v. Board of Education, 330 U.S. 1 (1947).
10. *Congressional Record*, 4, p. 175 (1875).
11. Bennett, John C., *Christians and the State*, Scribner, New York, 1958, p. 232.
12. Pfeffer, Leo, *Church, State and Freedom*, Beacon Press, Boston, 1953, p. 189.
13. *Ibid.*, p. 189.
14. *Ibid.*, p. 187.
15. Stokes, Anson Phelps, *Church and State in the United States*, Harper & Row., New York, 1950, Vol. III, p. 421.

16. Lundberg v. County of Alameda, et al, 46 C2d 644; 298P. 2d 1 (1956). Appeal dismissed, 352 U.S. 921 (1956).
17. *Op. cit.*, II, p. 680.
18. See for example De LaSalle Institute v. United States, 195 Fed. Supp. 895, Northern District Calif., 1961, where tax-exemption was denied to business activities not judged to be "educational and religious."
19. *Op. cit.*, pp. 234-235.
20. "An Unreligious View," *Religion and the Schools*, Fund for the Republic, New York, 1959, pp. 79-96 at p. 88.
21. Cited in Stokes, III, p. 297.
22. Cited in Stokes, III, p. 265.
23. (Thorpe, *op. cit.*, V. 2648) quoted in Stokes, III, p. 265.
24. *Ibid.*, III, p. 266.
25. *Ibid.*, III, p. 266.
26. Arver v. United States, 245 U.S. 366, 389, 390 (1918).
27. United States v. Kauten, 133 F.2d 703 (1943).
28. United States v. Schwimmer, 279 U.S. 646 (1929).
29. Girouard v. United States, 328 U.S. 61 (1946).
30. United States v. Macintosh, 283 U.S. 605 at 625 (1931).
31. *Ibid.*, p. 635.
32. Girouard v. United States, 328 U.S. 61 at 64 (1961).
33. Cohnstaedt v. Immigration and Naturalization Service, 339 U.S. 901 (1950).
34. West Virginia State Board of Education v. Barnette, 319 U.S. 624 (1943).
35. "What's New in the Work of the Church and the Chaplain in Correctional Institutions?" Bulletin No. 11, issued in November 1961 by the United Prison Association of Massachusetts.
36. Michigan Constitution of 1908, Art. 5, #26.
37. Washington Constitution of 1889, Art. 1, #11.
38. Quoted in Stokes, III, p. 108.
39. Bulletin No. 11 cited footnote 35 at p. 3.
40. *Ibid.*, p. 4.
41. Cited in Stokes, III, p. 143.
42. Bennett, *op. cit.*, p. 234.
43. The information in this section is taken from an address, "The Military Chaplaincy," by Marion J. Creeger, Executive Secretary, General Commission of Chaplains, National Council of Churches, printed in Reports of the Third Assembly, by the Board of Social and Economic Relations of the Methodist Church, 1959.

44. Werner, Ruth M., *"Public Financing of Voluntary Agency Foster Care,"* Child Welfare League of America, Inc., New York, 1961, pp. 141-142.
45. *Ibid.,* p. 142.
46. *Services in Public and Voluntary Child Welfare Programs,* Helen R. Jeter, 1962, Children's Bureau, U.S. Dept. of Health, Education and Welfare.
47. *The New York Times,* Feb. 22, 1962.
48. See Hearings, p. 573.
49. *Ibid.,* pp. 573-574.
50. *Ibid.,* p. 628.
51. *Ibid.,* p. 347.
52. *Ibid.,* p. 590.
53. *Ibid.,* p. 591.
54. *The New York Times,* May 23, 1960.
55. Brader, Spencer E., "Public Financing and Church Responsibility," *Lutheran Social Welfare Quarterly,* No. 2, 1961, pp. 19-27.
56. *Ibid.,* p. 19.
57. *Ibid.,* p. 26.
58. Cited by Tussman, *The Supreme Court on Church and State,* Oxford Univ. Press, New York, 1962.
59. Engel v. Vitale, 370 U.S. 421 at 437 (1962).
60. *The New York Times,* May 29, 1962.
61. Kentucky Building Commission v. Effron, 220 S.W.2d 836 (1949).
62. Craig v. Mercy Hospital, 45 S.2d 809 (1950).
63. "Hill-Burton Act after Five Years," *America,* February 9, 1952, pp. 499-507.
64. Abernathy v. City of Irvine, 355 S.W.2d 159, Review Denied, 31 U.S. Law Week 309 (1962).
65. Pfeffer, Leo, *Creeds in Competition,* Harper & Row, 1958, p. 49.
66. Bradfield v. Roberts, 175 U.S. 291 (1899).
67. Quick Bear v. Leupp, 210 U.S. 50 (1908).
68. Cochran v. Louisiana State Board of Education, 281 U.S. 370.
69. Everson v. Board of Education, 330 U.S. 1 (1947).
70. McGowan v. State of Maryland, 81 S.Ct. 1101 (1961).

CHAPTER TWO. *Religion in Public Education*

1. Everson v. Board of Education, 330 U.S. 1, pp. 23-24 (1947).
2. Pfeffer, Leo, *Church, State and Freedom,* Beacon Press, Boston, p. 288 (1953).

3. McCollum v. Board of Education, 333 U.S. 203 at 236 (1948).
4. Curran, Francis X., S. J., *The Churches and the Schools*, Loyola Univ. Press (1954); Dunn, William K., *What Happened to Religious Education*, Johns Hopkins University Press (1958).
5. Shaver, Erwin L., "The Weekday Church School—Opportunity and Challenge," Information Service, Department of Research and Education, Federal Council of Churches, Vol. XXI, No. 22, May 29, 1943.
6. Fosdick, Harry S., *School and Society*, Vol. 66, Nov. 1947, pp. 401-406.
7. *Ibid.*, pp. 402-403.
8. Cited in V. T. Thayer, *The Attack Upon the Secular School*, p. 59, Beacon Press, Boston, 1951.
9. Report of the Committee on Religion and Education of the American Council on Education, ACE Studies: Reports of Committees and Conferences, Vol. XI, No. 26, Washington, April, 1947.
10. *Ibid.*, pp. 19-30.
11. *Ibid.*, p. 15.
12. *Ibid.*, pp. 46-47.
13. *The Function of the Public Schools in Dealing with Religion:* A Report on the Exploratory Study Made by the Committee on Religion and Education, American Council on Education, Washington, 1953, pp. 6-7.
14. See, for example, a harshly critical evaluation at pp. 61-69 in V. T. Thayer, *The Attack upon the American Secular School*, Beacon Press, Boston, 1951.
15. For background and discussion material on this study document see *Religious Education* July-August, pp. 265-296.
16. *Religious Education*, July-August 1960, p. 266.
17. *Ibid.*, p. 267.
18. *Ibid.*, p. 267.
19. "Observations from a Catholic Viewpoint" by Neil G. McCluskey, S. J., *ibid.*, pp. 273-278 at 276.
20. Quoted in *Religious Education*, March-April 1954, pp. 102-103.
21. Everson v. Board of Education, 330 U.S. 1, at p. 59 (1947).
22. "Safeguarding Religious Liberty," (Statements of Policy and Position on Religion and Public Education and Other Aspects of Church–State relationships Jointly Adopted by the Synagogue Council of America and the National Community Relations Advisory Council and issued by their Joint Advisory Committee), New York, 1957.
23. *Ibid.*, p. 7.
24. *Ibid.*, p. 6.

237

25. *Ibid.*, pp. 8-10.
26. *Ibid.*, p. 8.
27. *Ibid.*, p. 5.
28. *Ibid.*, p. 7.
29. Williams, George H., "Church–State Separation and Religion in the School of Our Democracy," adapted from an address delivered at the Eleventh Annual Spring Conference of the Jewish Community Council of Metropolitan Boston, *Religious Education*, Sept.-Oct., 1956, pp. 369-377.
30. *Ibid.*, p. 371.
31. *Ibid.*, p. 371.
32. *Ibid.*, p. 371.
33. *Ibid.*, p. 371.
34. *Ibid.*, p. 370.
35. *Ibid.*, p. 370.
36. *Ibid.*, p. 371.
37. Gilbert, Arthur, "Religion in the Public School—A New Approach to the Jewish Position," an address delivered before the Jewish Community Council Institute on Separation of Church and State, Detroit, April, 1960, *Religious Education*, July-August, 1961, pp. 297 ff.
38. *Ibid.*, p. 297.
39. *Ibid.*, p. 299.
40. *Ibid.*, p. 301.
41. *Ibid.*, p. 301.
42. Rabbi Gilbert questions "The Technique of the Jewish Community which so easily threatens court suit as the most telling weapon in its dialogue with the Christian Community on this issue," *ibid.*, p. 301.
43. See Leo Pfeffer, *Creeds in Competitions*, Harper & Row, New York, 1958.
44. *Op. cit.*, p. 5.
45. See Maritain, *Man and the State*, University of Chicago Press, 1951.
46. *Op. cit.*, p. 6.
47. "Unchanging Duty in a Changing World," issued by the Administrative Board of the National Catholic Welfare Conference, reprinted in Denver *Register*, November 26, 1961.
48. *Public Schools and Moral Education*, Neil Gerard McCluskey, S. J., Columbia University Press, New York, 1958.
49. *Ibid.*, p. 261.
50. *Ibid.*, p. 264.
51. *Ibid.*, p. 267.

CHAPTER THREE. *Problems of Religion in Public Education*

1. "Moral and Spiritual Values in the Public Schools," Educational Policies Commission, National Education Association, Washington, 1951.
2. See 30 United States Law Week, 3309-3310, April 10, 1962.
3. *Ibid.*, p. 3310.
4. Miller, William Lee, "The Fight over America's Fourth 'R'," *The Reporter*, March 22, 1956, pp. 20-26.
5. *Ibid.*, p. 21.
6. Engel v. Vitale, 370 U.S. 421, 430 (1962).
7. Quoted in "Religion in Public School Education" by Joseph F. Costanzo, S.J., 31 *Thought*, Summer 1956, 1-29 at 2.
8. *The New York Times*, March 29, 1955.
9. *Op. cit.*, note 61, p. 3.
10. *Ibid.*, p. 4.
11. *Ibid.*, p. 5.
12. See note 3, Chapter II.
13. "Moral and Spiritual Values in the Public Schools," p. 4.
14. Dewey, John, "Intelligence in the Modern World," (Ratner Ed., New York, The Modern Library, 1939, p. 706). The quotation is from an essay "Religion and Our Schools" first published in *Hibbert Journal*, July 1908.
15. See *The New York Times*, August 23, 1956; Sept. 13, 1956; October 5, 1956.
16. Manwaring, David R., *Render unto Caesar: The Flag-Salute Controversy*, University of Chicago Press, 1962, pp. 3-11.
17. "Moral and Spiritual Values in the Public Schools," p. 3.
18. Murray, John Courtney, S. J., "America's Four Conspiracies," *Religion in America*, pp. 1-41, Meridian Books, New York, 1958.
19. *Ibid.*, p. 34.
20. Torcaso v. Watkins, 367 U.S. 488, (1961).
21. Chamberlin v. Dade County Board of Public Instruction, 143 So.2d 21 (Fla. 1962).
22. See Plaintiff's Memorandum on the Law—p. 55 in case supra, note 21.
23. "The Treatment of Minorities in Secondary School Textbooks," Lloyd Marcus, Anti-Defamation League of B'Nai B'rith, New York, 1961.
24. *Ibid.*, p. 10.

25. Murray, John Courtney, S. J., "Dr. Morrison and the First Amendment: II," *America*, March 20, 1948, p. 683.
26. Dierenfield, R. B., "The Extent of Religious Influence in American Public Schools," *Religious Education*, May-June, 1961, pp. 173 ff.
27. *Ibid.*, p. 173.
28. *Ibid.*, p. 167.
29. *Ibid.*, p. 167.
30. *Ibid.*, p. 167.
31. "Christian Education Today: A Statement of Basic Philosophy," The International Council of Religion Education, Chicago, 1940, p. 35.
32. McCollum v. Board of Education, 333 U.S. 203 (1948); Zorach v. Clauson, 343 U.S. 306 (1952).
33. McCollum v. Board of Education, 333 U.S. 203, 209, 210 (1948).
34. Record of oral arguments in McCollum v. Board of Education, p. 28.
35. *Ibid.*, p. 28.
36. McCollum v. Board of Education, 343 U.S. 306, 323 (1952).
37. Kurland, Philip B., "Of Church and State and the Supreme Court," 29 *University of Chicago Law Review*, Autumn '96,' pp. 1-96 at p. 73.
38. Drinan, Robert F., S. J., "The Novel 'Liberty' Created by the McCollum Decision," 39 *Georgetown Law Review* 216 (1951); "The McCollum Decision, Three Years After," *America*, February 24, 1951.
39. Everson v. Board of Education, 330 U.S. 1, (1947).
40. Minersville et al v. Gobitis, 310 U.S. 586 (1940).
41. West Virginia State Board of Education v. Barnette, 319 U.S. 624 (1942).
42. *Op. cit.*, note 34 at p. 39.
43. *Ibid.*, p. 30.
44. *Ibid.*, pp. 50-51.
45. *Ibid.*, p. 60.
46. See Brief of the Synagogue Council of America in re McCollum v. Board of Education, p. 1.
47. McCollum v. Board of Education, 333 U.S. 203, 240 (1948).
48. *Ibid.*, p. 210.
49. *Ibid.*, p. 212.
50. *Ibid.*, p. 231.
51. *Ibid.*, p. 212.
52. *Ibid.*, p. 211.
53. *Ibid.*, p. 232, cited from Everson v. Board of Education, 330

U.S. at 59 (1947).

54. Palko v. Connecticut, 302 U.S. 319, 325 (1937).
55. "The Supreme Court as National School Board," 14 *Law and Contemporary Problems*, pp. 3-22 (1949).
56. "Separation of Church and State in the United States: A Summary View," *Wisconsin Law Review*, pp. 427-478 at p. 471 (1950).
57. "The Case of Religious Liberty," *Religion in America*, p. 95, Meridian Books, New York, 1958.
58. McGowan v. Maryland, 366 U.S. 420, 440 (1961).
59. Engel v. Vitale, 370 U.S. 421 at 430, (1962).
60. *Ibid.*, p. 445.
61. Zorach v. Clauson, 343 U.S. 306 at 325 (1952).
62. Pfeffer, Leo, *Creeds in Competition*, p. 74, Harper & Row, New York, 1958.
63. Zorach v. Clauson, 343 U.S. 306 at 317 (1952).
64. *Ibid.*, p. 317. The Administrative Board of the National Catholic Welfare Conference in its annual statement issued on November 20, 1948, affirmed its determination to work for the reversal of the McCollum decision. See *The New York Times*, November 21, 1948.
65. "The Supreme Court as National School Board," 14 *Law and Contemporary Problems*, pp. 3-22, (1949).
66. "Educational Cooperation Between Church and State," 14 *Law and Contemporary Problems*, pp. 61-72 (1949).
67. See "Church and State," Vol. 1 thru Vol. 7, Newsletters of POAU, Vol. 5, No. 1, p. 4, January, 1952.
68. *God in Education*, Scribner's, New York, 1951, pp. 99-118.
69. "Due Process and Disestablishment," 62 *Harvard Law Review* (1949).
70. Corwin, *op. cit.*, p. 21.
71. Murray, John Courtney, S. J., "Law or Prepossessions?," 14 *Law and Contemporary Problems*, 949, pp. 23-43, at p. 40-41.
72. Pike, *op. cit.*
73. Zorach v. Clauson, 343 U.S. 306 at 325 (1952).
74. Pfeffer, Leo, *Creeds in Competition*, p. 49.
75. *Ibid.*, p. 49.
76. "Some Current Issues in Church and State," 12 *Western Reserve Law Review*, Dec. 1961, pp. 9-33 at p. 11.
77. Kauper, "Church, State and Freedom: A Review," 52 *Michigan Law Review*, p. 829, 839 (1954).
78. *Christians and the State*, p. 227.
79. "A Problem of Culture" in *Religion and the Schools*, Fund for the Republic, 1959, pp. 64-78 at p. 69.

80. All of the quotations taken from the one majority opinion of Mr. Justice Douglas in the Zorach case will be without footnotes.
81. Zorach v. Clauson, 343 U.S. 306 at 316 (1952).
82. "Religion and American Society," a statement of principles prepared by a group whose members were: William Clancy, Education Director of the Church Peace Union; Arthur Cohen, vice president of the World Publishing Company, in charge of Meridian Books, which he founded; Robert Gordis, associate professor, Jewish Theological Seminary of America; William Gorman, former associate director of the Institute for Philosophical Research; F. Ernest Johnson, former member of the executive staff of the National Council of Churches of Christ; Robert Lekachman, associate professor of economics at Columbia University; William Lee Miller, associate professor of social ethics in the Yale Divinity School; and Mark DeWolfe Howe, professor of law at Harvard University, who resigned from the work in June, 1959. Edited by John Cogley, chairman. Issued by Center for the Study of Democratic Institutions, Santa Barbara, California, 1961, 79 pp.
83. "Educational Cooperation Between Church and State," 14 *Law and Contemporary Problems,* pp. 61-72, at 67 (1949).
84. See Johnson and Yost, *Separation of Church and State in the United States,* University of Minnesota Press, 1948, p. 33.
85. Clithero v. Showalter, 284 U.S. 573 (1930).
86. Doremus v. Board of Education of Hawthorne, 342 U.S. 429 (1952).
87. Weiss v. District Board, 76 Wis. 77, 44 N.W. 967 (1890).
88. People ex rel. Ring v. Board of Education, 245 I, 11. 334 (1910).
89. Herold v. Parish Board of School Directors, 136 La. 1034, 60 So. 116 (1915).
90. State ex rel Linger v. Weedman et al, 226 N.W. 1348 (1929).
91. Doremus v. Board of Education, 5 N.J. 435, 75 A2d 880 (1950).
92. 20 *U. S. Law Week* 3206, Feb. 5, 1952.
93. Schempp v. School District, 177 F.Supp. 398 (E.D.Pa. 1959).
94. Chamberlin v. Board of Public Instruction, 143 So.2d 21 (Fla. 1962).
95. Murray v. Curlett et al and Board of School Commissioners of Baltimore City, 179 A2d 698 (Md. 1962).
96. 24 P.S. Penna. 15-1516 (1949).
97. *Ibid.*
98. Schempp v. School District, 177 F.Supp. 398 (E.D.Pa. 1959).
99. *Ibid.,* p. 401, n. 14.

100. *Ibid.,* p. 404.
101. *Ibid.,* p. 405.
102. *Ibid.,* p. 405.
103. *Ibid.,* p. 407.
104. School District v. Schempp, 364 U.S. 298 (1960).
105. Schempp v. School District, 201 F.Supp. 815 (1962).
106. See note 95 supra.
107. *Ibid.,* p. 701.
108. Zorach v. Clauson, 343 U.S. 306, 313 (1952).
109. Murray v. Curlett, 179 A2d 698, 702 (1962).
110. Chamberlin v. Board of Public Instruction, 143 So.2d 21 (Fla. 1962).
111. See Arthur E. Sutherland, "Public Authority and Religious Education," in *The Study of Religion in the Public Schools,* American Council on Education, Washington, D.C., 1958.
112. "Religion and American Society," Center for the Study of Democratic Institutions, Santa Barbara, California, 1961, p. 73.
113. Engel v. Vitale, 370 U.S. 421, 433 (1962).
114. *Ibid.,* 10 N.Y.2d 174 at 182, 76 NE2d 579 at 582 (1962).
115. *Ibid.,* 370 U.S. 421 at 434 (1962).
116. Engel v. Vitale, 18 Misc.2d 659 N.Y. 191 N.Y.S.2d 452 (1959).
117. *Ibid.,* 18 Misc. 2d 659 at 690, 191 N.Y.S. 2d 453 at 487.
118. *Ibid.,* at 694-695.
119. Engel v. Vitale, 11 A.D.2d, 340 at 345, 206 N.Y.S.2d 183 at 188 (1960).
120. Engel v. Vitale, 10 N.Y.2d 174 at 180, 176 N.E.2d 579 at 581 (1961).
121. *Ibid.,* 10 N.Y.2d 174 at 183.
122. *Ibid.,* 10 N.Y.2d 174 at 189.
123. *Ibid.,* 10 N.Y.2d 174 at 191.
124. *Ibid.,* 10 N.Y.2d 174 at 191-192.
125. Engel v. Vitale, 370 U.S. 421 at 445 (1962).
126. *Ibid.,* p. 442.
127. *Ibid.,* p. 430.
128. *The New York Times,* June 26, 1962, p. 16, column 7.
129. Palko v. Connecticut, 302 U.S. 319, 325 (1937).
130. Howe, "The Constitutional Question" in *Religion and the Free Society,* Fund for the Republic, New York, 1958, pp. 49-63, at p. 55.
131. All quotations are from the one majority opinion of Mr. Justice Black in the Engel case and will be without footnotes.
132. Engel v. Vitale, 370 U.S. 421 at 437 (1962). All following quotations are from Mr. Justice Douglas' concurring opinion and are without footnotes.

133. "The Study of Religion in the Public School," American Council on Education, Washington, D.C., 1958, p. 32.

CHAPTER FOUR. *The Church-Related School*

1. Childs, John L., "American Democracy and the Common School System," *Jewish Education*, Vol. 21 (1949), pp. 32-37.
2. Quoted in Will Herberg, "The Sectarian Conflict over Church and State," Vol. 14 (Nov. 1952) 450-462, at p. 456.
3. Conant, James B., *Education and Liberty*, Harvard University Press, Cambridge, Mass., 1953, pp. 81-82.
4. Brubacher, John S., *Modern Philosophies of Education*, 2d ed., McGraw-Hill Book Company, Inc., New York, 1950, p. 142.
5. Hearings on March 21-29, 1961 before the General Subcommittee on Education of the Committee on Education and Labor, House of Representatives, 87th Congress, First Session, on H.R. 4970, Part 2 at pp. 1024-1025.
6. Herberg, Will, "The Sectarian Conflict Over Church and State," *Commentary*, November 1952, pp. 450-462, at 461.
7. Pierce v. Society of Sisters, 268 U.S. 510 (1925).
8. Gitlow v. People of New York, 268 U.S. 652 (1925).
9. Pierce v. Society of Sisters, 268 U.S. 510 at 535 (1925).
10. *Ibid.*, pp. 534-535.
11. *Ibid.*, p. 535.
12. Cited in Pfeffer, *Church, State and Freedom*, Beacon Press, Boston, 1953, at p. 433.
13. *National Education Association Research Bulletin*, Vol. XXXIV, No. 4, Dec. 1956, p. 208.
14. Everson v. Board of Education, 330 U.S. 1 at 51 (1947).
15. *Ibid.*, at 59.
16. For details on the Ohio struggle see p. 662-673 in Gabel, n. 17 infra.
17. Gabel, Richard J., *Public Funds for Church and Private Schools*, Catholic University of America, Washington, D.C. (1937).
18. Kentucky Constitution (Bill of Rights) §5 (1891).
19. Anderson v. Swart, 167 A.2d 514, cert. denied 366 U.S. 925 (1961).
20. 16 Vermont Statutes Annotated 793(a).
21. *Ibid.*, (b).
22. Art. 3, Ch. 1, Vermont Statutes.
23. Judge Hill's opinion is not reported officially but may be found in

the record as printed for the use of the Supreme Court of the
United States at p. 29.

24. Everson v. Board of Education, 330 U.S. 1. at pp. 15-16.
25. *Ibid.*, p. 18.
26. Swart v. South Burlington Town School District, 167 A.2d 514, at
    514 (1961). All further quotations from the Swart decision
    are from this source.

CHAPTER FIVE. *Benefits to Pupils in Private Schools*

1. Niebuhr, Reinhold, *Essays in Applied Christianity*, Meridian
   Books, New York, 1959, p. 220.
2. Mitchell v. Consolidated School District 21 et al, 17 Wash.2d 61,
   135 P.2d 79 (1943).
3. Visser v. Nooksack Valley School District, 33 Wash.2d. 699
   (1949) 207 P.2d 198 (1949).
4. Powell, Theodore, *The School Bus Law*, Wesleyan University
   Press, Middletown, Conn., 1960.
5. *Ibid.*, p. 240.
6. Snyder v. Newtown, 147 Conn. 374, 161 A.2d 770 (1960).
7. Pfeffer, *op. cit.*, p. 476.
8. Zellers v. Huff, 55 N.M. 501, 236 P.2d 949 (1951).
9. 60 *Harvard Law Review* 793, 800 (1947).
10. Squires v. Inhabitants of the City of Augusta, 155 Me. 151, 153
    A2d 80 (1959).
11. *Op. cit.*, p. 223 (note 27).
12. State ex rel. Reynolds v. Nusbaum, 115 NW.2d 761 (Wisc.
    1962).
13. Matthews v. Quinton, 362 P.2d 932, appeal refused by the U.S.
    Supreme Court 368 U.S. 517 (1962).
14. Chapter 39, SLA 1955, Sec. 1(b).
15. McVey v. Hawkins, 364 Mo. 44, 258 S.W.2d 927 (1953).
16. Jones, Harry, *Religion & Contemporary Society*, Macmillan, New
    York, 1963.
17. Cochran v. Board of Education, 281 U.S. 370 at 374, 375.
18. Bennett, John C., *Christians and the State*, p. 249.
19. Chance v. Mississippi State Textbook Board, 190 Miss. 453 at
    457, 200 So. 706 at 713 (1941).
20. Dickman v. School District No. 62C, 366 P.2d 533 (Oregon
    1961).
21. United States Law Week, Vol. 31, p. 3117 (cert. den.) sub. nom.
    Carlson v. Dickman (1962).
22. Lippmann, Walter, *A Preface to Morals*, Macmillan, New York,
    1929, pp. 77-78.

CHAPTER SIX. *Federal Aid to Education*

1. Mitchell, William A., "Religion and Federal Aid to Education," 14 *Law and Contemporary Problems*, 113-143, at p. 115 (1949).
2. S. 717, 79th Congress, 1st Session (1945).
3. Freeman, Roger A., "Federal Aid to Education," 10 *Social Order*, 170-179, April 1960.
4. Statistics taken from a U.S. Census survey cited by Hon. Abraham Ribicoff, Secretary of Health, Education and Welfare at p. 9 of *Hearings* on H.R. 4970 noted *supra*.
5. Snyder v. Town of Newtown, 147 Conn. 374, 161 A.2d 770 (1960).
6. See Dr. William W. Brickman in *School and Society*, December 2, 1961; Lloyd Money in *College and University Business*, December 1961.
7. 42 U.S.C. 242(a).
8. See "Church and State," *Wall Street Journal*, March 29, 1961, p. 10, 40 U.S.C. 484(j) and (k) 1958.
8a. It is most significant that *The New Republic* reversed the position on federal aid to Catholic schools which it took in 1961. In the March 2, 1963, issue of *The New Republic* a strong, well-reasoned editorial urges the granting of state aid to assist the secular purposes of church-related schools.

   In the March 23, 1963, issue of the same liberal weekly a lengthy editorial elaborates on the new position of *The New Republic* and makes a detailed answer to the critics of the reversal in policy of *The New Republic*.
9. *Hearings, op. cit.* Part 2, p. 711.
10. "The Constitutionality of the Inclusions of Church-Related Schools in Federal Aid to Education," 50 Georgetown Law Journal, pp. 399-455 (Winter 1961).
11. *Ibid.*, p. 437.
12. Handbook of Catholic Education, ed. by National Catholic Welfare Conference, 1961.
13. Sacks, Benjamin, *The Religious Issue in the State Schools of England and Wales, 1902-1914*, University of New Mexico Press, 1961, p. 223.
14. Encyclical on Education by Pope Pius XI, Text.
15. Zorach v. Clauson, 343 U.S. 306 at 314 (1952).
16. Everson v. Board of Education, 330 U.S. 1, at 59 (1947).
17. Reynolds v. United States, 98 U.S. 145 (1878).

18. McGowan v. Maryland, 366 U.S. 420 (1961).
19. Barnette v. Board of Education, 319 U.S. 624 (1943).
20. *Ibid.*, p. 660.
21. Niebuhr, *Applied Christianity*, p. 223.
22. Pierce v. Society of Sisters, 268 U.S. 510 at 535 (1925).
23. Bennett, *Christians and the State*, p. 246-47.

CHAPTER SEVEN. *Sunday Laws, Sabbatarians and the Constitution*

1. See American Jewish Year Book, 1962, noted in *The New York Times*, August 4, 1962.
2. Brief of General Conference of Seventh-Day Adventists, in Gallagher v. Crown Kosher Market, in the U.S. Supreme Court, 1960, p. 2.
3. McGowan v. Maryland, 366 U.S. 420 at 576 (1961).
4. People v. Friedman, 300 N.Y. 694, 91 N.E.2d 724 (1950); cert. den. 341 U.S. 907 (1951).
5. *America*, March 8, 1958, p. 649.
6. McGowan v. Maryland, 366 U.S. 420 (1961); Two Guys from Harrison-Allentown, Inc., v. McGinley, 366 U.S. 582 (1961); Gallagher v. Crown Kosher Markets, 366 U.S. 617.
   Braunfeld v. Crown Kosher Markets, 366 U.S. 599 (1961);
7. Commonwealth v. Chernock, 336 Mass. 578, 145 N.E.2d 920 (1957).
8. Hennington v. Georgia, 163 U.S. 299 (1896). Petit v. Minnesota, 177 U.S. 164 (1900).
9. See 73 *Harvard Law Review* 729 at 734 (1960) and other law review articles critical of Magruder's opinion.
10. Crown Kosher Super Market v. Gallagher, 176 F.Supp. 466 at 475 (D.Mass. 1959).
11. *Ibid.*, p. 475.
12. Two Guys from Harrison-Allentown v. McGinley, 179 F.Supp. 944 (1959).
13. *Ibid.*, p. 951.
14. Braunfeld v. Brown, 366 U.S. 599 at 606 (1961).
15. McGowan v. Maryland, 366 U.S. 420 at 445 (1961).
16. All citations from note 15 through 27 are taken from the Sunday law cases noted above.
28. Ohio's Laws, Title 37, Chapter 3773.24 (1961).
29. See "Sunday in the Sixties," *Public Affairs Pamphlet No. 327*, by Richard Cohen, 1962.
30. Ward, Hiley H., *Space-Age Sunday*, Macmillan, New York, 1960.

CHAPTER EIGHT. *Conclusions and Recommendations*

1. Katz, "Religious Perspectives in American Culture," Volume 2 of the four-volume *Religion in American Life*, Princeton University Press, 1961, p. 54.
2. Margolin, Ephraim, Review of "Religious Perspectives in American Culture" (see note 1), 72 *Yale Law Journal*, 212-216 at 215, November, 1962.
3. Kauper, Paul G., "Church and State: Cooperative Separatism," Vol. 60, *Michigan Law Review*, 1961, pp. 1-40, at p. 4.
4. Kurland, Philip B., *Religion and the Law*, Aldine Publishing Co., Chicago, 1962.
5. Johnson, F. Ernest, "A Problem of Culture," in *Religion and the Schools*, Fund for the Republic, New York, 1959, p. 64.
6. 55 *American Political Science Review*, 777-791 at 789 (1959).
7. Sutherland, "Establishment According to Engel," 76 *Harvard Law Review*, 25-52, November 1962 at p. 27.
8. Drucker, Peter F., "Organized Religion and the American Creed," *The Review of Politics*, Vol. 18 (July 1956) pp. 296-304, at p. 297-298.
9. *Ibid.*, p. 303.
10. *Ibid.*, p. 296.
11. *Ibid.*, p. 299.
12. Niebuhr, Reinhold, *Essays in Applied Christianity*, Meridian Books, 1959, p. 211.
13. Woodruff, Douglas, *Church and State*, Hawthorn, 1962, p. 122.
14. Niebuhr, Reinhold, *The Children of Light and the Children of Darkness*, Scribner, 1944.

Bibliography

The following titles are probably the best contemporary book-length treatments of the church–state problem in America.

1. *The Supreme Court on Church and State*, edited by Joseph Tussman, Oxford University Press, 1962, 305 pp.

   This collection of the texts of the 29 major decisions on church and state of the United States Supreme Court is an excellent and indispensable handbook. It is ideal for study groups, reading assignments for senior high school or college classes and for intercredal clergy dialogue. This volume, however, does not contain the Sunday law decisions of May 29, 1961, nor the prayer decision of June 25, 1962.

2. *Christians and the State*, by John C. Bennett, Scribner, 1958, 302 pp.

   Dean Bennett of Union Theological Seminary has written in this volume one of the most balanced and sympathetic Protestant books on church–state problems in America. This study rejects the theory of an *absolute* separation of church and state, endorses health and welfare benefits for parochial schools but rejects direct state aid for these institutions.

3. *Church, State and Freedom*, by Leo Pfeffer, Beacon, 1953, 675 pp.

   Written by the general counsel of the American Jewish Congress and the articulate advocate of an "impregnable wall of separation" between church and state, this volume is a complete, well-ordered analysis of America's statutory and decisional law on church and state. The author's thesis is that *absolute* separation between church and state will bring about the most complete religious freedom for all. This volume should be read in connection with Mr. Pfeffer's more popular study, *Creeds in Competition* (Harper and Row, 1958, 178 pp.).

4. *Of Church and State and the Supreme Court*, by Philip B. Kurland, University of Chicago Press.

This reprint of an article published by Professor Kurland in the Autumn 1961 issue of the *University of Chicago Law Review* is a most valuable review and evaluation of all the principal decisions of the U. S. Supreme Court on church and state. Professor Kurland's thesis is that the First Amendment means that government "cannot utilize religion as a standard for action or inaction . . . either to confer a benefit or to impose a burden." He finds his thesis supported by some but not all Supreme Court decisions but urges that the application of his thesis would bring justice to all parties. This study is remarkably well done and merits the most careful consideration.

5. *Philosophy of the State as Educator*, by Father Thomas Dubay, S.M., Bruce, 1959, 237 pp.

This study of the rights and duties with regard to education of the church, the state and Catholic parents is noteworthy.

6. *Catholic Viewpoint on Church and State*, by Jerome G. Kerwin, Hanover House (Doubleday), 1960, 192 pp.

This readable study by an outstanding Catholic political scientist has the limitations inherent in its broad coverage but the excellence of being an over-all treatment of contemporary church–state problems.

7. *Catholic Viewpoint on Education*, by Father Neil G. McCluskey, S.J., Hanover House, 1959, 192 pp.

By far the best current summary of the controversy over public aid for parochial schools this volume (now in paperback) is ideal for discussion groups or for courses in education in high school or college. Father McCluskey's eight chapters cover every major educational issue in the church-state field. The volume can be read in connection with the author's study, *Public Schools and Moral Education* (The influence of Horace Mann, William Torrey Harris and John Dewey), Columbia Univ. Press, 1958, 315 pp.

8. *Religion in America*, edited by John Cogley, Meridian, 1958, 288 pp.

A valuable volume containing essays on many aspects of church and state by Reinhold Nieʋuhr, John Courtney Murray, S.J., Leo Pfeffer, Wilbur G. Katz, Will Herberg,

James Hastings Nichols, Walter J. Ong, S.J., Stringfellow Barr, Gustave Weigel, S.J., Abraham Heschel and Paul Tillich. A broad spectrum of opinion is here obtainable, with particularly outstanding material on the issue of state aid for nonpublic schools.

9. *Hearings on Federal Aid to Schools*, March, 1961. Before the Subcommittee on Education of the Committee on Education and Labor, House of Representatives, 87th Congress, 1st Session, on H.R. 4970—2 Vols., 1052 pages.

These two volumes are literally a treasury of excellent material on every aspect of Federal aid to education. Full texts of statements by Monsignor Hochwalt, Secretary Ribicoff (as well as the brief of the Department of Health, Education and Welfare), all Protestant statements and those of the American Jewish Congress and the American Civil Liberties Union. A good bibliography of church–state literature is contained on pp. 938-939 of Part 2. These volumes *may* be available through one's Congressman or from the U. S. Government Printing Office.

10. *The Constitutionality of the Inclusion of Church-Related Schools in Federal Aid to Education*, 50 Georgetown Law Journal, (Winter, 1961), pp. 399-455.

This article is a brief prepared by the legal department of the National Catholic Welfare Conference in reply to a brief issued by the Department of Health, Education and Welfare to support the Administration's postion that "across-the-board" grants and loans to parochial schools would be unconstitutional. The NCWC brief is a thorough, well-reasoned presentation of all the major legal and constitutional issues involved in Federal aid to Catholic schools. A very valuable document.

Index